HERE I AM, LORD

Published by Barbour Publishing, Inc., P.O. Box 719, Uhrichsville, Ohio 44683
www.barbourbooks.com

Our mission is to publish and distribute inspirational products offering exceptional value and biblical encouragement to the masses.

Member of the
Evangelical Christian
Publishers Association

Printed in the United States of America.
5 4 3 2 1

HERE I AM, LORD

*Daily Meditations to Deepen Your
Relationship with the Heavenly Father*

ANITA CORRINE DONIHUE

BARBOUR
PUBLISHING

Dedication

To the reader:
May God richly bless your prayer life
through these devotions.
May you always be ready to respond to Him
with a heartfelt "Here I Am, Lord!"

Introduction

O come, let us worship and bow down:
let us kneel before the LORD our maker.
For he is our God;
and we are the people of his pasture,
and the sheep of his hand.
PSALM 95:6–7 KJV

What a privilege it is to come into the presence of our Lord God. The simple things in life—like a favorite chair, the kitchen sink, a flower and vegetable garden, our bedside, or sometimes even the bathtub—become private altars of prayer. Simple places like a backyard patio, a hillside, a spot by a quiet stream, or the inside of our car become holy sanctuaries where we are blessed by God's awesome presence.

In this busy world, we find treasured slips of time to enjoy communing with God, our Father and best Friend. Each time we come to God and say, "Here I am, Lord," He listens to our joys and concerns. He comforts us and nurtures our hungry, thirsty souls through His Scriptures. His encouraging words whisper to our hearts, giving us the strength and guidance we need each day. We discover adventures with Him beyond our imagination.

Join me for a yearlong journey of discovery in this daily devotional. Every month, we'll focus on a different aspect of our relationship with the heavenly Father:

> January—to Receive You
> February—to Honor You
> March—to Know You
> April—to Serve You
> May—to Enjoy You
> June—to Hear You
> July—to Tell You

August—to Share You
September—to Ask You
October—to Trust You
November—to Praise You
December—to Worship You

I pray that you'll be challenged and encouraged by our time together.

JANUARY 1

In Search of You

Here I am, Lord. As I begin this new year, I look back to another beginning: one when I accepted You as my Savior. Oh, how I love being with You.

Once, I wasn't sure if You knew me. I seldom talked with You. I'm thankful for my friend who invited me to ask You to be my Savior. Although I didn't understand how it could be possible, I felt a longing in my heart to receive You.

I feared such a big decision. *I* wanted to control my life. I preferred everything mapped out, certain. I wondered how I could trust You to direct me when I didn't even know You. I wasn't sure about turning my entire existence over to Someone I hadn't seen.

I didn't do well with the way I lived before receiving You, Lord. Should I have died then, I wonder what my eternity would have been. I questioned why You wanted to be my Savior, and if You would care about me, through good or bad. I feared You might desert me, especially when I messed up.

Thank You for leading me to find You, dear Lord. Or did You find me? I'm so glad You revealed what it meant to receive You as my Savior. In Jesus' name, amen.

> *"I am the way, the truth, and the life.*
> *No one comes to the Father except through Me."*
>
> JOHN 14:6 NKJV

to Receive You

Getting to Know about You

I'm grateful for how You kept urging me to get to know You, Lord. Once, my whirlwind life tossed me about like a rag doll. No matter how hard I tried, I couldn't solve my dilemmas. Things were just too difficult to untangle. I longed for joy and peace, but I could find none. Even though I hadn't yet received You as my Savior, You still showed me Your unfailing love and mercy. That's when I wanted to know more about You. Thank You for caring for me and *really* hearing my prayers.

Still, I wondered if there was more to praying than repeating the same words over and over—more than asking You for help out of my problems.

When I sought *You*, Lord, You guided me to Your Bible. I'm still overwhelmed by the way Your Holy Spirit whispered, *"Come unto Me. Receive Me as your Lord and Savior."*

Thank You for tugging on my heartstrings, so I knew You were near. Through Your Son Jesus, You were only a prayer away. It was like the air I breathed. I couldn't see You, but I began to perceive You were real.

Thank You for never giving up on me, Lord. How appreciative I am for the way You showed me how to know more about You.

Therefore he is able to save completely
those who come to God through him,
because he always lives to intercede for them.

HEBREWS 7:25 NIV

Why Did I Treat You So?

While sipping a cup of tea in a restaurant today, Lord, I happened to notice a couple having lunch with their teenage boy and girl. Sadly, the teenagers showed impudent and argumentative attitudes toward their parents and each other. No matter how the parents tried to relate and make a pleasant lunch, the teens responded rudely.

I reflected back to the know-it-all behavior I sometimes displayed toward my parents during my teenage years and hung my head. How sorry I am for the grief I caused them. Why did I hurt them so? Forgive me, Lord.

I recalled the flippant attitude I also once had toward You before I became a Christian. No matter how much You tried to relate to me and guide me in the right way, I rebelled. Whenever I heard You whisper to my heart, I refused to listen. When You showered Your love upon me, I shrugged it off. I wanted everything my way.

Why did I treat You so? I caused grief for You, myself, and those around me. I'm sorry for my flippant, thoughtless ways, Lord. Thank You for not giving up on me. Thank You for forgiving and loving me.

For you were continually straying like sheep,
but now you have returned to the Shepherd
and Guardian of your souls.

1 PETER 2:25 NASB

Yielding to You

Before I yielded to You, I was incredibly stubborn, Lord. At church, the pastor explained how to accept You as my Savior. He invited people to pray at Your altar. It seemed the pastor could peer into my soul and was talking directly to me.

I held off coming to You too long. When we all stood and prayed, my hands gripped the pew in front of me until my knuckles turned white. Still, You kept calling me.

Everywhere, all the time, I heard You talk to my heart. You patiently waited, while I turned my life into more confusion and disaster. I could sense You reaching out Your hand to me. Finally, I gave up and grabbed hold.

That night by my bedside where I knelt and prayed, I wholeheartedly gave You my life. There, You led me to Your throne of grace. What a new and amazing experience it was. Although I had prayed to You before, I was finally meeting You personally as my Savior. You, who are Master of everything, came into my heart.

A huge burden lifted from my shoulders when I gave You my wasted, sin-controlled life. An indescribable joy filled me. I could hardly wait to tell all my friends and family what You did for me.

So from now on we regard no one
from a worldly point of view.
Though we once regarded Christ in this way,
we do so no longer.

2 CORINTHIANS 5:16 NIV

Simplicity of Surrender

Once I chose to ask You into my heart, it became simple to surrender to You. Somehow, You managed to melt my willful ways and help me open my eyes to Your unwavering love for me. When I gave up my will to You, the things that once tugged me away from You faded to total insignificance. I didn't feel I lost anything. Instead, I became aware that I gained everything. For the first time, I realized You truly cared about me. You knew how I felt. You kept my wants and dreams in mind. Most of all, You recognized what was, and what was not, best for my life.

How sweet Your ways became to me. Everything in my life, good and bad, I freely gave to You. I felt sorry to be laying the mess I had made of my life before You. I was amazed that You picked up my fragmented pieces without hesitation. Immediately, You took me into Your loving presence just the way I was. You were able to reach into my soul and write Your name upon my open, pliable heart at last.

Thank You, Lord, for gently tugging at my stubborn heartstrings and for helping me experience a simplicity of surrender to You—my Lord, my Hope, my all.

> *"For whoever desires to save his life will lose it,*
> *but whoever loses his life for My sake will find it.*
> *For what profit is it to a man if*
> *he gains the whole world,*
> *and loses his own soul?"*

MATTHEW 16:25–26 NKJV

Repenting Prayer

Father, I had no idea how it could be possible to be "born again." Through reading Your Bible and hearing my Christian friend explain that I had been physically born as a baby, I learned I could be born again spiritually into the family of God. I slowly started to understand and opened my heart's door, just a crack.

I knew I had sin in my life just like everyone else in this world. The only way I could come to You was through Your Son, Jesus. I wondered what I would need to do so I could receive Jesus as my Savior.

Thank You for the way my friend taught me to pray a repenting prayer. I was already sorry for my sins. All I had to do was tell You so and ask You to forgive me. In a flash, You *did* forgive me. Then I asked Jesus to become my Savior and for Your Holy Spirit to come into my life.

It was amazing how You made me Your born-again child. I had become a brand-new baby Christian. What a thrill it was to know You as my heavenly Father, Your Son as my Savior, and experience Your Holy Spirit in my life. Thank You, Father, for helping me to pray a repenting prayer and ask You into my heart.

Peter said. . .
"Repent, and let every one of you be baptized
in the name of Jesus Christ for the remission of sins;
and you shall receive the gift of the Holy Spirit."

ACTS 2:38 NKJV

I Wish I Could See You

There was a time, Lord, when I felt seeing was the only way to believe. Although I couldn't see You, I'm glad I took that fearful step and accepted You as my Savior. Once I did, my whole world began to change. No longer did I go aimlessly through life. You gave me a purpose. You gave me love; I received that love and gave it back to You. You gave me a drive to share with anyone who listens all about what You did and are still doing for me.

When night falls, I know Your sun will return the next day. The moon also revisits at evening. When clouds hover overhead and the sun cannot be seen, I know it is there. Though unseen, I know You are here, too.

But I wish I could *see* You, Lord. I wish I could slip my fingers into Your nail-scarred hands. I long to gaze into Your eyes or touch the hem of Your robe. Once, I felt this way because I wanted to be sure You were real. Now I *know* Your loving presence dwells within me. But I still wish I could get just one glimpse of Your face.

Now, Lord, I will follow You by faith, not by sight. The more I walk and talk with You, the more I know You. Although I have never seen You, I thank You for being my Savior. Thank You for helping me to walk by faith and not by sight.

> *"No one has seen the Father except*
> *the one who is from God;*
> *only he has seen the Father. I tell you the truth,*
> *he who believes has everlasting life."*
>
> JOHN 6:46–47 NIV

Another Chance

Why did You have the patience to keep calling me? No matter how far I ran, You gave me another chance—and another—to receive You. Am I important to You?

My dear child, I love you with an everlasting love. You are dearer to Me than you can imagine. I am the Good Shepherd. You are My sheep. When you were lost, I followed you like a sheep gone astray. I didn't give up until you were safely in My fold.

Do You really know me?

I understand you better than anyone. I see when you sit and rise. I perceive your joys, your concerns, and everything you think. I knew you before you were formed in your mother's womb. I am even aware of how many hairs are on your head.

Will You always be with me?

No matter how high you ascend into the sky, no matter how deep you descend into the seas, I am here. And I shall lead you.

Will You love me through good and bad times?

Nothing can separate you from My love. Not tribulations, persecution, or famine—none of these can keep My love from you. Death or life or evil cannot. The angels will not. Be certain you are My child, whom I love and adore.

Thank You for another chance, Lord.

But the lovingkindness of the Lord is
from everlasting to everlasting,
to those who reverence him;
his salvation is to children's children of those who
are faithful to his covenant and remember to obey him!

PSALM 103:17–18 TLB

All Things Became New

Before everything became new through You, Lord, I felt ashamed to tell people I loved You. I gave only a trite answer: "Yes, I'm a Christian." That was because I hadn't fully given You my heart, my all. After that night, the old things in my life were gone. Everything became new. No longer was I alone. From then on, Your presence filled me every day. It wasn't a big dramatic experience. I just knew You were there, loving and helping me.

Because Your Holy Spirit dwelled within me, my likes and dislikes changed. My life became Your temple. My heart, Your dwelling place. I lost interest in what I used to do that didn't please You. I still cared about my old friends. But I found a greater satisfaction in drawing closer to my newfound Christian acquaintances. They were always good about encouraging me in my walk with You. Best of all, You had become my Savior, my dearest Friend.

Thank You for never leaving me. Thank You for loving me through the good and bad times. Before I gave You my life, I was lost. Now I praise You, dear Lord, for I am found. Once I was spiritually blind, but now I see. I look forward to being Your child for the rest of my life.

> *Therefore, if anyone is in Christ,*
> *he is a new creation;*
> *the old has gone, the new has come!*
>
> 2 CORINTHIANS 5:17 NIV

No Strings Attached

Father, some time ago I received a beautiful picture drawn and colored by my granddaughter, Talia. She spent a lot of time on it, making it look just right, autographed with the message: "To Nana with love, Talia." She made the picture for me because she loves me. No strings attached. Not expecting anything in return but my love. I treasure the picture hanging on my refrigerator.

I think of the free gift You gave me—the priceless gift of salvation. All I needed to do was ask You into my heart. Because I did, You have given me a life full of joy. A life in which You provide victory over circumstances and abundantly shower me with Your loving care.

How grandly blessed I am to have You as my heavenly Father and Your Son as my Savior. You aren't miles away. Your Holy Spirit is with me all the time. Thank You for adopting me as Your child and allowing me to receive You with no strings attached.

You are my Light and my Salvation. Because of You, I shall not fear. You are my strength, my life. To You be all power. I want to give You glory in everything I do and say. I want to reflect You, Father—You who made me Your own.

The free gift of God is
eternal life in Christ Jesus our Lord.

ROMANS 6:23 NASB

Everlasting Freedom

Everywhere I turn, Lord, I hear people talking about the importance of freedom. Thank You for allowing me to live in a country where we can to go to school, learn, and travel across our land. Thank You for the privilege of being able to worship You.

However, I see a different bondage in our world. It's enslavement to sin, sadness, and self-destruction. Once, I was a slave to all this. It was like I carried a huge suitcase with me everywhere, filled with regrets, failure, bitterness, and wrongs I could never make right.

Then I met You, and You became my Master and Lord. All I had to do was hand over my heavy burden to You. Before I knew it, You were sorting and throwing out the things not pleasing to You. Never would I have a part of any of them again.

I'm no longer a slave to sin. Instead, I have You as my dearest Friend. You, dear Lord, have made me free—free to love and serve You forever. You helped me escape the awful things that once weighed me down. No longer am I buried under guilt and shame. No longer do I feel worthless, for You have told me I am priceless to You.

Thank You, Lord, for giving me a life, everlasting and free.

Jesus replied, "I tell you the truth,
everyone who sins is a slave to sin.
Now a slave has no permanent place
in the family [of God],
but a son belongs to it forever."

JOHN 8:34–35 NIV

Your Son Took My Place

The news story of a young hero tugged at my heartstrings. A twelve-year-old boy, playing along the riverbank, slid into the wintry icy water. Was it Your timing for the young man to be walking on the bridge and to see the whole thing happen? Thank You for how he quickly ran down and rescued the boy. That man risked his own life to save the youngster. Thank You, Father, for helping them both to reach the shore safely.

If I ever need to rescue someone, grant me quick thinking and the strength to do so. Give me enough courage and love to risk my life for another.

Would I be willing to sacrifice one of my family members to save another, Father? Do I have enough love to pay for someone's sins, serve time in prison, or die in his or her place? I don't know.

I can't realize the pain You experienced when You sacrificed Your Son to die a criminal's death. Jesus took our place so we can all be free from sin and have everlasting life. He died for me and my loved ones. I praise You for Your loving mercy. Because of Your sacrifice, I can come directly to You in prayer and enjoy Your fellowship. First, You gave me Your love. Now, I give You mine in return.

*And the real life I now have within this body is
a result of my trusting in the Son of God,
who loved me and gave himself for me.*

GALATIANS 2:20 TLB

Too Good to Be True?

There have been more disappointments in my life than I can count, Lord. Sometimes circumstances almost destroyed me. When this happened, I had fair-weather friends who turned their backs on me just when I needed them most. But there were others who truly cared and stuck by me through thick and thin.

When I heard You calling me, I wondered if You were too good to be true. Why should Your promises be different from the promise of those who failed me? Was it worth answering Your knock at my heart's door?

Once I answered, Your love and faithfulness went beyond measure or comprehension. There are still disappointments and heartache. Yet through each one, You remain with me—guarding, guiding, helping me along the way.

Now I bring someone else to You, Lord. My life was never as difficult as hers. Please help her. No matter her past or present, I know *You* are her answer.

I pray for her to receive You as her Savior and Friend. Help her to turn everything over to You and trust You to work all things together for good.

Teach her to share her deepest concerns and secrets with You as You once taught me. Help her hear the loving whispers You place within her heart and to experience Your unfailing friendship.

[Jesus said,]
"If anyone hears me calling him [or her]
and opens the door, I will come in."

REVELATION 3:20 TLB

It Makes Sense

Lord, before I knew You personally, becoming a Christian didn't make sense. How could this new life be so fantastic? What if You made everything different for me? I wasn't sure if I wanted to become a Christian and change. Before I knew You, I had learned about Your gift of salvation, but I couldn't comprehend it.

Finally, I answered Your constant knocking at my heart's door and asked You in. After You became my Savior and filled me with Your Spirit, You became real in my life. Now I experience and enjoy Your presence and love. My head knowledge of You has been transformed to a heart knowledge.

The things I had learned about You became a part of me. You understand my every feeling. You know my every need. You hear my prayers and talk to my heart. You help me make decisions when I ask You for guidance. You, Lord, have become the very core of my being. You are my life, my all.

Thank You, Lord, for helping me make sense of Your being my Savior. Thank You for abiding in my heart and taking me to be Your very own treasured child.

"Because he loves me," says the LORD,
"I will rescue him;
I will protect him, for he acknowledges my name.
He will call upon me, and I will answer him;
I will be with him in trouble,
I will deliver him and honor him.
With long life will I satisfy him
and show him my salvation."

PSALM 91:14–16 NIV

How Can You Forgive Me?

Father, I want to say how sorry I am for the things I did wrong before I started following You. I wasted so many years. How can You ever forgive me?

Is there anything I can do to make it up? Will years of good deeds pay my debt? No matter how much I try to do right, I can never repay You.

I already forgave you, My dear one. You don't need to make everything up. Your sin is gone forever. All I want is your love.

Are You happy with me, Lord? I'm really trying. Let me feel Your presence.

I am here. I never left you. You are the apple of My eye. As you love and obey Me, you continually make My heart glad.

Come to Me. Listen to Me. Hear My words so You may live a life of joy unspeakable. You are My child, and I am your God.

Thank You again for forgiving me. Thank You for loving me, for being my heavenly Father. When I feel overwhelmed with regrets, let me remember Your forgiveness.

> *I said, "LORD, be merciful to me;*
> *Heal my soul, for I have sinned against You."*
>
> PSALM 41:4 NKJV

> *Let the wicked forsake his way,*
> *And the unrighteous man his thoughts;*
> *Let him return to the LORD,*
> *And He will have mercy on him;*
> *And to our God,*
> *For He will abundantly pardon.*
>
> ISAIAH 55:7 NKJV

How Can I Forgive Myself?

Although You've forgiven me, Lord, regrets of my wasted years still haunt me. I can pardon others, but I'm having trouble forgiving myself. Help me, please. There's no way I can change my past. I've asked others for their mercy. I've even tried making things right. Teach me, now, to let things go.

The Bible says the two greatest commandments are to love the Lord with all your heart, soul, and mind; and love your neighbor as you do yourself. Does that mean loving myself is part of Your commandments? I think it does.

As You forgive me, I will endeavor to forgive myself. In so doing, I open my life to Your emotional and spiritual healing. No longer will I allow myself to be burdened by former things. Instead, I will trust You to make my life new.

When I make wrong choices, I'm grateful for how You pull me back to the right way. Thank You for Your constant love and guidance during these times.

Thank You, Father, for granting me the ability and compassion to forgive myself. If the remorse returns, I know it isn't of You. I will focus on Your love instead and enjoy Your grace and mercy.

Jesus said to him,
" 'You shall love the LORD your God with all your heart,
with all your soul, and with all your mind.'
This is the first and great commandment.
And the second is like it:
'You shall love your neighbor as yourself.' "

MATTHEW 22:37–39 NKJV

You Gave Me Faith

Before I received You as my Savior, I didn't have faith that You could save me and make me Your child. I don't know why I doubted, Lord. Perhaps I simply couldn't comprehend Your love. Each time I was close to accepting You, I held back, unsure of Your desire to come into my heart.

Thank You for my friend who explained the way of salvation to me. Thank You for her letting me know faith wasn't something I could conjure up for myself. It could come only from You. She told me faith was like a grain of mustard seed—so tiny but one that can grow into a plant four to six feet tall. What I needed to do was exercise enough faith to invite You in. Now I realize You were waiting for me all along.

When I did this, the floodgates of Your blessings opened. In no time, my minuscule mustard seed–sized faith blossomed and grew beyond measure! Thank You, Lord, for the way I heard about Your wonderful love for me; for showing me in Your Bible how You died for my sins to save me; and for talking to my heart. Without a doubt, I am saved by grace through You—Jesus Christ, my Lord. I praise Your name! For now I belong to You.

> So then faith comes by hearing,
> and hearing by the word of God.

ROMANS 10:17 NKJV

> [Jesus said,] "Your faith has saved you. Go in peace."

LUKE 7:50 NKJV

Mercy Received and Given

I will bless You, O Lord, for Your mercy. I will remember all You do. Praise You for Your forgiveness. Thank You for healing my body, mind, and soul.

I'm grateful for the way You shower me with Your kindness. When I am weary, You strengthen me. When I am oppressed, You console me.

I'm continually humbled by how merciful and gracious You are. When I struggle and try to do things right, You are patient and understanding. How amazing is the way I can come to You and enjoy Your presence. How marvelous is Your mercy. You have removed my sins and cast them as far as the east is from the west. You love me like an upright parent cherishes a little child.

Your kindness is everlasting. Your truth shall endure throughout my future generations. Because I follow You, I look forward to You keeping Your righteous hand upon my children's children. How I thank You for doing this, for I have dedicated them to You. In the same way I receive mercy from You, let me give compassion to others. Teach me to be quick to forgive, to look beyond the faults and see each need.

Thank You for Your mercy and for teaching me to be merciful.

But from everlasting to everlasting
the LORD's love is with those who fear him,
and his righteousness with their children's children—
with those who keep his covenant
and remember to obey his precepts.

PSALM 103:17–18 NIV

JANUARY 19

Fully Committed to You

I recall when You repeatedly spoke to my heart, Lord, asking me to make You Lord of my life. Although I had accepted You when I was a child, I knew I hadn't totally committed my all to You. I often tried riding the fence between right and wrong. I wanted to follow the things of this world and still claim to be a Christian.

Thank You for those who showed me that being a halfhearted Christian was robbing me of a victorious life with You. Oh, how much I would have missed had I not given You my all.

At last, I let go of my past, my hurts, my bad habits, my wants. When I did, You forgave and healed me. Then You helped me grow closer to You. Step-by-step, my desires, dreams, and goals changed. I started seeing life through Your eyes.

Things of this world faded in light of Your splendor and holiness. Tinsel and glittering lights were replaced with the brilliance of Your awesome presence. It became a new way, filled with love, forgiveness, uprightness, hope, and purpose.

Hold on to my heartstrings each day, Lord, so I will never return to such an existence as before You saved me. Fill me to the brim with Your wisdom and steadfastness. May my life always be fully committed to You.

Therefore be imitators of God as [His] dear children.
And walk in love, as Christ also has loved us
and given Himself for us,
an offering and a sacrifice to God
for a sweet-smelling aroma.

EPHESIANS 5:1–2 NKJV

You Are the Strength of My Life

When my friend asked You into his heart, I think Your angels burst into chorus. Thank You for giving him a new birthday, a spiritual one in accepting You. Thank You for giving me new life, as well. Doing good doesn't gain Your favor. It's simply loving You, because You forgave our sins and showed us a better way.

Once, my life was soiled and distorted. Now I am made clean, without a spot or wrinkle. I love You so much, Lord. How can any of us remain pure in Your eyes?

My little child, always remember I am the Way. I will give you the strength you need each day. Keep reading My Word and heeding its lessons. They will guide you along the right path. Think about them. Store them in your mind and heart so you won't sin against Me. Each time you seek Me you shall find Me. Abide in Me, and I shall abide in you.

Because I delight in You, O Lord, I will follow Your teachings. I will trust in Your promises day and night. They are more valuable to me than silver and gold. In all my ways I will acknowledge You. Thank You for being my Savior, for renewing my faith and staying power each day. Thank You for being with my friend, too.

The LORD is my light and my salvation—
whom shall I fear?
The LORD is the stronghold of my life—
of whom shall I be afraid?

PSALM 27:1 NIV

Thank You for My Baptism

Father, what an awesome experience it must have been for those who witnessed Your Son, Jesus, being baptized. When I first read about it, I felt as though I were there. I wondered why someone so holy needed to be baptized. Jesus never had to repent of any personal sins. Still, He set the example for me.

I wish I could have seen the Savior rise from the water and witnessed Your Holy Spirit descend like a dove and settle on Him. I wish I could have heard Your words thunder, *"This is My beloved Son, in whom I am well pleased."*

After learning this, I realized I must be baptized. I wanted to tell my friends and loved ones my sinful life had died—how You washed my heart clean and flung my wrongs into the deepest sea.

I'll never forget my first step into the baptistery water, Father. I glanced at the congregation and saw those who had faithfully taught me of Your love. When asked if I loved You, I gave an enthusiastic yes. Then into the water and up I came. I felt Your dovelike holy presence settle upon me. From that time on, I have never been the same.

Thank You for the example of Jesus and for the privilege of following Him.

As soon as Jesus was baptized,
he went up out of the water.
At that moment heaven was opened,
and he saw the Spirit of God descending
like a dove and lighting on him.
And a voice from heaven said,
"This is my Son, whom I love;
with him I am well pleased."

MATTHEW 3:16–17 NIV

I Will Serve You

Lord Jesus, I know You grieved as You saw my life heading for sin and destruction. How oblivious I was of Your offer to make me Your child. Then You began speaking to me over and over to turn from my wrongdoing and choose life, abundant and free. Once I heard the way of salvation, I had to make a choice. Would I serve and obey You or become a slave to sin?

I looked around me at the glorious things You created—the earth and sky, the sun and moon, the mountains, trees, and valleys. How could such things accidentally have fallen into place and synchronized so perfectly?

How heavily it weighed upon my heart when You made known that the wages of sin are eternal death. But Your free gift is eternal life through You, my Lord Jesus Christ. All I needed to do was trust You, God's Son, to save me and make me one of Your own.

Now I realize no one can serve two masters. I must either love or hate You. Or I must love or hate the devil. I choose You, Lord! It is You I shall follow and serve all the days of my life.

[Jesus said,] "No one can serve two masters;
for either he will hate the one and love the other,
or else he will be loyal to the one and despise the other.
You cannot serve God and mammon [riches]."

MATTHEW 6:24 NKJV

[God said,] "Choose life, that both you and your descendants
may live; that you may love the LORD your God,
that you may obey His voice, and that you may cling to Him,
for He is your life and the length of your days."

DEUTERONOMY 30:19–20 NKJV

Power beyond Measure

It doesn't seem long ago, Lord, when Bob and I stood in a southern Washington park near the Toutle River and watched Mount St. Helens blow its top. I felt small to see plumes of ash erupt and burst into the sky, filling my vision. Like mighty cotton balls, they rolled toward the valley. Hot mud rumbled down the river, taking out everything in its path. The deadly flow caused huge trees to flatten like miniature dominoes.

Reality set in, then fear. Thank You for how Bob and I barely made it over the bridge so we could return home. Later, we found the eruption had displayed more power than an atomic bomb. Ash had pushed high enough to leave the atmosphere, completely circling the world.

Each time I wonder how much power You have to solve my little problems, I realize Your measureless capabilities are far greater than any earthly force. Your power freed me from sin. No matter the circumstances, Lord, You are my refuge, my strength. You are always here to help me in good times and in trouble. Because of this, I won't be afraid.

When the earth shakes and mountains swell and slide into the sea; when turbulent waters thunder, destroying all in their paths, You are still in charge. Your powerful hands created it all. You created and rescued me.

> *The LORD of hosts is with us;*
> *The God of Jacob is our refuge. . . .*
> *Be still, and know that I am God.*
>
> PSALM 46:7, 10 NKJV

My Dearest Friend

What silly games I played, running, trying to hide from You, Lord. It makes me think of when my children were small, learning to play hide-and-seek in our living room. One counted while the other hid. Our younger son thought he couldn't be found if his head was out of sight.

"You can't find me," his diminutive voice sang.

All the while we could see his little body sticking out from behind a couch or coffee table. It was so amusing, Lord. In the same way, I once thought I could hide from You.

Like the prodigal son, I was determined to do things my way. I had no idea what it meant to have You as my Friend. No matter where I strayed or tried to hide, You followed me, calling me to come back to You.

Now I have come to You and am set apart. You, Lord, are my dearest Friend. How thankful I am that You love me and have accepted me as Your own.

I finally see what real love and friendship are: not love the world talks about, but a selfless, unconditional love—a holy *agape* love, coming from You.

Thank You for becoming my dearest Friend. Now we can walk and talk and listen to one another throughout each day.

[Jesus said,]
"And you are my friends if you obey me."

JOHN 15:14 TLB

Everyday Friend

Thank You, dear Father, for being my Friend every hour of every day. I praise You for Your constant presence, for the way You walk with me and talk to my heart.

When I get so involved that I'm not aware of Your presence, thank You for still being near. Loving. Helping. Protecting. Guiding.

I love You so much, more than I can even express. How grateful I am for Your becoming my heavenly Father and being with me all the time, in any circumstances.

My little child, I am always here with you. My love and friendship are unconditional and never failing. I love you with an everlasting love.

In good times, I rejoice with you. In your trials, I hurt for you and comfort you as a little one is consoled by his mother.

When you are hungry, I feed you. When you are thirsty, I give you a drink from My vast well of living water. When you are frightened and confused, I am here to encourage and lead you. I will never abandon or forsake you during your storms of life. Each time you call on Me, I am here, in your heart. I am your Friend, now and forever.

> *"Fear not, for I am with you;*
> *Be not dismayed, for I am your God.*
> *I will strengthen you,*
> *Yes, I will help you,*
> *I will uphold you with My righteous right hand."*

ISAIAH 41:10 NKJV

In You I Believe

Today I prayed with someone and showed him how to receive You. It was so exciting. I felt like I was helping to bring a new life into this world. I could almost hear Your angels singing in celebration over one more soul coming to You. Thank You, Lord Jesus, for allowing me to be part of such a marvelous event. How I praise You for talking to my friend's heart and gently helping him to trust in You. I'm thrilled to see the joy and peace in his face now that he knows You as his Savior.

It doesn't seem that long ago since I, too, took my first tiny step of faith and accepted You as my personal Savior. What a difference it has made for me. I can't imagine ever going through life without You. Receiving You was like taking a breath of fresh, cleansing air. After I did, I felt remarkably clean through and through. Because I took this step of faith, You made a new life for me, a life filled with joyfulness and harmony. Each day I'm getting to know and trust You more. Now we share sweet communion. You are my Savior, my all. Thank You, Lord, for helping me believe in You.

"Believe in the Lord Jesus,
and you will be saved."

ACTS 16:31 NIV

Your Family

Thank You for adopting me into Your family, Father. Along with my earthly lineage, You have made me a part of the heritage of God.

Like several of my friends who have chosen to adopt and love their children, I realize You also have done this with me. Now I have a relationship with You—and am related to You, as well. This is beyond my scope. How glorious. How awesome!

What a blessing it is to be somewhere and recognize another who loves You, because of Your Spirit's reflection in his or her life. When this happens, it never ceases to fill me with awe. Brothers and sisters in the Lord, they say. What a marvelous inheritance I've gained in my new family of God. Thank You for the many ways we learn to care. May we always treat one another kindly, with patience and love.

Just like with my family from birth, there may be times of disappointment and hurt. When these times come, I pray for direction, forgiveness, and healing. Even though I'm a part of Your family, I know we still struggle with shortcomings. Help me to still reflect Your pure, unwavering love.

Thank You for being the Head of my Christian family and being the source of my comfort and strength.

> *But to all who received him,*
> *he gave the right to become children of God.*
> *All they needed to do was to trust him to save them.*
> *All those who believe this are reborn!—*
> *not a physical rebirth resulting from*
> *human passion or plan—*
> *but from the will of God.*
>
> JOHN 1:12–13 TLB

A Brand-New Life

I am continually filled with wonder when I think of my brand-new life with You, Lord. In receiving You, I have been able to experience all You give me. How I praise You for this.

Now You call me by name. You have made me Your own. Each time I pass through difficult waters, I know I will not be swept away; for You are with me, holding my hand. When I go through fiery trials, You walk before me as my Shield and Defender.

You are my Lord, my God—the Holy One who rules over all. You created me in Your image. You made me for Your glory. To You I give honor and adoration and praise. To You I give the whole of my life.

I'm grateful for the way You show me how to put the past behind and press forward into the new life You now provide. I wonder what lies ahead. I look forward with great anticipation as we walk life's road together.

Because you are my Lord, I will trust everything to You. Help me remember to depend not only on my own understanding. I will acknowledge You and follow as You direct my paths.

"Do not remember the former things,
Nor consider the things of old.
Behold, I will do a new thing,
Now it shall spring forth;
Shall you not know it?
I will even make a road in the wilderness
And rivers in the desert."

ISAIAH 43:18–19 NKJV

Abundant Life through You

I'm here again with another question, Father. What does it mean to have life more abundantly? How can You perceive my every want and need? Do You know what is best for me even better than I do? I feel unworthy to receive all Your blessings.

You have searched me and know me so well. You notice me when I lie down and when I awaken. You understand my every thought. You care about my every need and longing.

I praise You for putting a protective hedge around me in times of uncertainty and danger. I'm grateful for how Your sure hand is holding mine, for how You provide me with Your wisdom and quick thinking. All You give is too wonderful for me to fathom. I praise You, Lord, for Your constant, tender care.

Thank You for the material comforts You provide. I'm starting to realize, after all, that there is more to abundant life than money and possessions. It includes unselfish love and caring, victory over temptation and trials—the ability to discern and make right decisions.

Help me listen to You so I can avoid self-made problems and experience Your blessings and calmness of mind. Thank You, Father, for the abundant life You provide and for placing me in the center of Your care.

[Jesus said,]
"My purpose is to give life in all its fullness."

JOHN 10:10 TLB

Thank You for Receiving Me

I thank You, Lord Jesus, that along with my receiving You as my Savior, You took me into Your arms and received *me* as Your own. I know You loved me before I was ever born. I can't comprehend how You prayed for me in the Garden of Gethsemane, knowing full well You were about to die for my sins.

I read in my Bible that before You died, no one could come directly to Your Father except chosen priests. In the temple, there was a Holy of Holies, with a huge, thick curtain keeping those who loved the heavenly Father from coming directly into His presence. It was because they weren't free from sin. When You died on the cross, that huge, thick curtain (or veil) mysteriously split from top to bottom! Those who accepted You as their Savior were no longer separated from the holy presence of the Father. For You sacrificed Yourself on the cross and washed away with Your blood the sins of those who accepted You.

Because You died for me and I asked You into my heart, I can come to You anytime, anywhere, and be welcomed into Your presence. Thank You, Lord, for receiving me as Your child.

Therefore, since we have a great high priest
who has gone through the heavens,
Jesus the Son of God,
let us hold firmly to the faith we profess. . . .
Let us then approach the throne of grace with confidence,
so that we may receive mercy and
find grace to help us in our time of need.

HEBREWS 4:14, 16 NIV

What a Difference You Have Made

I knew You had made a huge difference in my life, Lord; but I never realized how much until one of our visits with my parents. They decided to dig out some old home movies. I was shocked to see my old self. The way I felt about things back then showed all over my face. It was difficult to believe I was that person. Now I'm no longer the same, thanks to Your love.

I remember feeling I could never measure up to the rules and regulations of a Christian, so why try? Now I enjoy grace and truth, provided through You, Lord Jesus. I obey You because I love You with all my heart, soul, and strength.

How awesome the way mercy and truth met the moment I accepted You as my Savior. An indescribable relief filled me. You, O Lord, through Your loving-kindness, have replaced my hopelessness with joy, my defeat with triumph over sin!

Yes, I sinned and fell short of Your glory. But I'm thankful that You now declare me "not guilty" because I received You. I'm grateful that old person is gone forever, never to return. Thank You for the difference You have made in my life.

And of His fullness we have all received,
and grace for grace.
For the law was given through Moses,
but grace and truth came through Jesus Christ.

JOHN 1:16–17 NKJV

to Honor You

Who Can Compare to You?

How wonderful You are, my God. How awesome it is to come into Your presence. I worship You with joyfulness and thanksgiving, for I know You are my Lord, my God. You are the Creator of everything. You wrapped Your fingers around the mountains and formed their highest points. You reached down and dipped Your hand into the depths of the earth. You scooped out huge cavities and filled them with oceans, lakes, and rivers. You skillfully shaped the dry ground.

You took the care to plan my distinct being, before I was even formed in my mother's womb. With a puff of breath and a thump to my chest, You set my heart and lungs into motion. You made me the person I am. Thank You for allowing me to be Your child and for being my heavenly Father.

Who can compare to You, my God? There is no other so great. You are all-knowing, forever loving. Your mercy to me shall endure forever, even beyond my earthly life! Your indisputable love shall last throughout future generations. Forever, You shall be exalted among the nations. Forever, You shall be exalted over the earth!

I come to You and bow down, for You are my Lord, my Maker. You, Lord, are the true God. There is no other who can compare to You.

O LORD God Almighty, who is like you?
You are mighty, O LORD,
and your faithfulness surrounds you.

PSALM 89:8 NIV

You Surpass All Else

Whom can I call, my Lord, besides You? You surpass everyone, everything in heaven, and all the galaxies, my God. You matter most, for You are my strength and my portion. You are my source of food and drink. You are my Lord and Savior forever! When I despair, You lift me up. You are my greatest joy. How lovingly You watch over me as Your own. In You rests my spiritual inheritance. In You I place my every hope.

O holy God, You exceed all else. How immense and powerful and awe-inspiring You are! Before You, there was no other. No one shall come after You; for You, Lord, are the Beginning and the End. You and You alone are Lord over all. Aside from You, I have no origin.

Before the ancient days, You were there. Before heaven and earth, You were, You are, and You ever shall be. When You speak, Your will comes to pass. No one else can reverse it; for You are Creator and Ruler over everything. Your mouth declares all truthfulness. Your never-ending words cannot be rescinded.

Before You every knee shall bow, and every tongue shall confess, "In the LORD alone are righteousness and strength" (Isaiah 45:24 NIV). You alone, O God, surpass all else!

Because Your lovingkindness is better than life,
My lips shall praise You. Thus I will bless You.

PSALM 63:3–4 NKJV

I Belong to You

Thank You, Father, for allowing me to belong to You. I praise You for adopting me as Your own. Since I accepted Your Son, Jesus, as my Savior, I am no longer separated from Your holy family. I desire to honor You all the days of my life and cling to You as a branch does to the vine. You are my Vine, and I am one of Your branches. It is only in being grafted to You that I'm able to accomplish anything of eternal value. I can do whatever You ask of me through You, Jesus Christ, my Lord.

Because You took me in as Your own, I will praise You from my inmost being. With all my heart, I give honor to You. Thank You for loving me as the apple of Your eye— for hiding me in Your strong arms and protecting me from wrong. I will never forget Your many blessings.

Thank You for Your forgiveness. When I come to You, You pump life into me the same way subsistence goes from the vine to the branches. I praise You for making Your ways known and showering me with Your compassion and graciousness. I am Your child and You are my heavenly Father. With every fiber of my being, I give honor to You.

Keep me as the apple of Your eye;
Hide me under the shadow of Your wings.

PSALM 17:8 NKJV

Let My Thoughts Honor You

When the temptations and confusion of this world press around me, Lord, let my thoughts be focused on what pleases You. May my mind meditate on Your teachings throughout my day and night. Let me drink in Your priceless words of Scripture. Hide them in my memory bank, I pray, so I may apply them to my daily life. Grant me strength and guidance through Your Holy Spirit, to honor You in what I watch, read, and observe. May all of this be delightful and pleasing to You.

When the dry winds of stress flurry around me, I will not be consumed, for my spiritual roots sink deeply in You. With Your help, my leaves shall not wither. They shall produce the priceless fruits of Your Spirit: unselfish love, joyfulness, harmony, patience, kindness, goodness, faithfulness, sensitivity, and self-control.

I will think on all Your marvelous works and reflect on the mighty things You do, for Your ways, O God, are holy. I marvel at how You display Your astounding power. I treasure the recollections of the many instances You have placed Your blessings upon me.

Let me meditate on You every day. Guide my decisions. May each one bring respect to You. Guide my mind and heart, I pray. In all my ways, I want to honor You with pure, obedient thoughts, words, and deeds.

> *But his delight is in the law of the LORD,*
> *And in His law he meditates day and night.*

PSALM 1:2 NKJV

My Heart Is Your Home

Oh, how I praise You, Lord, for entering my heart and making my soul Your dwelling place. It goes beyond my comprehension. I praise You for showering me with Your loving-kindness. You looked beyond my sins and saw my needs. When I bowed in repentance before You, You washed my heart clean and made me as pure as fresh snow.

Welcome to my heart, Your home, dear Lord. May it honor You in every way. Wherever I go, whatever I say or do, I know You are with me—fully aware of my every move. When I start to go the wrong way and You nudge me, give me strength to turn around and leave. My heart is Your home, Lord. May no person or thing be allowed through its door unless it is honorable to You.

Search the corners of my heart so it remains a holy place for You to dwell. Help me rid myself of unpleasant dust bunnies hidden from human eyes. Fill the corners with Your loving, holy presence. With my whole heart I seek You so I won't wander from Your way. I will treasure Your wise words and hold them within me so I will not sin against You. I pray for You to always grant me Your presence in my heart, Your home.

Create in me a new, clean heart, O God,
filled with clean thoughts and right desires.

PSALM 51:10 TLB

FEBRUARY 6

At Night, I Think of You

It's the end of a long day, Father. There have been struggles, but You were there with me all day long. Though my body aches from weariness, my heart feels glad to come to You in prayer. Ah, sweet rest, dear Lord. My head sinks into the pillow. How magnificent Your watchful presence is. Thank You for the way Your Holy Spirit surrounds me. Songs of praise fill my mind. My body relaxes. My heart is fixed on You.

How wonderful are all Your promises to love and care for me. How much more wonderful are the ways You have kept Your word. My mind is filled with everything I know about You. Thank You for watching over me while I sleep. In the night shadows, I lift my heart in adoration. You are my strength. You are the One who rejuvenates me while I rest.

My soul clings to You while You hold me close to You throughout the night. I commit my thoughts, even my dreams, into Your care. Each worry I place at Your feet. Each request I leave in Your sure care. In all my meditations I will honor You. For You are holy. Holy. Holy are You, O my God.

Good night, dear Lord. I love You. Thank You for loving me.

By day the LORD directs his love,
at night his song is with me—
a prayer to the God of my life.

PSALM 42:8 NIV

My Mind Turns to You in the Morn

Good morning, Lord. Thank You for last night's rest and providing me with a fresh start today. Thank You for hearing my prayers and acknowledging my deepest concerns. I love this time when all is quiet—when I hear You speak to my heart and pay heed to the whispers from my lips. How grateful I am to be able to lay my requests before You and wait in trusting expectation for Your will.

Thank You for allowing me to come into Your presence. I bow before You in reverence. Lead me in Your ways of righteousness. Throughout my day, I will take refuge in Your counsel and be glad, for Your wisdom is greater than any other. I shall keep You foremost in my thoughts and give You the sacrifice of my will. In all things, I exalt Your name.

With each task I seek to accomplish, each decision I must make, I will reflect and honor You, O Lord. You are my strength, my Shield, my Rock, and my Defender. I praise You for going before me—for being at my right hand and my left, before and behind me. Each time I face uncertainties, thank You for straightening my path.

Praise You, Lord, for being within my mind and heart.

O LORD, in the morning thou dost hear my voice;
in the morning I prepare a sacrifice for thee, and watch.

PSALM 5:3 RSV

My Lips Give You Honor

May my prayers give You honor, dear Lord. May what I say to others make You glad. Guard my tongue so gossip and cutting remarks are replaced with words that soothe and heal. Help me speak the truth. Help me seek answers, instead of escapes from problems. I will have no part of cursing or tainted language. Instead, I look to You for words of innocence, purity, and caution—filled with life and health.

You are holy, Lord. You are the essence of life and all that is good. In You I find hope, a purpose to do right, and words filled with exultation. My heart is full of gratitude. I praise Your holy name. Your righteousness and saving grace are measureless. Wherever I go, I want to tell others how wonderful You are. Over and over You put a new song of praise in my mouth. Because of this, others hear and come to You. How awesome! How marvelous, the way Your Spirit works!

How delightful are the words from Your Bible. Whenever I speak them and pay homage to You, they are sweeter than honey to my lips. Accept my words of adoration, O Lord. Continue to teach me Your ways. Let all I say give honor to You.

> *My mouth is filled with your praise,*
> *declaring your splendor all day long.*
>
> PSALM 71:8 NIV

Harmonizing Praise

Praise You, O Lord. I feel Your love stay within me. Like a beautiful melody coming full circle, our love and communication weave back and forth between us. Holy, holy, holy are You, Lord. I'm blessed to receive You and give You praise. How fulfilling to talk things over—You and I. You tune my heart. I strike a chord. You give me words. I lift them back to You in honor and gratitude—praise in perfect harmony.

You are my one true God. You created everything and worked it all together. You wrought heaven and earth. Perhaps the angels sang as You made it all. You caused everything to have life. You brought me into this world. You heard my first cry. Though no one else could understand my squall of protest, You did; for You know me inside out.

From the moment I burst into this world, You hummed a soothing lullaby only I could hear. All through my years, I have heard You strike the chords in my heart and give me reason to love and praise You. You, dear Lord, have taken good and bad times and mixed them skillfully together for good with Your loving hand. You, my Author and Composer, have written our harmonizing songs of praise.

We love Him because He first loved us.

1 JOHN 4:19 NKJV

My Eyes Behold Your Splendor

It's barely daylight, Father. I can hear the wind whistling about and rain pelting the roof. I look out the window and marvel. Tall pine and fir trees are silhouetted against a slate gray sky. Sunlight rays break through sheets of rain. They weave in and out among huge tree trunks, streaking their amber reflections back toward heaven. Your colossal chariots of clouds glide on wings of the winds. The sun's yellow glow disappears above the gray umbrella as quickly as it came. Winds seem to whisper messages that You made it all. I can no longer see the sun but am aware it is there. Although I can't see You, I know You are here, as well. You are closer than the air I breathe. You fill my heart, my entire being.

You caused brilliant purple and white mountains to jut upward. Precarious peaks give You glory. Waterfalls crash to rivers below. Rivers work their ways toward the ocean, as though they have a life and will of their own. Riotous ocean waves swell and ebb in perfect timing. Rubbery-skinned whales frolic in mystifying indigo depths. Waterways flow into gentle streams, where animals and birds come to drink. What my eyes behold fills me with mind-boggling ecstasy. I praise You, Father, for You made it all.

> *O Jehovah, how manifold are thy works!*
> *In wisdom hast thou made them all:*
> *The earth is full of thy riches.*
> *Yonder is the sea, great and wide,*
> *Wherein are things creeping innumerable,*
> *Both small and great beasts.*
> *There go the ships;*
> *There is leviathan,*
> *whom thou hast formed to play therein.*

PSALM 104:24–26 ASV

I Give You Glory

With all my heart, I praise You. With every fiber of my being, I give You glory. Each morning, I thank You for being so good to me. Your loving-kindness is better than life itself. Each evening, I rejoice in Your remaining near. I pray that every living thing will give You glory. May my body, mind, and soul be holy and glorify You. When I think of the many things You do for me, there is so little I can do in return. No matter what comes my way, I will praise and glorify You.

Worthy are You, O Lamb of God. Worthy are You to receive power and riches and wisdom and strength and honor and glory. Even the heavens declare Your glory. Your name is majestic throughout the galaxies and over all the earth. Young and elderly sing Your praises. Only You are glorious and mighty enough to triumph over wrong.

Who am I that You are mindful of me? Am I only a speck of dust in Your vast creation? What of my loved ones? Do You care about them? And their children and grandchildren? I know You care, for You died on the cross to save all who believe in You.

I give You glory and adulation and praise, Lord. Through all my days, I will honor You.

Sing to the Lord, all the earth! Sing of his glorious name!
Tell the world how wonderful he is.
How awe-inspiring are your deeds, O God!
How great your power!

PSALM 66:1–3 TLB

Let My Memories Honor You

Something happened today that triggered some terrible memories, Lord. Before I knew it, my mind flooded with anxiety, hurt, and bitterness. Then You brought words of comfort to mind. Although the time I recalled was terrible, You helped me commit to memory the incredible way You rescued victory from defeat.

In the midst of life's trials, let me honor You with the memories of Your love and compassion. I praise You that You are there for me in all circumstances. Let me bless You, O Lord, with my memories. May I always consider the marvelous benefits You have given me. Thank You for how You forgave my iniquities and saved me from a life of waste and self-destruction. Let me never forget the many times You have crowned me with Your tender mercies and loving compassion.

When things were tough financially, You provided for my needs. During times of illness, You helped me get well and renewed my strength. How grateful I am for the way You showed me kindness and patience when I made unwise decisions. Thank You for Your forgiveness and for helping me start over. How grateful I feel for the ways You have guided me through situations and made my faith stronger because of them. How blessed I am, Lord, for treasured memories provided by You.

> *I bless the holy name of God with all my heart.*
> *Yes, I will bless the Lord and not forget*
> *the glorious things he does for me.*
> *He forgives all my sins. He heals me.*
> *He ransoms me from hell.*
> *He surrounds me with lovingkindness and tender mercies.*
> *He fills my life with good things!*
>
> PSALM 103:1–5 TLB

I Honor You in Worship

My heart races as I seat myself in Your sanctuary. I feel like I came through the church doors with roller skates on! Family and church responsibilities fill my thoughts. Are my clothing and hair all right? Here comes my sweet friend.

The organ is playing the prelude. I want to bow my head and think of You. Help me, Lord. Thank You for giving me the loving strength to greet my friend, offer her a seat by me, and tell her I'll visit later. I want to honor You with my worship, Lord. Quiet my heart and mind. Let me think of You. Ah, yes. Now I sense Your peace.

How lovely is Your sanctuary, O Lord. How blessed it is to meet You here. After a hectic, trying week, my soul yearns to worship You here. Help me forget about looking or feeling important. Feed my hungry soul, I pray.

Forgive me, Lord, for my distracted thoughts. I'm here to seek You and be Your servant. Better is this day in Your house of praise than a thousand anywhere else. I will bless You now as I come into Your presence. More than anything, I want to worship and honor You.

O Lord, you have freed me from my bonds
and I will serve you forever.
I will worship you
and offer you a sacrifice of thanksgiving.

PSALM 116:16–17 TLB

FEBRUARY 14

I Honor You with My Love

I love You so much, Lord. Yet no matter how great my love, it can't compare to the love You give me. I want to honor You with my love. Show me how to care for others with the same unselfish kindness You give me. Fill me with Your Holy Spirit. Use me to give them Your love. As You direct my life, You generate my sensitivity.

You *are* love, O Lord. As I live in You, I learn to care more for others; for You live in me. I feel the warm compassion of Your Holy Spirit within me everywhere I go. I love You because You first loved me. I want to honor You by doing whatever You ask and not expect any recognition in return. Because You died for me, You have helped me give up my old selfish life I once had. Now it is centered on the things that honor and please You. Help me remember to care for others as much as You do for me. Grant me enough love to look beyond the faults and see the needs— in the same way You did mine. Instead of being selfish, I want to become generous. Instead of being bitter, I want to show compassion. I want to revere You, Lord, and love the same way You do.

> *So you see, our love for him comes*
> *as a result of his loving us first.*

> 1 JOHN 4:19 TLB

I Will Listen and Honor You

This is a cold winter night, Lord. Layered heavy blankets of snow have fallen outside without making a sound. Our teakettle whistles, blending its cheerful noise with soft, whooshing air from the furnace. My husband sings praises to You while doing the dinner dishes. "Rest," he told me. How sweet. How thoughtful he is.

I lean back in my chair and listen to the purr of our kitty curled up on my lap. I think of the day before, when our grown sons, daughters, and grandchildren filled our home with fun and laughter. The words "I love you" gently rang through the house before they all left. What beautiful music it always is to my ears. It's the music of caring, security, and love. Thank You for reminding me to slow down and listen.

I love these sounds, Lord. But I love even more the words that come from You. They are filled with unlimited perception and consideration, guiding me to do right. They show me what to say to the discouraged and weary and to those who need to know You.

Your words are powerful, cutting through falsehood to truth—sharper than a two-edged sword. No wonder Your Bible is called the sword of the Spirit. Help me listen and apply Your words to my heart. I want to honor You in all I hear and do and say.

My son [and daughter], if you receive my words,
And treasure my commands within you,
So that you incline your ear to wisdom,
And apply your heart to understanding. . .
Then you will understand the fear of the LORD,
And find the knowledge of God.

PROVERBS 2:1–2, 5 NKJV

I Honor You with My Hands

There's a special event approaching in our church. People from miles around will be coming. It will take a lot of work to get our little building ready. I felt tired just thinking about it. Still, You nudged me to help, so here I am at the workday. I'll do what I can, Lord, with willing hands. Help the few of us who turned out to work swiftly and efficiently. Multiply our efforts, I pray. Help us work together with glad hearts.

I can't believe it, Lord. More people are arriving to help. As we work, visit, sing together, and share our lunches, our load lightens. It's actually kind of fun. Thank You for our many hands volunteering as one.

The special event turned out to be a great blessing, Lord. Now, during the cleanup, tired but willing hands pitch in again. Amid dish-soap bubbles, I hear the hum of vacuuming and the clanging of folding chairs; and I sense Your warm approval.

I want to honor You in prayer and lift my hands in praise. I want to sing Your praises and clap my hands with joy. I also want to honor You by helping others. Let my hands do much and bring glory and honor to You.

*Praise the LORD, all you servants of the LORD
who minister by night in the house of the LORD.
Lift up your hands in the sanctuary and praise the LORD.*

PSALM 134:1–2 NIV

*And as for you, brothers [and sisters],
never tire of doing what is right.*

2 THESSALONIANS 3:13 NIV

My Feet Shall Honor You

It doesn't seem that long ago, Lord, when our little church prepared for children's Vacation Bible School. Our handful of workers decided to walk door-to-door in the neighborhood, inviting children to come. It was scary, Lord. We wondered what kind of reception we would receive. I'm glad we remembered to unite in prayer before we left. It was then that You gave us courage, strength, and the right words to say.

My most precious memory is of eighty-year-old Jessie. Though crippled with arthritis, she came along with us. She kept a smile on her face all the time. At the end of the day, she said she had tired feet but a warm heart. Thank You, Lord, for Jessie and others like her. Thank You for her willingness to teach a class. Several children gave their hearts to You through that Bible school.

Use my tired feet to honor You, dear Lord. Grant me good sense, and guard my paths as I serve You. As You direct my steps, may You take delight in each one I take. Make my feet as beautiful as Jessie's. Should I lose my focus and stumble, help me up and lead me on, I pray. Lay out Your map, and go before me so I can follow. Wherever You lead, may I bring glory and honor to You.

"How beautiful are the feet of those who
preach the Gospel of peace with God
and bring glad tidings of good things."
In other words,
how welcome are those who
come preaching God's Good News!

ROMANS 10:15 TLB

You Are All-Knowing

I just turned off the news, Father. I couldn't stand to watch it any longer. Life is filled with uncertainties in times like these. We learn of wars; rumors of wars; financial struggles and famine; storms, volcano eruptions, and earthquakes; crime and hatred. I realize this is history repeating itself, but it's still frightening. What will happen to this beloved world I hold so dear? What about my loved ones?

Thank You for urging me to turn off the news and turn in Your Bible to Your *good* news. None of these things we face as individuals or as a struggling nation and world are unfamiliar to You, Father. You are all-knowing. Only You have the answers to what we are going through. You are the One we can depend on to bring us through each crisis. In my darkest of times, You chase away the night and bring out the dawn and hope for the future.

I praise You, Father, for You know everything. You even understand and love individual hearts of humankind all around the world. I take comfort and thank You that You are always in control and are watching over and guiding us in times like these.

> *"Cease striving and know that I am God;*
> *I will be exalted among the nations,*
> *I will be exalted in the earth."*
> *The LORD of hosts is with us;*
> *The God of Jacob is our stronghold.*

PSALM 46:10–11 NASB

My Endeavors Honor You

I used to have lofty dreams and goals of my own desire. No matter how hard I tried, things didn't turn out right. That was before I met You and asked You to become Lord of my life.

When I gave everything to You, including my endeavors, my life changed. Now I desire what is pleasing to You. I dream the dreams and set the goals You and I talk about together. I don't want to go off on a tangent anymore. Now I set goals in compliance with Your will. You know me well, Lord; and You recognize what is best for me. I praise You for giving me a life filled with peace, joy, and fulfillment.

In all these things, I delight in You. To You I commit my ways. May my greatest endeavor be to love others as You love me. Each day I pray for You to help me make righteous choices so I can glorify You. I don't feel frustrated when others succeed, and I'm not leaping over giant buildings! You have a plan for me. No longer do I stew in anger over some who carry out wicked schemes. Instead, I stand and wait in eager anticipation of *Your* plans! With all my strength, through all my days, let my endeavors honor You.

Commit everything you do to the Lord.
Trust him to help you do it and he will.
Your innocence will be clear to everyone.
He will vindicate you with the blazing light of justice
shining down as from the noonday sun.

PSALM 37:5–6 TLB

FEBRUARY 20

Our Friendship

Here I am again. It's that special time I get to talk with You—just You and me, Lord. I feel as though I'm sitting at Your feet, telling You all about my day. Thank You for being my dearest Friend.

Those close to me are more precious than gold. But You, Lord, are priceless. I love You and want to honor You with my friendship. When I felt others didn't care, You understood and loved me. You recognized worth in me and developed my abilities. I love how we walk and talk together. I tell You my deepest secrets. You take time to listen. Thank You for never being too busy for me. Each day You unfold new lessons and help me mature. In turn, I listen to You and learn.

Thank You for looking for the best in me, Lord. When I feel I lack beauty, You make me lovely inside. When I struggle and fail, You help bridge the gap.

Now You speak to my heart. I know Your voice. I stop and listen. I trust in You and will do whatever You ask, for You are my Friend and know what is best. In this quiet time, I enjoy the fellowship we have with one another and want to honor You.

> *I am listening carefully to all the Lord is saying—*
> *for he speaks peace to his people,*
> *his saints [and to me].*

PSALM 85:8 TLB

The Calling

It started as a nudge, when I first felt You calling me. It was so subtle, I barely noticed. Still, You kept beckoning. You had a plan of what You wanted me to do for You. You gradually placed things in my mind and gave me a dream. I wondered if (or how) it would fit into my future. Little did I realize that when You call someone, You have Your own ways and timing to make it happen. Long before I became aware of Your bidding, You were preparing me.

You soon gave me a burning desire to follow Your lead. It was constantly in my heart and mind. How could it come about? I trusted You and felt complete peace. There is no element of time with You, Lord, and no challenges are too difficult.

The day came when You showed me how to answer Your call. I wanted to follow, step-by-step. It was hard, Lord, but You helped and led me. Your mission for me still isn't easy, and I ask for Your help. You grant me the strength and wisdom I need. Perhaps I'll never know the miracles wrought in the lives of others because of Your calling to me. In all I say and do, may I give You honor and praise.

[Jesus said,] "Whoever serves me must follow me;
and where I am, my servant also will be.
My Father will honor the one who serves me."

JOHN 12:26 NIV

My Time Is Yours

Here I am, Lord. No matter how I tried today, I was behind schedule. I frantically struggled to do three things at once, desperately attempting to catch up. I want to honor You by not taking on too much in my life, but things have a way of taking over. Before I know it, I'm frustrated, grumpy, and feeling pushed away from You and the ones dearest to me.

Now I bring this calamity of a schedule to You. Take my time and make it Yours. Help me find ways to save minutes rather than wasting them. Show me how to weigh my priorities. When others want me to accept responsibilities I know will overwhelm me and aren't of You, help me to graciously say, "No, thank you." Be the guardian of my strength. Show me how to set limits. Remind me, Lord, to reserve time for You, my family, and my dearest friends. Prompt me also to make more time for myself.

Show me how to enjoy the moments You give. Help me bring back order instead of frantically racing against the clock. Grant me wisdom to manage time rather than allowing it to manage me.

When I'm tempted to take on too much again, nudge me, Lord, and I'll obey. I want to honor You with my time and let it belong to You.

> *I will praise the LORD, who counsels me;*
> *even at night my heart instructs me.*
> *I have set the LORD always before me.*
> *Because he is at my right hand,*
> *I will not be shaken.*

PSALM 16:7–8 NIV

May My Attitude Honor You

Something happened today at work, Lord, that brought out the worst in me. It wasn't such a big thing. It just happened to be one of my pet peeves. I tried to handle the situation politely. Unfortunately, my phony two-faced attitude spoke louder than my words. I should have prayed about this.

Then on the way home, I stopped by the store. There was a perfect parking space. If I maneuvered my car just right, I could slip in and beat the other driver waiting for it. The frustrated look on that person's face made me feel lower than dirt. The worst happened at home, when my negative mind-set spilled out on my family.

So here I am, Lord, meeting You in my quiet place. Neglecting time with You has taken its toll on me. Please forgive me. Help me to make things right with others as much as possible. Let my starving soul feed upon Your Word. Search my heart and cleanse me of the things not pleasing to You. Create a way of thinking in me that pleases You. Fill me with Your strengthening Holy Spirit. Thank You for Your forgiveness and love, Lord.

As I go about my day tomorrow, remind me to ask for Your help. Renew a right attitude within me, Lord, so I can honor You.

Create in me a clean heart, O God;
and renew a right spirit within me.

PSALM 51:10 KJV

Let My Appearance Give You Honor

As a teenager, I tried to look like my friends. My appearance showed the condition of my heart. It wasn't right with You, Father. I had little regard for how You wanted me to look. After I gave You my heart and grew closer to You, I realized You had a better way for me. I learned how my appearance could honor You. I no longer copied the lifestyles of this world. Instead, You gave me a fresh newness in all I did and thought. I wanted others to see You in my life.

Now grown and married, I try to look nice for my husband. As years pass and youth fades, You're showing me that beauty goes deeper than outward appearance. It doesn't come from fine clothing, stylish hair, or luxurious jewelry. They're nice. But true beauty comes from my inner self, then shows on the outside.

I want to be recognized by my smile and the kindness You put in my eyes. May those around me detect Your Spirit dwelling in me. Someone asked me not long ago why I look so happy. It was easy to tell them—because I have You in my heart.

Lord, give me the unfading loveliness of a gentle, quiet spirit. May it be of great value and bring honor to You.

> *Charm is deceptive, and beauty is fleeting;*
> *but a woman who fears the LORD is to be praised.*
> *Give her the reward she has earned,*
> *and let her works bring her praise at the city gate.*

PROVERBS 31:30–31 NIV

My Gift of Praise

What can I give You, Lord, that You haven't already imparted to me? All I have to offer are honor and praise. I come before You on my knees with adoration and thanksgiving. I praise You for the wonderful things You do for me. I am grateful for Your loving care.

I praise You for the words You teach me—for how they enrich my life and give me wisdom. Thank You for all the things on this earth You have provided for me to enjoy. Thank You for creating me and being my Father. I praise You for purchasing my soul with a great price and saving me through Your Son, Christ Jesus. I praise You for allowing me to represent You by being a Christian. I praise You for the presence of Your awesome, strengthening Holy Spirit.

Wherever I go, I will tell others of the glory of Your name and what You do in my life. Each day I will boast of Your constant, holy ways. Each day I will tell the discouraged to take heart because You love them, too. Through the good and the bad of life, I will continually speak of Your glory and grace, for *You* are my joy, my triumph, my security. In You, Father, I place my trust. In all things, I bring You honor and praise.

I will praise You, O LORD, with my whole heart;
I will tell of all Your marvelous works.
I will be glad and rejoice in You;
I will sing praise to Your name, O Most High.

PSALM 9:1–2 NKJV

Let Me Honor You in Song

The worship service is about to begin. Our song leaders are in their places. The entire sanctuary vibrates with Your holy presence. Weariness, distractions, and concerns are shed from me as I stand to honor You in song. You alone are worthy, O God. To You I raise my voice and sing.

I will sing to You, O Lord, for You have been kind to me. You have helped me trust in You and Your unfailing love. You have turned my sorrows into gladness and clothed me with Your infinite joy. Because of this, my heart shall not be silent. You, O Lord, are my awesome God. I will sing thanks to You for as long as I live.

Cleanse my heart and fill me with Your righteousness. You are holy. Holy are You, O God. We praise You with the stringed instruments and the drums. We praise You with the tambourines and the cymbals. I will lift my voice in adoration to You with a new song.

You, Lord, are honorable, just, and true. You are praiseworthy in all You do. I give glory, laud, and honor in song, and praise to Your blessed, holy name.

> *Sing to the LORD a new song;*
> *Sing to the LORD, all the earth.*
> *Sing to the LORD, bless His name;*
> *Proclaim good tidings of His salvation from day to day. . . .*
> *For great is the LORD, and greatly to be praised.*

PSALM 96:1–2, 4 NASB

A Holy Life

I long to live a holy life for You, Lord Jesus. Yet the more I've tried, the more I have failed. Like Paul, I desire to do what's right. But in a short time, I've often messed up. What I've done isn't the good I want to do. And the wrongs I don't want to do keep cropping up. I love Your ways, dear Lord, and want to be like You.

You overcame sin and temptation while You were here on earth. You are the Son of God. Still, Your human example helps me. You went off alone regularly to talk with Your Father. The Bible says You know Him well, and He knows You. Is this what gave You strength? While spending forty days in the desert fasting and praying to Your Father, You overcame temptation. Filled with the Holy Spirit, You conquered its lure with Scripture. Now I understand, Lord. I realize being tempted isn't a sin. Help me fight temptation with Scripture from my Bible. Fill me with Your Spirit, and remind me to run like crazy from all appearances of evil.

You know me, Lord, and I know You. When I mess up, thank You for Your forgiveness and for helping me start over. I will fix my thoughts on You and remember how to honor You with a holy life.

"Consecrate yourselves and be holy,
because I am the LORD your God.
Keep my decrees and follow them.
I am the LORD, who makes you holy."

LEVITICUS 20:7–8 NIV

I Honor You with My Giving

It's time to budget a portion of my income for You, Lord.
You have blessed me more than I ever could have imagined.
How thankful I am. This amount to confer is big. Can I afford to give it to You? I can't afford not to. I want to honor
You with this offering. Everything I have belongs to You
and is only loaned to me. I present it to You as a token of
gratitude for all You do. How amazing it is that You manage to bring it full circle and bless me all the more.

There was a time finances were tight. I wondered how
the bills could be paid. Still, I knew a portion of my earn-
ings belonged to You. So I gave, believing You would help
provide. I praise You for how You met my needs at the end
of the month, and with money to spare. I felt You leading
me to plant a giving-seed of faith, and I started to give You
more. Each time I prayed You would bless my offering and
help it to reach others for You. How good it is to see it used
for Your glory.

Help me to always be faithful in my offerings, Lord.
Let it be done with glory and honor to You.

> *So let each one give as he purposes in his heart,*
> *not grudgingly or of necessity;*
> *for God loves a cheerful giver.*
> *And God is able to make all grace abound toward you.*

2 CORINTHIANS 9:7–8 NKJV

You Are Worthy

How worthy You are to receive my honor and praise. It is I who feel unworthy to come before You. Thank You for welcoming me into Your holy presence. How gracious You are for showering Your blessings on those who trust in You. How great is Your goodness. When I am in distress, I cry out to You, and You hear me. You reach down from on high and rescue me. When all seems impossible, You show the way.

Let everyone praise and honor Your name. For You alone are deserving of praise. In all my ways, I will honor You, O Lord. You are worthy to receive reverence and adoration. You are the essence of splendor and glory. Through You all things are created and have their being. You have created everything for Your pleasure. May You take delight in one such as me.

Your ways are perfect. The words You speak are flawless. There is no other God besides You. You live. You are now. You shall be forever. Blessed are You, the Rock of my salvation.

You are King of all kings, Lord of all lords. May You be exalted throughout the earth. I bow before You in humility and praise. My life I give to You, O God, for You are worthy—so worthy. I give You tribute, honor, and praise.

"O Lord, you are worthy to receive the glory and the honor and the power, for you have created all things.
They were created and called into being by your act of will."

REVELATION 4:11 TLB

I Long to Know You More

When I watched my husband get out of his van tonight, I could tell his day had been good, Lord. He marched quickly toward the front door with his chin up, his shoulders straight, and a big smile on his face. I know him well after being married for over forty-four years. He understands me, too—sometimes better than I do myself.

I recognize the ways of my sons and daughters and grandchildren. A certain posture, a tilt of the head, or a shuffling of feet give me clues. Most of all, I see a lot in the expressions of their eyes.

I long to know You like that, Lord. Let me listen as You whisper to my heart. Help me to see things through Your eyes. My daughters-in-law have taught me to ask, "What would Jesus do?" in this or that situation. Help me to remember this, I pray.

When I first received You into my life, I realized things I did that saddened You. Thank You for forgiving me and helping me to change. I still feel I have a long way to go. Show me how I make You glad, Lord. Help me draw closer to You each day. I pray for Your Spirit to commune with mine as I get to know You more.

> *"Oh, that we might know the Lord!*
> *Let us press on to know him,*
> *and he will respond to us as surely as*
> *the coming of dawn or the rain of early spring."*

HOSEA 6:3 TLB

71

You Are My Heavenly Father

Do You always understand how I feel, Father? Are You happy for me when I'm in high spirits? Do You really empathize with me when I'm sad? Do You know how I feel when frustration and anger in me reach a boiling point? Are You with me when I bolt up in bed at night from a bad dream? Surely You know and care; for each time I call on Your name, I experience peace. I sense Your pleasure when I share my joys with You. Whenever I cry for help, You calm me and give me peace.

My little child, I know you better than you do yourself. I have searched your heart and am aware of everything about you. My presence is with you when you fall asleep and when you awaken. I see when you come and go. I perceive the words you are about to say before you speak. I am familiar with all your ways.

I go before and behind you. I keep My hand upon your head and watch over you. No matter where you are, I am there, holding tightly onto you. I do this because I love you, and you belong to Me.

Thank You for being my heavenly Father. Thank You for knowing and loving me.

As a father has compassion on his children,
so the LORD has compassion on those who fear him;
for he knows how we are formed.

PSALM 103:13–14 NIV

Before I Was Born

Father, when I was a child, I dreamed of being a parent someday. I wondered how many children I would have. What would they be like? Would I have boys or girls? I wanted to be the best parent ever. Did You know me before I was born? Was I a soul in heaven You loved and cared for? Did You plan for me to be brought here? At this place? This time?

I feel You once wrapped me securely in Your loving arms, long ago. Being with You in heaven seems familiar. Was this my first home?

Even before you were conceived in your mother's womb, I knew you and consecrated you as My own. You were no mistake. Before all time, I had a plan for you. I created your inmost being as I carefully knit you together. In the depths of that secret place, I took your tiny, unformed body and molded it into something wonderful. I formed your nose, your fingers and toes—even your strands of hair. I knew your every little crease and fold. You are My masterpiece, My unique and lovely soul. I loved you before time. I love you now and forever.

I am grateful, Father, for Your planning and wanting me. I'm so glad You made me.

> *My frame was not hidden from you*
> *when I was made in the secret place.*
>
> PSALM 139:15 NIV

In Your Image

What a thrill we received when each of our children was born, Father. I still remember their first cries—unique, individual. I can almost feel their tiny fingers wrapped around mine and see their daddy's proud gaze. And how those babies looked! A special combination of my husband and me.

Was I created like You, Father? How can I be the image of You, my awesome God? How fearfully and wonderfully made I am!

I created both male and female in My image. You are a reflection of Me. You are My very own dear one. I have made you to be My offspring—My child. In Me, you live and move and are.

It was no accident, the time and place you were born. From the beginning, I set My special plan for you into motion. It is true things would not always go smoothly for you. But all through your life, I have and will be with you as your heavenly Father. Even though you are in My image, I give you free will. Choose to remain close to Me and reflect My purity, My child. I want you to be filled with joy and for you to experience the calling I give you.

Thank You, Father. In You, I will live and move and exist!

"For in him we live and move and have our being. . . .
We are his offspring."

ACTS 17:28 NIV

You Know My Number of Hairs

I'm amazed how You number my hairs, Father. On days I'm frustrated and feel like pulling some out, I must keep You pretty busy! You know me on the outside, and You surely understand me through and through. You share my pain when I lack confidence. You weep with me when I mourn. You nudge me to show mercy to those who wrong me. You help me find peace amid stress. Thank You for meeting my needs—for teaching me to rejoice during times of trouble.

I praise You for peace of heart and mind. How awesome, the way You allow me to come into Your presence. How good You are to change my heart, Father. When I am unsure, You encourage me. When fiery trials come, You go before me. Instead of worrying, I will remember the flowers and the fields and how You even see when one sparrow falls. How grateful I am that I matter more to You than these, for I am Your child.

I want you to tell others these things I reveal to you in quiet, dear child. This way they, too, can get to know Me more.

How wonderful You are, Father, for knowing me so well.

> *[Jesus said,] "What is the price of five sparrows?*
> *A couple of pennies? Not much more than that.*
> *Yet God does not forget a single one of them.*
> *And he knows the number of hairs on your head!*
> *Never fear, you are far more valuable to him*
> *than a whole flock of sparrows."*

> LUKE 12:6–7 TLB

Your Plans for Me

Walking with You is the most excellent journey I've ever taken, Father. The adventure is trusting You when I can't see around the next bend. More than anything, I want to stay within Your will. I want to be sure my plans are in line with Yours. You are in charge. I search for Your will through prayer. I explore the lessons in Your Bible. Remind me to seek wise advice of Christians and focus on Your purpose, instead of notions of those who don't know You. You are my heavenly Father. You know what is best.

I belong to You and am confident in Your plans for me. You promise in Your Word that Your direction will help and never harm me. No matter life's circumstances, Father, Your ways shall stand firm and true.

I have so many wonders and blessings in store for you, My child, that you will not be able to count them—plans for the present and more for the future. Not only are they for you, but for your children, your children's children—even for those who have not yet been born! My hand is already on them, too. Seek Me, and I will tell you great and incredible things you have yet to know.

Thank You, Father. I will fit into Your plans, for You are my God.

"For I know the plans that I have for you,"
declares the LORD,
"plans for welfare [well-being] and not for
calamity to give you a future and a hope."

JEREMIAH 29:11 NASB

Love Everlasting

You're so compassionate in the way You give Your love. How thankful I am for Your being my eternal Father. Thank You for calling me Your child. You even know my name. Your love goes beyond limits. It's unconditional. It's never-ending. When I'm at my best, I feel Your care. When I feel down and complain, You are still near. Even when I make poor decisions, You help me through and set my feet on the right path. You are dear to me, Father. I love You so much. At Your feet I bow, awaiting Your direction. There's no other like You. Now and forever, You will be first in my life.

Before time, in the present, and forever, I, your heavenly Father, cherish you with an inexhaustible love. With tenderness, I draw you closely to Me. I do this, My dear one, so you may know My Son. Each time You demonstrate love, I am glad. From everlasting to everlasting is My love for you, because You revere Me and act upon My precepts. I will always shower My compassion upon you, for I am your Lord and Redeemer.

I will remember Your promise of choosing me from the beginning. Thank You for Your love and encouragement. I praise You, Father God. I love You with the love You first gave me.

> *The Lord had said. . .*
> *I have loved you, O my people,*
> *with an everlasting love;*
> *with lovingkindness I have drawn you to me.*
>
> JEREMIAH 31:3 TLB

Perfect Father

Father, I always wanted to be a perfect parent. Our children are my loves, my pride, my hope for the future. No matter how I try, though, I can't do everything right. In spite of my errors, I'm grateful for the good in our children. Thank You for healing hurts and helping to make things right. Always keep us close, Father.

Thank You for my dad. How dear he is to me. Thank You for the way we love and appreciate each other. I treasure the times we have together.

But You are far greater than my family, for You are my heavenly Father. You are perfect, kind, merciful, and just. Thank You for caring about and forgiving me.

You are holy. You are my Father and my God. And Your only begotten Son, Jesus Christ, who paid the ultimate sacrifice with love and mercy, is my Lord and Savior! Your Son loved me so much, He took my sins upon His shoulders. He died and triumphed over wrong. Now, I praise You for allowing me to come directly to You in prayer.

Once, I chose to give you life through a physical birth, My child. Now, I give you a spiritual birth, through Jesus. I and My Son are One; and you, My child, are Mine.

Thank You for giving me a new life in You.

All honor to God,
the God and Father of our Lord Jesus Christ;
for it is his boundless mercy that has given us
the privilege of being born again,
so that we are now members of God's own family.

1 PETER 1:3 TLB

I Love to Know You, Jesus

I praise You for being my Savior and Redeemer, Lord Jesus. Thank You for having enough love for me and all of humankind to take our sins upon Yourself. You gave Your life on a cross made for thieves. How frightening it must have been to those present when the earth shook and huge rocks shattered. How glorious then, when people were healed. Even Christians who had died were brought back to life.

How grateful I am that You won over sin and split the thick veil in the temple from top to bottom! No longer were believers separated from the Holy of Holies. Neither does the veil keep me from coming directly to You and our Father in prayer. Death didn't keep You in its grip. Instead, You came alive after three days. Now You are in heaven with our Father.

In all my ways I exalt You, Jesus. I praise You for how You also abide in my heart. Not only are You my Savior, but You are my Friend, my Counselor, my Teacher. Thank You for changing my life. Thank You for providing hope to my descendants through Your saving grace. I commit them to You, O Lord. May they always know, love, and obey You. I love to know You, Lord. You are more than life to me.

> *For I know whom I have believed*
> *and I am convinced that He is able to guard*
> *what I have entrusted to Him until that day.*

> 2 TIMOTHY 1:12 NASB

You Are My Help

Thank You for this quiet week at the ocean, dear Lord—just You, me, and my writing. I was making great progress, but then it happened. Everything locked up on my portable computer. The screen turned a haunting blue. I was scared, Lord, but thankful I had saved most everything on a disk. Nothing happened, no matter what I tried.

Finally, I prayed. I felt complete trust. I didn't even cry. I didn't know anyone in this little town, Lord. There wasn't even a computer store. This was quite a challenge. I wondered if someone could help me. I needed a miracle. I asked You to direct me, and You did.

I started writing in a notebook. The words flowed. I sensed Your presence. After a few hours, the library came to mind. The librarian checked my disk, offered the use of a library computer, and helped me phone a store several miles away. You know what happened next, Lord. While I was on the phone, a technician who happened to be repairing a library computer overheard me. Before long, he not only fixed my computer, but taught me how to solve the problem myself.

Thank You for these kind people and for Your much-needed help.

My help comes from the LORD,
Who made heaven and earth.

PSALM 121:2 NKJV

MARCH 13

Let Me Learn from You, Lord

I wrote down the lessons the computer technician taught me today and saved them, Lord. Sometimes I try to solve problems and do things the hard way without asking for Your help. Then You remind me You are here to teach me.

Let me learn Your valuable lessons, Lord. Thank You for charting my path, for instructing me when to go or stop and where to rest. Keep my heart pliable as I search for the things of You. You are my refuge and strength. You are my forever-present help in my times of need and advice.

I come to You in prayer. Help me search out the things You have for me to learn. I open my Bible and pore over Your timeless, wise words. You, Lord, are the Way, the Truth, and the Life. I constantly want to study Your lessons and store them in my heart. May I find Your approval as You guide me in understanding the Truth.

I take delight in teaching you, My child. Each day as you learn My truth, it shall free you from the bondage of this world. Call upon Me. Keep reading My Word. In turn, I will answer you and tell you great and marvelous things.

Teach me, Lord, and I will listen.

> Lord, I am overflowing with your blessings,
> just as you promised.
> Now teach me good judgment as well as knowledge.
> For your laws are my guide.

PSALM 119:65–66 TLB

No Reservations Needed

Lord, here I am at work. Are You with me? I'm starting to panic. Please, let me feel Your closeness in the midst of this absolute chaos! Nothing seems to be going right. No matter which way I turn, I can't find a solution to all the problems I'm dealing with. I'm tired, Lord. My patience is wearing thin. Help me, please.

I bring my needs to You in faith, believing You are stepping in and helping me through. Calm my emotions; quicken my tired body and mind, I pray. Make my actions wise, swift, and sure. Surround me with Your presence, I pray.

I feel myself beginning to relax. Ah. . .I know You are near. Now my focus is on You and Your direction. Thank You.

Conditions are better now. I can sense Your presence. Even those around me have calmed down, and our work is coming into order. Why didn't I think of these solutions before? It is, of course, because my help comes from You, the maker and solver of all things.

Thank You for allowing me to call on You anytime, anywhere. I don't need reservations to talk with You; nor will You put me on hold. I praise You again and again for Your constant, abiding presence.

Then you will call upon me and come and pray to me,
and I will listen to you.
You will seek me and find me when you seek me
with all your heart.

JEREMIAH 29:12–13 NIV

MARCH 15

You Are My Way

The garden path to Happy and Minnie Green's outhouse was a short distance but felt more like a mile, Lord. As a child, I didn't know there were outhouses until I spent a summer with this family. It wasn't bad during the daytime—lined with wildflowers, quack grass, and crickets. But my nine-year-old feet stopped in their tracks when darkness approached. Flashlight in hand, the older daughters accompanied me. Their cheerful presence and my thoughts of You helped chase scary shadows away.

As an adult, I'm not so afraid to walk in the dark now, as long as there are plenty of streetlights. But I'm often fearful of the darkness of life's uncertainties. This is one of those times, Lord. I can't see what lies around the next bend. I must make some important decisions. I'm afraid and apprehensive. Please lead and direct me. I love You with all my heart. I will trust You and not depend on my own limited comprehension. Take away my fear. Light my way. Lead me to make right choices, to do what I can and leave the rest in Your capable hands.

Fear not, dear child. I am here. I am your Light. Follow Me. You will not walk in darkness but will have My Light of life, for I am the Way.

You, Lord, I will follow.

> *[Jesus said,] "I am the light of the world.*
> *He who follows Me shall not walk in darkness,*
> *but have the light of life."*

JOHN 8:12 NKJV

Proof of the Positive

It made my day, Lord, to have lunch with a friend of mine. She is one of the most positive people I've ever been around. Her life is a total plus. If it's raining, she talks about the fresh-smelling air. If her car breaks down and she has to walk to work, she mentions the great exercise she had that day. She plays a game of how many people she can make smile in an hour. One of them is me. She sees the upside to everything. My friend is walking proof of Your Scripture, Romans 8:28. She trusts You that all things, good or bad, really do work out for good when we love You.

She's that way with her children. I often hear her saying, "I love you," "I believe in you," or "I'm proud of you." She tells them, "Do the right thing," rather than "Don't mess up." She helps build self-confidence and character in everyone she meets. A small note card in her kitchen window says it all: "I can."

Thank You for my friend, Lord. She is living proof of the positive. She must get it from You. You often say in Your Bible what to do: "Follow Me." "Let your light shine." "Love one another." I can almost hear You telling me, *"Do* be a proof of the positive."

[Jesus said,] "Don't hide your light!
Let it shine for all;
let your good deeds glow for all to see,
so that they will praise your heavenly Father."

MATTHEW 5:15–16 TLB

Choose Life

Lord, my fifth-grade school year was the most difficult I experienced while growing up. My feet were too big. I was the tallest one in the whole school (with the exception of one teacher). I felt awkward and not very smart. My grades were slipping, and I was developing a bad attitude about everything in general.

Thank You for my teacher, Mrs. MacDonald. She took me aside and gave me a firm talking to. Ironically enough, *she* was the tallest person in school. Mrs. MacDonald told me I was very pretty in God's sight. But she reminded me that a poor attitude eliminated any good looks! She made it clear I was the one who needed to make the choices. No matter the circumstances. No excuses. She hoped I would make good ones and begin building a positive life. Even though a lot was wrong, she reminded me it was never too late to change. I now see Your positive hand in that.

Mrs. MacDonald's lesson to choose a better life reminds me of You, Lord. Thank You for being my Savior and helping me to choose the right paths of blessings rather than ones resulting in regrets. Thank You that it is never too late to make a change for the good—a change in which I choose life.

> *[Jesus said,]*
> *I am come that they might have life,*
> *and that they might have it more abundantly.*
>
> JOHN 10:10 KJV

Thank You for Your Patience

Remember when my son Jonathan and I were shopping in that T-shirt store, Lord? He was still a teenager. Jon found a shirt for me with an enthusiastic-looking roller-skating turtle on the front. He said it described me perfectly. The caption under the picture spoke words I heard so often that I believe them: "Knowing me is to love me."

I bought that shirt and wore it until it turned to rags. I'd buy another, if I could. To me, Jonathan's words are a compliment. Thank You for his being proud of my never-give-up determination and faithfulness. Although I don't sprint wherever I go or move mountains in a day, he and the rest of my family love me.

One of my favorite children's books, Lord, is *The Tortoise and the Hare*. The author must have had people like me in mind. How comforting to know that those of us who move a little (or a lot) slower are still serving You. I'm glad all the animals made it on Noah's ark, including the turtles. Thank You for being tolerant enough to wait for them.

Remind me when I become frustrated or discouraged with my progress to look back at what You have helped me accomplish and the perseverance You've taught me. Thank You, Lord, for being patient and loving me.

I keep working toward that day when
I will finally be all that Christ saved me for
and wants me to be.

PHILIPPIANS 3:12 TLB

Thank You for Your Friendship

The most wonderful thing in all the world is knowing You, Lord, my Savior and my Friend. The Bible says a true friend stays nearer than a brother. You are that kind of friend to me. Thank You for being with me day and night.

You entered my heart and set up housekeeping. You tell me the truth, even when I don't like to hear it. You patiently counsel me in right ways. You never cause me to stray, Lord, for You do not tempt. You provide zeal for my life and help me keep a positive outlook. I discover morsels of wisdom from Your words.

When I am weary, You wrap Your arms around me and give me rest. You nourish and restore my soul. When I go through deep waters, You wade ahead and hold on to me with Your strong, firm hand. Whether I am on the mountains or in the valleys of my life, You listen to my every word and care. You are more than my Friend. You are the Lover of my soul.

Let our souls entwine as one, Lord. Come what may, help me yield and trust in You. I will cling to Your counsel and follow You. At day's end, I will rest securely in Your safekeeping, for You are my treasured Friend.

> *[Jesus said,] "I have called you friends,*
> *for all things that I heard from My Father*
> *I have made known to you.*
> *You did not choose Me,*
> *but I chose you and appointed you."*

JOHN 15:15–16 NKJV

Let Me Touch Your Hem, Lord

This thing I'm going through, Lord, is almost beyond my endurance. I'm pressed in on all sides. No matter which way I turn, I ache with indescribable pain and cry until there are no more tears. Why must I face such things? I don't know if I can take much more.

You are my Savior, my Strength and Defender. Although I'm discouraged and afraid, I will still trust in You. Let me touch the hem of Your garment, Lord. Let me hold its threads in my fingers. Help me tie a knot in the strands and not let go of my hope in You!

Come to Me, you who are heavy laden. You are My dear child. Know for certain, there are no troubles you face that others have not gone through before you. I will take these things and make a way of escape for you. Take my yoke. Place it on your shoulders. It will not make your load heavier. I am helping you carry it so your burden will become lighter and easier. Rest upon My everlasting arms, for they are under you all the time. Here is the hem of My garment. Touch it. Feel My presence. In your weakness, know My strength and healing.

Thank You, Lord Jesus, for the hem of Your garment and for Your loving touch.

[Jesus said,] Take my yoke upon you, and learn of me;
for I am meek and lowly in heart:
and ye shall find rest unto your souls.
For my yoke is easy, and my burden is light.

MATTHEW 11:29–30 KJV

Teach Me How to Fish

After all You do for me, Lord Jesus, I want to tell everyone how glorious You are. But I'm unsure. I'm afraid. I read about the way You walked by the Sea of Galilee. You found Simon (later to be called Peter) and his brother, Andrew, fishing. You bid them to lay down their nets and follow You, asking them to attract men instead of fish. At once, the fishermen stopped what they were doing and went with You. They listened and didn't hesitate.

Remember when I was a child and my dad patiently tried to teach me to fish, Lord? He and my mother loved fishing. I attempted it but could never get past putting the worm on the hook. Then our grandsons came along. Somehow they have the touch. They cast out their lines and wiggle them a little, and the fish gravitate to them. Perhaps the ability is inherited from their great-grandparents.

Lord, I want to be a fisher of men (and women). Please teach me how. Every time I try telling others about You, I stumble over my words. No one pays attention to me. Just like when I tried catching fish, I don't have the touch. Help me, Lord. Show me how to cast out my spiritual line and draw others to You.

Jesus called out to them,
"Come, follow me!
And I will make you
fishermen for the souls of men!"

MARK 1:17 TLB

I Send You a Comforter

Thank You for Your Holy Spirit, Lord. Thank You for coming into my heart. Fill me and refill me to overflowing. Train me to reach souls for You. Help me to recall the teachings from Your Word.

When I start to tell someone about Your love, remove the fear I struggle with and replace it with Your peace of mind. Surround me with Your presence. Because I love and trust in You, I ask for You to provide the right words. Anoint my words with Your power so they won't come back hollow or meaningless. Lord, let each person I talk with hear You instead of me.

You are not alone, dear child, for My Father and I send you a Helper. He abides with you now and forever. He is the Spirit of truth, the Holy Spirit. I and the Father and the Spirit are One, working in perfect, holy harmony. The people who do not know Me or the Father will not recognize the Holy Spirit. But you know Him, because you have invited Me as Savior into your heart.

Thank You, dear Lord, for Your Holy Spirit. Thank You for being my Helper, my Comforter, my Strength, my Guide. Thank You for blessing my words with Your great power.

[Jesus said,] "And I will pray the Father,
and He will give you another Helper,
that He may abide with you forever. . .
but you know Him, for He dwells with you
and will be in you."

JOHN 14:16–17 NKJV

MARCH 23

My Journey with You

I'm so excited about Your Holy Spirit filling my soul, Lord. I feel I'm about to take the most exciting trip of my life— a spiritual journey with You as my Captain. I'm anxious to serve You—anytime, anywhere. What can I do for You? How I long to be useful.

In one way, I can hardly wait. In other ways, I feel unworthy of being Your servant. I'm only a regular person. Your greatness is measureless. I don't know if I can fulfill the callings You have awaiting me. Still, I will trust and obey You. Direct me as You will, Lord.

Don't be afraid, dear child. From now on, My Holy Spirit goes with you all the time. You shall be a fisher of souls. When you are weak, I shall give you strength. When you are afraid, I shall give you courage. When you are uncertain of what to do, I shall lead you.

I will trust in You, Lord, and not fear my own frailties and limited reasoning. Remind me, I pray, not to get ahead of Your will. May my motives and actions be pure and pleasing to You. Thank You for Your Holy Spirit, Lord. I'm ready now to start my journey with You.

> *"As I was with Moses, so I will be with you;
> I will never leave you nor forsake you."*
>
> JOSHUA 1:5 NIV

Fill Me

Fill me with Your Holy Spirit, Lord. Search my heart. See if there is anything You would make right. Know my thoughts. Renew my mind and lead me into Your everlasting ways.

Help me shed the weights that will hold me back from being a victorious and joy-filled Christian. Cleanse me with Your holy power. Wash me through and through, my Lord. Plant seeds of Your Holy Spirit within me that will produce Your love, joy, and peace of mind and heart. Grant me patience, kindness, and purity. Cause me to be faithful, no matter how difficult things become. Teach me gentleness and self-control.

Once I thought I could do all these things through my own strength of will. Now I know I am able to have these spiritual fruits only through the power of Your Holy Spirit who dwells in me. No longer am I oppressed by temptations and fears, for You are closer than life itself. You dwell within me. You crucify my sinful nature and give me victory in You. Let me keep in step with Your Spirit and synchronize my will with Yours. Thank You for filling me with Your Spirit, dear Lord. I yield my all to You.

May the God of hope fill you with all joy
and peace as you trust in him,
so that you may overflow with hope
by the power of the Holy Spirit.

ROMANS 15:13 NIV

Thank You for Making Yourself Known

Thank You for the Christian retreat I went to, Lord. New friendships made, Bible studies, excellent speakers, and great music made me feel good inside. After that, the retreat leader asked everyone to take an hour only to talk with and listen to You.

I said a lot, Lord. You patiently listened. Pretty soon, I finished with an "amen." I remember glancing at my watch and being surprised to find only twenty minutes had passed. It was then I realized You wanted me to know You more. For the next forty minutes, I searched Your Bible for guidance. I stopped and listened to You speak to my stagnant heart. How blessed I was that day, Lord, as You unraveled the tangles in my life and began weaving them into an orderly, Holy-Spirit–filled tapestry. I left the retreat filled with peace, power, and purpose to take more time with You.

I was so hungry to know Your Spirit more. Thank You for giving me the insight and determination to do something about it. It takes planning and a little less sleep (or less television the night before) for me to meet You in the quiet of each morning. Oh, how fantastic it is as we communicate and You make Yourself known to me more every day. Thank You, Lord.

Be still, and know that I am God.

PSALM 46:10 KJV

Your Hallowed Presence

It's early morning, Lord. Nighttime's chill permeates the house. I turn up the heat and sit near the window. I want to take time with You. A gray dawn gives way to a new day. I hear Your silent voice speak Your words of assuring love to my listening heart. Thank You for meeting me here.

Even breathing from my family nearby mingles with the warming furnace air. I glance down the list I've tucked in my Bible and bring my requests before You. Thank You for answered prayers. With each one, my faith grows. You are loving and caring. I tell You my joys, concerns, and deepest secrets. I ask Your direction. You give me clarity of mind and peace of heart. Your Bible spells out precepts so clearly. Thank You for helping me.

I place circumstances I don't understand at Your feet. My hurts and confusion I bring to You. When things don't go my way, I will trust You. You perceive them, Lord. You are all-knowing. Thank You for caring about what's important to me.

The alarm clock is ringing. How quickly time has passed, Lord. Abide with me through this day. Let me feel Your guiding Holy Spirit in everything I deal with. Bless my loved ones, I pray. Keep them in Your care. Thank You for Your hallowed presence.

[Jesus said,] "But when you pray, go away by yourself,
all alone, and shut the door behind you
and pray to your Father secretly, and your Father,
who knows your secrets, will reward you [openly]."

MATTHEW 6:6 TLB

How Can I Overcome?

Thinking of what my life used to be like before knowing You leaves me weary, Lord. I grieve to see others who are lost and don't know You. This sinful existence, supposedly full of fun and excitement, is only a farce—an empty mirage. It leads to sadness and ruin. Thank You for saving me from it.

Yet I face challenges. At times, sin and sorrow press in from every side, no matter which way I turn. How can I overcome these ordeals I must cope with? Give me strength enough to resist the devious temptations put before me. As I do, please let others listen to what I'm trying to tell them about You. I love You, Lord, and want to overcome these things through You.

I shall overcome, dear one. I am your Fort, your Rock, and a strong Tower to which you can run. I am like the strong horn of a mighty fighting bull. I will defend and buffer you, no matter the difficulty.

Thank You, Lord God, for Your promise that no temptation, no problem, is too great when I obey You. Thank You for helping me each time I call Your name. I praise You for empowering me with Your Holy Spirit and providing the right words when I tell others about You. In You I completely trust.

> [Jesus said,]
> "But when the Holy Spirit has come upon you,
> you will receive power to testify about me with great effect,
> to the people in Jerusalem, throughout Judea,
> in Samaria, and to the ends of the earth,
> about my death and resurrection."

ACTS 1:8 TLB

You Give Me Zeal

Where does this passion to tell everyone who will listen about Your wonderful love come from, Lord? Is it from Your Holy Spirit dwelling within me? I feel an urgency to win souls for You. Not because I think I have to. I simply long for others to experience the bountiful blessings of having You in their lives.

Like an all-encompassing, loving Friend and Counselor, You are here. You provide me with a fire and zeal that almost cause me to burst, unless I'm able to pass them on in either actions or words.

I don't know why You bless me so, dear Lord. I'm just a simple person who wants to love and serve You with all my heart. I am awed by how You give me an enthusiasm and a deep inner joy and hope, no matter what circumstances I face. As long as I focus on You and the Scriptures and take my mind off the things of this world, I have hope with peace of heart and mind.

Thank You for teaching me how to be patient in facing problems, to be faithful in prayer to You during the good and bad. I praise You for keeping my fervor and zeal for You alive and well. To You, Lord, be honor and acclamation and power. Amen.

[Jesus said,]
"And behold, I am sending forth
the promise of My Father upon you;
but you are to stay in the city until you are
clothed with power from on high."

LUKE 24:49 NASB

Cling to the Vine

I want to be a blessing to everyone I'm around, Lord. A lot of times I do all right. But when I'm with people I live and work with day after day, it's a lot harder. They know my every attitude. No matter how hard I try, I can't reflect You without Your Holy Spirit working through me.

I read in my Bible that You are the Vine, and my heavenly Father is the Gardener. It also says I am one of Your branches. You grafted me to You when I became Your child. I choose to remain close to You, Lord. Thank You for pruning away the things in my life that are undesirable to You. May I please You in all my ways and bring forth spiritual fruit that comes directly from You. Please show me how.

My dear child, I abide in you, and you abide in Me. If you remain in Me, you will produce much of My fruit. Apart from Me, you are not able to yield any of it. No matter your good intentions, your efforts will be a waste. Cling to Me. Draw life from Me. And I will help you bring forth the sweet-tasting fruit of My Spirit.

I will cling to You, Lord—my Vine, the source of all that is good and holy.

> *[Jesus said,] "I am the vine, you are the branches.*
> *He who abides in Me, and I in him, bears much fruit;*
> *for without Me you can do nothing."*

> JOHN 15:5 NKJV

Fruit of the Holy Spirit

Once I tried to have the fruits of Your Spirit in my life by working hard to achieve them—one at a time. It didn't take long for me to realize I couldn't do it that way. Thank You for showing me this fruit comes only from Your Holy Spirit dwelling within me.

Fill me, Lord. Take my talents, my time. Bless the work of my hands. Grant me the spiritual gifts You would have me receive. More than anything, help me yield my will to Yours.

I pray for Your Spirit to work within me, dear Lord. Let me abide in You. In turn, live within my heart and direct me. Tell me where to go and what to do in accordance with Your will. Let my life be a living proof of Your presence abiding within me. Cause Your spiritual fruit to grow in abundance.

My child, I shall produce in you love, joyfulness, harmony of heart and mind, selflessness, kindheartedness, uprightness, faithfulness, sensitivity, self-control. Love Me with all your heart and your soul and your strength. When you are guided by My Holy Spirit, you will be able to do what pleases Me.

Plant the seeds of Your fruit within me, Lord. Tend the garden of my heart. Make it grow and flourish for Your glory.

But the fruit of the Spirit is love, joy, peace,
longsuffering, kindness, goodness, faithfulness,
gentleness, self-control. Against such there is no law.

GALATIANS 5:22–23 NKJV

MARCH 31

Selah

Here I am, Lord, walking the track in our neighborhood park. March winds whip and push against my legs. Not a problem. This intensifies my workout. The blasts of air whistle a baffling symphony. I reach the first bend. Trees yield to the hearty gusts. My heartbeat and breath quicken, along with my pace. One foot in front of the other. Keep going.

Thank You for walking with me, Lord. Your presence is like this wind. It, too, comes in powerful gusts, filtering through every part of my life. It sings holy melodies, more beautiful than I can describe. My heart echoes back in synchronized harmony. You are so marvelous, I can scarcely take in Your presence.

Here comes the rain, Lord. No matter. It smells clean. Let the cleansing showers of *Your* Holy Spirit also fall upon me. Ah, how blessed. How pure. I praise You, O Lord, for Your awesome presence.

I round another bend to the final stretch. My breathing is labored. But I'll keep going. Look toward the eastern sky, Lord! Your rainbow of promise! Yes, I know You put it there. I feel like it's for me.

Here we are at the end of our trek, Lord. I pause. The winds and rains cease. I hear You quietly whisper to me, *"Selah. Pause. Reflect on Me."*

> *My soul, wait thou only upon God;*
> *for my expectation is from him. [Selah].*

PSALM 62:5 KJV

How Can I Repay You?

to Serve You

Lord, I lift my heart to You in thanksgiving and praise this evening for how You were here with me today. While being faced with several problems to untangle, You showed me the answers once again. Thank You, Lord.

I glance over my prayer list from this past year and am amazed at how many petitions You answered then—just like You did today. I recall the nearly impossible challenges I faced and how You repeatedly brought me through victoriously.

I feel undeserving, Lord. How can I repay You for the incredible things You do? Will serving You every hour of every day, with all the strength I can muster, make up for Your blessings? Not a chance. Will selling my worldly possessions repay You? Your blessings are priceless. I love You, Lord. Show me what I can do for You.

You need not repay Me, dear one. I merely want you to love Me with all your heart and soul and mind. Give yourself, holy and pleasing, to Me. I am the Potter. You are the clay. Allow My Spirit to fill and mold you so you can pass My love on to others. As My Father sent me, I therefore send you.

Thank You for calling me to serve You, Lord. Let Your plans and ways be mine.

[Jesus said,] "You did not choose Me, but I chose you and appointed you that you should go and bear fruit, and that your fruit should remain, that whatever you ask the Father in My name He may give you. These things I command you, that you love one another."

JOHN 15:16–17 NKJV

Serving You with My Love

Who can compare to You, dear Lord? There is no other I love more. How I treasure my times in communication with You. But I want this love I have to *do* something for You. Although You're in my heart, I can't touch or see You. How can I serve You with my love?

My child, when you give others your love, you do so as to Me. Do not be afraid to shake the hand or hug the unlovely. Imagine that person being Me. Love by feeding the hungry, and you feed Me. Offer a drink of water to the thirsty, and you do so to Me. Lovingly open your home to someone, and you welcome Me, as well. Give your clothing to one in need, and you give it to Me.

Take time from your busy days to visit the sick. Go to those in prison and tell them of My love for them. Never mind the clanging doors that slam shut behind you. You are there to help set their spirits free. Reach out and watch over the aged in rest homes. When you love all of these, you are giving love to Me.

I will serve others with love as unto You, Lord.

> *[Jesus said,] "For I was hungry and*
> *you gave me something to eat,*
> *I was thirsty and you gave me something to drink,*
> *I was a stranger and you invited me in,*
> *I needed clothes and you clothed me,*
> *I was sick and you looked after me,*
> *I was in prison and you came to visit me."*

MATTHEW 25:35–36 NIV

Sacrificial Love

It doesn't seem long ago, Lord, when I was six months pregnant with our youngest son. I became deathly ill with hepatitis A and B. I was hospitalized. No one was allowed to touch me except Bob. Relatives and friends were contacted. Thank You for their concern and prayers.

Among many were people who showed a sacrificial love, Lord. One was my mother. Around the clock for days, she contacted everyone she could think of who knew me to pray and send a card. Flowers and cards came from all over the country, many because of my mother's quick actions of love. Their expressing care encouraged me. It played a major part in helping me get well. Thank You for my mother and those who were thoughtful.

How I longed for the touch of a friend. Then a young lady, a pastor, and Bob came to visit. Bob and these friends joined hands and gathered around my bed to pray for me. Bob took one of my hands. The young lady reached for my other one. I remember recoiling, Lord, and warning that she wasn't to touch me. "The Lord will protect me," she explained.

Thank You for how she sensed my need and gave me her loving touch. Grant me strength also to serve with that kind of sacrificial love.

Dear friends, let us practice loving each other,
for love comes from God and those who are
loving and kind show that they are the children of God,
and that they are getting to know him better.

1 JOHN 4:7 TLB

Ceaseless Love

Father, I hear You calling me to shower this person and her children with my love. I did this before with someone else. I wrapped my arms around the mother and her children You know so well and passed Your love on to them. I took time to recognize their concerns and needs. I encouraged them and taught them about You. Then without warning, they moved away. They didn't even say good-bye or thank you. I'm still saddened and really miss them.

I don't want to get hurt again, Father. Still, I know You are calling me to help again. Grant me a ceaseless love without fear of being hurt again. Help me to look beyond my disappointments and acknowledge the needs of others.

You were hurt by some. Still, You blessed many. Only few showed their thanks. I know I'm here to serve You by caring for those You send my way. Help me not to expect appreciation or pats on the back.

Help me, dear Father. Bless this family. Guide them so they may get to know and love You. And, Lord, please be with and watch over the ones I still miss and care about. Teach me to always love with an unconditional, ceaseless love.

> *[Love] bears all things,*
> *believes all things,*
> *hopes all things,*
> *endures all things.*
> *Love never fails.*

1 CORINTHIANS 13:7–8 NKJV

I Will Serve You with Joy

Thank You, dear Lord, for helping me overcome my fear to love again. I'm grateful for my new friend and her children. They bring delight and joy to my heart. Am I doing enough for her, Lord? She is certainly a blessing to me.

What a pleasure to see her and her family growing in You. I had no idea that You could use her to help me. My schedule is so full, Lord. I knew she needed help financially, so I've started paying her to give me a hand with my housework. What a lifesaver she is. She's so thorough and fast!

Along with this, You've brought healing to my heart by my knowing her. I'm not afraid of giving my love away now. I realize I'm Your servant. Let any praise go to You. I don't have to worry about how long You place someone in my care, for You have a plan.

I may be the one who sows the seed or feeds and waters. Once in a while, I might be fortunate enough to reap the harvest and see a soul come to You. Either way, I thrill when I hear of one more person accepting You as Savior. Thank You for the joy of serving You.

For You, O LORD,
have made me glad by what You have done,
I will sing for joy at the works of Your hands.

PSALM 92:4 NASB

APRIL 6

Sharing My Life

I sense Your Holy Spirit working through me as I share my life with those whose paths I cross. Not as a project or duty to perform, but simply being available to Your will anytime, anywhere.

The other day I was in the grocery store, giving a word of encouragement. Today I stayed back a few minutes, listening to a coworker who was stressed. Tonight I felt the joy of being a mother to one of our grown sons, but he was also a sounding board—a confidant and friend.

It's becoming a way of life, Lord. Thank You for the delight You give. Each time I share a bit of myself with someone, I'm filled with gratitude and a warmth that spreads through my whole being.

Help me serve You with gladness. When I'm downcast, quicken my spirit. Let the joy of Your love and care flow through me. When I am worn out, strengthen me and meet the needs. When I don't have the answers, remind me to simply stop and pray with those in my path and leave the rest to You. I'm not here to solve their problems. You can do that. I'm here to love, care, and encourage. Thank You for giving me the privilege of living for You.

Always be full of joy in the Lord;
I say it again, rejoice!
Let everyone see that you are unselfish
and considerate in all you do.
Remember that the Lord is coming soon.

PHILIPPIANS 4:4–5 TLB

Your Joy Is My Strength

I can't believe I had to deal with so many sad and devastating situations in one day, Lord. I have a student at school who was just admitted to the hospital. She is so sick, the doctors don't know if she is going to survive. I listened to this child's parents talk about what is going on, and it pulls at my heartstrings. Please be with this little one and her family, dear Lord. Help her get well, I pray.

After work, I met with my friend who is going through more than I can comprehend. She's depressed and is often tempted to give up. I guess the best I can do is listen, look for ways I can lend a hand, and give encouragement. Be with her, I pray, and help her to keep trying.

Tonight I'm to attend a baby shower. Somehow You help me roll off the trials of the day and cast them on You. Somehow You free my mind so I can give my best to this sweet mother-to-be. I'm glad I can enjoy this festive occasion.

A deep, inward pleasure comes from You, Lord. Thank You for how Your joy is my strength. Thank You for taking my concerns and freeing me to give the vitality of this God-sent happiness to others.

The LORD is my strength and my shield;
my heart trusts in him, and I am helped.
My heart leaps for joy
and I will give thanks to him in song.

PSALM 28:7 NIV

More Than Words

There's this lady I know, Father, who looks tired and anxious every time I see her. She doesn't know Your Son as her Savior yet. I've been talking with her about You. But whenever we get into a conversation, she's interrupted by one of her children. How can I ever help her to get to know You if she doesn't have a moment to herself?

I remember what it was like when we were raising our children, Father. I loved being a mother and being a part of their lives. Still, I often wasn't able to get a full night's sleep. I seldom had some time I could call my own—even in the bathroom!

I'll never forget our dear friends Joan and Peggy, who offered to take the children for a weekend so Bob and I could get away. Once, we went to a motel only a few miles from home. The moment we walked in the motel door, I lay back on the bed and slept for two hours straight. That loving act of service meant more to me than all the kind words in the world.

Show me how I can put my words into action and help this exhausted mother. She needs some peace, Lord. Let my hands, my feet, and my time serve You.

> *So Jesus said to them again,*
> *"Peace to you! As the Father has sent Me,*
> *I also send you."*
>
> JOHN 20:21 NKJV

Offering of Tranquility

What a surprise, the way You answered my prayer, Father. I asked You how I could help a young mother. You opened so many doors, there was no way I could misunderstand Your direction.

First, I received some extra money I wasn't counting on. Then, two meetings I was scheduled to attend the following weekend were canceled. It was the same weekend our church had a couple's retreat planned. Surprisingly, the money I received was enough to cover the couple's cost, plus provide a little spending money.

When I told this mother and her husband, they looked so surprised, as though they couldn't believe it was true. I'm glad they could break away and bring their children to our home. We had a lot of fun together, Father. It reminded me of when our kids were growing up.

The best part was when the parents returned and told me they had accepted Jesus as their Savior. This was because of Your leading me to give a practical peace offering and allowing Your Holy Spirit to work.

Thank You for guiding me. Thank You for giving me the privilege of being a part of such a fantastic miracle happening in their lives.

Whatever you do, work at it with all your heart,
as working for the Lord, not for men,
since you know that you will receive an inheritance
from the Lord as a reward.
It is the Lord Christ you are serving.

COLOSSIANS 3:23–24 NIV

APRIL 10

Passing on Peace

Lord, this person is yelling at me! I didn't do anything to cause his problems. I want to bristle, shout some unkind remark, and walk out the door. Still, I sense You urging me to stop, listen, and patiently hear his anxious words.

The more I listen, the more I realize he isn't angry with me. He simply needs to talk out the situation with someone who cares. Help me to forget about the clock. Grant me strength and compassion, even when I hear his upsetting words of anger.

He's calming down, Lord. Thank You. He doesn't need my opinion—just a sensitive ear. The longer he talks, the more he seems to be viewing the situation reasonably. Please help him to make the right decisions.

May anything I say to him be words of peace and calmness. Let me remember not to be judgmental but to simply care. If it's Your will, make an opening so I can pray with him and ask for You to show him a way through.

I'm amazed how calm he is now, Lord. He's even thanking me for taking time to care. He's letting me pray with him! As we pray, Your harmony fills the air. Thank You for leading me to help bring him peace—a peace that passes all understanding.

[Jesus said,]
"I am leaving you with a gift—
peace of mind and heart!
And the peace I give isn't fragile like
the peace the world gives.
So don't be troubled or afraid."

JOHN 14:27 TLB

Serving with Your Patience

Father, I am so frustrated. No matter how many times I talk with this person I'm trying to help grow in You, she takes two steps forward then one or two steps back. She smiles and agrees but doesn't follow through with her walk with You. Sometimes I feel aggravated with her. I want to scold her or give a big speech and put her on a guilt trip. Help me, Lord. Grant me the patience only You can give.

I think of all the times You have been patient with me. Repeatedly, You try to show me Your ways. I struggle to do my best but keep messing up. In the same way, I often take those steps forward, then back.

Thank You, Lord, for Your staying power. You never give up on me. You never make me feel like a failure. Instead, You are constantly with me, helping me up so I can start over when I back-step. Thank You for how Your loving presence surrounds me, for how You forgive me more times than I can count. Then You gently whisper, *"Let's start again."*

When I help others, grant me Your patience to persist, to love, to forgive, and to help them start again. Remind me to look for the best in others like You do in me.

But the wisdom that comes from heaven is
first of all pure and full of quiet gentleness.
Then it is peace-loving and courteous.
It allows discussion and is willing to yield to others;
it is full of mercy and good deeds.
It is wholehearted and straightforward and sincere.
And those who are peacemakers will plant seeds of
peace and reap a harvest of goodness.

JAMES 3:17–18 TLB

APRIL 12

Your Well within Me

Things were challenging today, Father. Everything around (and in) me seemed to be off center. I felt on edge. Situations constantly rubbed me the wrong way. The world and all its circumstances pressed in on every side. It was drawing the spiritual life right out of me. Now I thirst for Your words and refreshing presence.

I remember the modest farm our family lived on in eastern Washington while our children were growing up, Lord. We had one small well to provide water for drinking, cooking, washing, and irrigating our garden.

We had little rain. But the more we used the well, the better it produced its fresh, cool water. Somehow You met our needs.

Now I'm here, Lord, asking You for a great big drink from *Your* spiritual well. Thank You for quenching and rejuvenating my parched, thirsty soul. Thank You for this special time we have together, when I can talk with You and draw from Your strength.

No matter how often I drink, no matter how much I pass on to others, the well of spiritual life-giving nourishment through Your Word and Holy Spirit never runs dry. I praise You for quenching my thirst and helping me to pass on Your living water to others.

> *[Jesus said,] "For the Scriptures declare that rivers of living water shall flow from the inmost being of anyone who believes in me."*
> *(He was speaking of the Holy Spirit, who would be given to everyone believing in him.)*
>
> JOHN 7:38–39 TLB

Enduring Encouragement

I remember when the teenage girl came into my church school class with tangled hair and an attitude to match. She looked as though she had just managed to pull herself out of bed—not really ready to face another day. She gripped a strong cup of coffee in one hand and her Bible in the other. She slouched in a chair and reflected total discouragement with the world in general.

Thank You for helping me so I could understand her better. You granted me patience to care when she was at her worst. It's easy to recall when I once felt like that, Lord. Circumstances caused me to become disillusioned with everything and everyone around me. And it certainly showed in the way I looked and acted.

Thank You for helping me draw on those memories. I'm grateful for Your giving me words of encouragement to speak that slowly penetrated her maze of discouragement and gave her hope. Thank You for guiding me to be sensitive enough to listen, care, and see the potential hidden within her.

I finally saw a glimmer of optimism come to her eyes. I'm grateful for her questions and for Your giving me the wisdom to answer them.

Thank You for blessing her and keeping her near You. In Jesus' name, amen.

[Love] bears all things, believes all things,
hopes all things, endures all things.
Love never fails.

1 CORINTHIANS 13:7–8 NKJV

APRIL 14

Harvest from Patience

Although the girl once in my church school class is grown now, I'm glad I continued praying for her. I'm especially happy after a letter from her came in the mail. Recently, I have felt discouraged, wondering how much I am accomplishing for You, Father. The letter arrived just when I needed encouragement the most.

She told me of the good job she has and that she's living in her own apartment. Best of all, she says she loves You and is going to church *and* teaching a church school class. Thank You, dear Father, for causing my patience and prayers to become fruitful. Thank You for using this Christian young lady to serve You. Provide her a prayer life filled with wisdom and a never-give-up patience. May she, too, experience a bountiful harvest from her efforts to win souls for You.

Now I have another challenging student. Please help him. I'm grateful for Your reminding me to look for the best in him and other youths who come my way. Bridge the gaps between us. Take over, Father. Show these young people Your unfailing, patient love. Thank You for giving me the privilege of teaching them. As I watch them grow, I look forward to harvesting more priceless young Christians for You.

[Jesus said,] "Look around you!
Vast fields of human souls are ripening all around us,
and are ready now for reaping."

JOHN 4:35 TLB

Right My Failures

Lord, I really messed up today. This person wanted to talk and talk and talk. She always does that. I seriously needed a break. I just wanted to go home. I brushed her off.

The hurt look on her face made me feel so guilty. Please forgive my impatience. Nudge me when You want me to listen awhile longer. Help me understand how she's feeling. Intervene with Your Holy Spirit and meet her needs. Give her peace of mind and heart. When the time is right, teach me how to care and still tactfully limit the length of our conversations.

Perhaps You're trying to show me I don't have to solve all her problems. You are God, and You can meet her needs better than I can. Remind me to pray with her, help the best I can, then leave the rest in Your hands.

Forgive me for not being mindful of Your guidance. You know my heart, Lord. I love serving You. Go behind me when my energy ebbs, when I'm unable to handle things in the best way. Right my failures, I pray. Thank You for being my strength and endurance. Thank You for the times You take over.

[God said,] "I am with you;
that is all you need.
My power shows up best in weak people."

2 CORINTHIANS 12:9 TLB

Gentle Service

When You met with Your disciples in the upper room for the Last Supper, You already knew who would betray You, Lord Jesus. You also had foreknowledge of those who would run away and not stand their ground for You.

It's difficult comprehending the gentle love and service You expressed by washing Your disciples' feet. You didn't eliminate Judas, Lord—and certainly not Peter. In spite of the things You knew, which were most likely breaking Your heart, You still continued loving and serving.

I can visualize You getting up from the meal and wrapping a towel around Your waist. I can almost hear the sound of trickling water while You poured it into a basin. If I had been there and felt Your strong yet gentle hands washing my dirty, sandy feet and drying them with the towel, I think I would have felt overwhelmed and unworthy, much like Peter.

My first reaction would be for You not to wash my feet. I should be the one who would wait on You. Yet this was part of Your plan. Like a servant, You once bathed Your disciples' dirty feet. As a Savior, You did more for them—and me. You cleansed our dirty, sin-filled souls.

Teach me, Lord, to serve with this same unfaltering love.

So he [Jesus] got up from the supper table,
took off his robe, wrapped a towel around his loins,
poured water into a basin,
and began to wash the disciples' feet
and to wipe them with the towel he had around him.

JOHN 13:4–5 TLB

Tender Hands

Every muscle in my body ached that night when I came home from work, Lord. My grown son, Bob Jr., was visiting from out of town and waiting up for me. I looked forward to our time for a good visit.

I still recall walking in the door, greeting his smiling face. I flopped on the couch by him and kicked off my shoes. Bone spurs, they were called. All I knew was pain in my feet. Before I realized what was happening, Bob Jr. took my feet in his big, gentle hands and started massaging them. I recoiled. They were hot and sweaty. But he kept rubbing them, gently talking and listening to the events of my night's work.

I thanked You and Bob Jr. for the unselfish love he showed me. I remember asking You to give me a love that would make me willing to go outside my comfort zone. And You have.

Over and over, You put me in unpleasant situations I'm asked to help with. Each time, I take a deep mental breath and remember that You are giving me gentle hands and feet to serve. Remind me to love and comfort. With each act of service, I give You the praise.

In everything you do,
stay away from complaining and arguing. . . .
Shine out among them like beacon lights,
holding out to them the Word of Life.

PHILIPPIANS 2:14–16 TLB

A Living Sacrifice

I often ponder how You, Lord Jesus, are alive in heaven at the right-hand side of Your Father. I'm grateful for Your bringing my needs to Him. At the same time, Your Spirit abides in my heart. Still, I think of the price You paid to free me from sin. Thank You for dying on the cross and sacrificing Yourself for me.

What would You have me do for You, dear Lord? If I should give my life for another, it wouldn't compare to everything You have done and are doing for me.

Just follow Me, My child. Be willing to give up anything in order to serve Me. Take up the cross I have for You to carry. Deny your own desires and aspirations daily in order to accomplish what I call you to do.

Help me put Your will ahead of my own wants and desires. I know when I do, I will gain joy and everlasting peace You offer me. I willingly dedicate my life to You, Lord. How wonderful it is to experience Your blessings and true happiness beyond measure.

Take everything in my life, Lord, and use it for Your glory.

> *Then Jesus said to His disciples,*
> *"If anyone desires to come after Me,*
> *let him deny himself, and take up his cross, and follow Me.*
> *For whoever desires to save his life will lose it,*
> *but whoever loses his life for My sake will find it.*
> *For what profit is it to a man if he gains the whole world,*
> *and loses his own soul?"*
>
> MATTHEW 16:24–26 NKJV

Let Me Share Your Goodness

I'm thankful, Lord, that after three days in the tomb, You didn't remain dead. Instead, You triumphed over sin and death and rose from that awful, cold grave. Before You died, You had the power to spread Your goodness everywhere You went. After You came back to life, You continued spreading kindness. Even now, You send Your Holy Spirit to help me. That same power to do good for others and overcome the sin and sadness of this world is here for me today. Thank You, Lord Jesus, for dying and rising again for me. Thank You for the constant, helpful presence of Your Holy Spirit who dwells within me.

Grant me Your strength and unconditional love as You lead me to spread Your goodness to others. Grant me new vitality in well-doing. Make my feet swift and my hands sure. All credit belongs to You. Whatever kindness I do is only significant and has eternal value if it comes through You. Because of this, let my every word and action be acceptable in Your sight, O Lord, my vitality and my salvation.

Every good gift and every perfect gift is from above,
and comes down from the Father of lights,
with whom there is no variation or shadow of turning.

JAMES 1:17 NKJV

Help Me Teach with Kindness

Lord, this student I'm teaching in school is sucking every ounce of patience out of me. No matter how I try, his mind seems to be elsewhere. How can I reach him with this important lesson? I know he's capable of learning it. He simply isn't doing his best. In desperation, I want to shout out numerous words filled with exasperation. Still, I sense Your presence, urging me to show kindness and love. Teach me how to understand his needs, I pray.

Well, here goes, Lord. Please help him. It's working! A time limit to complete lessons, a simple breakaway from the normal routine, and a learning game are making a difference. Most of all, a little loving assurance that I'm proud of him is helping a lot.

Thank You for Your wise direction, for helping this child—and me! Do You see his smile and the look of success in his eyes? I know You do. Thank You for giving me insight and kindness that can come only from You. Thank You for this child I'm teaching. I'm learning from him, too.

The next time frustration is taking over while I'm teaching, nudge me again, Lord. Guide me in ways to be firm but kind and understanding. Help the children I teach to see Your love in all I say and do.

> *And the Lord's servant must not quarrel;*
> *instead, he must be kind to everyone,*
> *able to teach.*

2 TIMOTHY 2:24 NIV

Teach Me Faithfulness

I just went through some depressing experiences, Father. I must be hard to get along with during these times. I felt so low, I wasn't able to think clearly. I'm sorry for the way I responded to You and others. Please forgive me. In spite of it all, I'm thankful for Your steadfast closeness.

I praise You, Father, for the wonderful ways You have shown Your faithfulness to me. Even when I'm at my lowest ebb, You are there—willing to help me. Thank You for never turning Your back, for looking for the best in me.

I'm grateful for those who have patiently stood by me through thick and thin. When I couldn't see a way through all my problems, my friends helped me sort things out. When I felt no one cared, they never deserted me. Thank You for their unwavering love and constant, selfless actions.

Show me how to be faithful like You. Help me stand by others when I may be the only one who is doing so. Grant me patience to help in whatever ways needed, even when they are depressed, unpleasant, or lost in spirit. Remind me to look for the best in them. Teach me how to love and care for them as You do me.

A true friend is always loyal,
and a brother [or sister] is born
to help in time of need.

PROVERBS 17:17 TLB

The Faithful Ones

When I learned during church that my aunt Virginia was gravely ill, I asked for Your help, Lord. I wanted to be at her side as quickly as possible. I had numerous duties to take care of after the service. There were people to greet, refreshments to serve, my church school classroom to clean up, dishes to do in the church kitchen, and much more. Faithful people jumped right in and took over for me!

I lost Aunt Virginia that day, Lord. Although I feel like a part of me was taken away, I know she was ready to go. She is in Your care. After I left her bedside and returned to the church to gather my things and go home, I realized how all of my work was faithfully done. I found out many were praying for our family during this time. Thank You for the incredibly dedicated members in our family of God.

I'm grateful for how they loved and encouraged me during the next few days. I always want to be the strong one. This time they insisted it was their turn. When I was down and filled with grief, they understood. They loved me with an unselfish, empathetic love. Bless these dear, faithful ones, Lord. I love them more than words can say.

If one part [of God's family] suffers,
every part [or person] suffers with it;
if one part is honored,
every part rejoices with it.

1 CORINTHIANS 12:26 NIV

Spirit of Self-Control

Father, this grocery store line is long tonight. I have an important meeting to be at in only a few minutes. What's holding things up? It seems like it's taking forever. I want to get impatient, but what good would it do? Please give me some self-control instead.

I can't see what's going on at the head of the line. It isn't moving. Be with whoever is having a problem up there and help her. Thank You for giving me the presence of mind to pray for that person instead of demonstrating a poor attitude.

Now I see, Father. It's one of Your children who is older. She's struggling to pay for her groceries but can't count the change. Thank You for the clerk helping her. Thank You for the person behind her who steadies her elbow as she stands there, and for the one who carries her groceries and walks her to the waiting cab outside.

I'm appreciative of Your helping me. Not only did I make it through the line quickly after that, but I had all green traffic lights and made it to my meeting on time. You are so good in how You help each of us through our problems.

In my elderly years, Father, I pray for other people to be patient and willing to help me.

For this very reason,
make every effort to add to your faith goodness;
and to goodness, knowledge;
and to knowledge, self-control;
and to self-control, perseverance;
and to perseverance, godliness;
and to godliness, brotherly kindness;
and to brotherly kindness, love.

2 PETER 1:5–7 NIV

Cause for Compassion

There are several people in our church who have mental or physical disabilities, Lord. Many days, several of our folks go the extra mile to help these dear ones in their times of need.

My schedule is jam-packed with numerous tasks during the mornings before church. No matter how much I try to get things done a day ahead, I'm always pressed before church and ask for Your help. Just about the time I'm making progress, though, I'm stopped by those who don't understand and want to chat a lot. This is when I feel Your call for compassion.

Though the lack of time frustrates me, I feel Your nudges to stop and care—more so, to tune in to the needs of those who have a hard time understanding and reasoning out different situations. Somehow You help me step back and look at these unique people from Your eyes. Thank You, Lord, for them. I can visualize them someday in heaven coming up to me, totally whole in mind and body. I hope they can tell me of some good memory they cherish of my having been in their lives.

They have so much to offer. Thank You for the love and dedication of each one. I often see the pride in their eyes as they exhibit faithfulness and love in doing small projects around our church.

> *Do nothing out of selfish ambition or vain conceit,*
> *but in humility consider others better than yourselves.*
> *Each of you should look not only to your own interests,*
> *but also to the interests of others.*

PHILIPPIANS 2:3–4 NIV

Am I Good Enough for You?

I want to serve You, Lord. Yet I occasionally feel inadequate. Am I smart or attractive enough? Sometimes I'm awkward in words and actions.

Others have more status. Many are more educated. I don't possess impressive material things. Sometimes I feel like others look down on me, as though they're much better. Perhaps they are, Lord. As I forge bravely ahead in serving You, I frequently hit a wall of negative thoughts: *I'm not good enough to really do this job well.*

Why did You call me to serve like this, Lord, when others are more capable? I know feeling this way isn't Your will. I want to heed Your call. Here I am, asking for Your help.

You must view yourself as I do, dear one. You are precious to Me. Each time you feel you are not good enough to serve Me, focus your mind, soul, and every fiber of your being on the things of Me. I am the One who calls you. I am the One who decides how capable you are of serving Me. Cast off the negative and trust in Me for help. I will have you do great things. Be filled with My Holy Spirit. I will give you power to serve.

Thank You for Your direction and confidence, Lord.

Therefore, holy brothers,
who share in the heavenly calling,
fix your thoughts on Jesus,
the apostle and high priest whom we confess.

HEBREWS 3:1 NIV

The Towel of Healing

Father, I can't imagine the hardships some experience in their lives. Today, while I helped finish cleaning our church kitchen, I talked and listened to someone who was ready to open her heart to me.

I must admit, Father, there have been times I felt impatient at how this dear lady was limping along spiritually. It seemed every time I crossed her path, she was making bad decisions. I know she loves You, but she is still taking two steps forward and one step back. I wanted to scold her and shame her into doing the right things. Then You spoke to my heart and encouraged me to love and listen and love some more—then pray a lot more.

Today she told me how much she appreciated my having patience and not belittling her. Tears streaked her cheeks as she began telling her story. Before I knew it, I was dabbing her eyes with a damp dish towel. We hugged and prayed together.

I do see some spiritual growth, Lord. Thank You for helping us each day. Thank You for reminding me not to wield the sword of correction but to use the towel of healing and compassion.

> Stop being mean, bad-tempered and angry.
> Quarreling, harsh words,
> and dislike of others should have no place in your lives.
> Instead, be kind to each other, tenderhearted,
> forgiving one another,
> just as God has forgiven you because you belong to Christ.

EPHESIANS 4:31–32 TLB

True Servanthood

Every time I saw this person, I cringed with a feeling of inferiority. Everything about her is so perfect. She's beautiful. No matter where she is or what time of the day it is, she never has a hair out of place. Not only that, Lord—she has the most beautiful clothes I've ever seen. She looks like she has walked out of a catalog! I often thought of her as a china doll—one brisk wind and she would tumble and break. That's what I assumed until the other evening when I went to visit a sick, elderly friend.

Homemade soup in hand, I rang the doorbell, and my friend answered the door. She tottered ahead of me with her walker and led the way to her dining room. When I glanced into my friend's kitchen, I was so surprised at what I saw, I almost fell over. There on her knees in the middle of the kitchen floor, scrub brush in hand, was my "china doll." She had a big smile on her face. She actually appeared to enjoy what she was doing. Despite all, her hair was still neatly in place.

A short time of visiting revealed that this polished lady doesn't have it as easy as I assumed. She had earned the money to put herself through beauty school by cleaning houses. She still pinches pennies and builds her beautiful wardrobe from savvy shopping at local thrift stores. She also confided her favorite thing to do is help those who are sick or down-and-out.

Forgive me, Lord, for judging. Help me to have humility and be as thoughtful as I have discovered she is.

Therefore, as God's chosen people, holy and dearly loved,
clothe yourselves with compassion, kindness,
humility, gentleness and patience.

COLOSSIANS 3:12 NIV

APRIL 28

The Secret Service

Here I am, Lord. I feel like I'm pulling a prank. My car is parked in the alley, where no one will notice it. It's early morning. I sneak up the steps of this family home. I know everyone is gone. I hope no one sees me doing this service. It will be known only to You and me, Lord. It's a secret.

This family is having a difficult time. The father's hours at work were cut back. Even though he works two minimum-wage jobs to help make ends meet, they barely get by. I realize You already know and care.

I just want to put my prayers for them to work by helping in this small way. How thrilled the family will be when they discover these boxes I'm depositing on their porch. It was fun to shop, to meet individual needs and probable wants of each family member. Now, I slip the envelope under the kitchen door, containing a short typewritten note of love and some cash. Best of all, they will never feel indebted to anyone for this secret service of love.

In doing this, Lord, I'm thankful for the inner joy it gives me to be a secret servant for You.

[Jesus said,]
"But when you do a kindness to someone, do it secretly—
don't tell your left hand what your right hand is doing.
And your Father who knows all secrets will reward you."

MATTHEW 6:3–4 TLB

129

The Loud Message of Kindness

It was a fleeting thirty years ago, Lord, when I learned a valuable lesson from my friend, Shirley. Crisp, white hospital sheets wrapped me in a sterile cocoon. I was so sick, I barely noticed what went on around me.

Cards came. Friends gathered to pray. I knew people cared, but Shirley's kind actions spoke loud and clear. When she stepped through the door, Your warm presence filled the room. She never seemed hurried as she sat by me. She talked little and listened a lot. She simply loved and cared.

Much later, I realized the sacrifice she had made, Lord. She had a large family. Her husband worked long hours. Shirley often took on the role of father and mother. Still, she broke away several times to be with me at the hospital.

You know that as well as being sick, I was pregnant. After my baby was born, I was so weak. Shirley took our newborn baby, our four-year-old son, and me into her home for several days so I could regain my strength. Her caring actions were the living example of Your sacrificial love.

I think often of this lesson and want to continue sharing Your message through practical acts of kindness. Then I will speak encouraging words.

We continually remember before our God and Father
your work produced by faith,
your labor prompted by love,
and your endurance inspired by
hope in our Lord Jesus Christ.

1 THESSALONIANS 1:3 NIV

What Can I Do for Another Today?

This is a new day, Father. Let me begin it by reaching for Your guiding hand. I want to do my best for You in all I do and say. What can I do for another today? Help me be sensitive and do unnoticed things for those around me. Help me be mindful of the opportunities to show acts of courtesy while driving to my job. Let me take an extra step in sharing the workload. Most of all, remind me at day's end to especially demonstrate love to my dear family.

It's strange how these things pump energy and warmth into me, Lord. Perhaps it is the approval of Your Holy Spirit working. Even if things go wrong and events all seem uphill, still I know You have used me as Your instrument to make life a little better for those around me.

Thank You for remaining close and showing me what I can do for others today. As You and I work together, I enjoy Your loving, kind ways more. Thank You for giving Yourself to me. Thank You for showing me how to give of myself.

> *[Jesus said,] "These things I have spoken to you,*
> *that My joy may remain in you,*
> *and that your joy may be full.*
> *This is My commandment,*
> *that you love one another as I have loved you."*

> JOHN 15:11–12 NKJV

I Meet You at Dawn

Good morning, Lord. It's still dark outside. I push myself out of bed, shuffle slippered feet to the kitchen, and brew a cup of tea. I want to meet with You at dawn. I step out the back door, steaming cup in hand. Ah. It's so wonderfully quiet—just You and me, Lord.

Dawn's silvery light silently pierces the darkness. I sense Your presence envelop me. Your whispers of love fill my soul. Turmoil and anxiousness leave. Your assurance and comfort take their place.

I love You with all my heart, dear Lord. I lift my praise and worship to You. Thank You for listening to my joys and concerns. I place them at Your feet and let them go. Now, I fix my heart on You and Your wondrous ways.

Look at the sun working its way up through the clouds, Lord. Brilliant shades of orange fill the sky. It causes me to think of You, the glorious Son of God. I walk along the flower beds. The roses drip silvery drops of dew and cause me to think of the tears You lovingly shed for me in the Garden of Gethsemane. How I love You, Lord.

Hush, My child. Quiet your thoughts, and listen to Me. Breathe deeply the freshness of My holy presence.

Yes, Lord. Here I am.

The Lord called Samuel.
And he answered,
"Here I am! . . .
Speak, for Your servant hears."

1 Samuel 3:4, 10 nkjv

You Are Altogether Lovely

How lovely You are, O Lord. You are the order in all Your creation. You cause the mornings, the days, and the evenings to rejoice in Your presence. Mountains show Your strength. You visit the ground with rainfall and make it yield. You provide grain, fruits, and vegetables for us to eat. You pour Your rain into ridges and settle them in furrows. You slow the drops to soft, refreshing showers that bless every growing thing.

You cover each season with goodness. Somehow You work them together. Your loving-kindness blankets the forests and pastures. You bring forth flocks of birds and countless varieties of animals.

Who in heaven or earth is so full of grace and glory? Who can compare to You? There is no other so great as You, whose very presence can cause the earth to tremble or calm my troubled heart. You make rock-hard ocean waves to crash, shifting turquoise waters from steel green to crystal-clear rivulets. You also cleanse and redirect my life.

You are altogether lovely, O Lord. How marvelous the way You shower Your love upon each of us, above and beyond anything else in this world's creation. You, who rule over everything, take the time to talk with and listen to me. Thank You for the caring way You always have time for me and minister to my heart.

Yes, he is altogether lovely.
This is my beloved,
And this is my friend.

SONG OF SOLOMON 5:16 NKJV

I Wait on You

Here I am, Lord. I need Your help. There are so many who need You. I'm stretched too thin. I can't do it all. I feel misunderstood and unappreciated. Am I seeking to do my will and not Yours? I know my vision of Your call is slipping. There is only one way I can regain it. I need to seek Your presence and wait on Your direction. In Your answer, I know I will regain the strength and confidence required.

As I pause before You, dear Lord, I enjoy Your understanding ways. Thank You for not looking down on me when I'm discouraged. Thank You for Your promise that You will renew my strength and cause me to mount up with wings like eagles. Only through Your wisdom, guidance, and power can I run and not be weary, walk and not faint.

Thank You for hearing my prayer and teaching me graciousness. You are my joy and strength. I'm grateful for Your helping me to look up, take courage, and press forward. Thank You for showering me with Your much-treasured compassion. I praise You for Your love, insight, and direction, and for giving me the good sense to wait on You and receive Your guidance.

Even the youths shall faint and be weary,
and the young men shall utterly fall:
But they that wait upon the LORD
shall renew their strength;
they shall mount up with wings as eagles;
they shall run, and not be weary;
and they shall walk, and not faint.

ISAIAH 40:30–31 KJV

More Than Enough for the Day

This has been a tight month financially, Father. Someone needed my help, though. I felt You led me to take action. Thank You for providing me the faith to give above my tithe. Everything I have already belongs to You. I'm grateful for Your promise to meet my needs, and that You know them even better than I do.

You always provide what I need each day, each month. You often give me more than I need. Thank You for Your bountiful blessings and for helping me trust in You. Because of this, I'm filled with Your peace and confidence.

I read how manna fell in Bible times. Just enough for each day. When the Israelites complained, You still remained with them. Like me, they sometimes learned things the hard way. You taught them patience and how to trust and depend on You.

Let me learn from their lessons. As I place my faith in You, I'm encouraged by Your promises to meet my daily needs. Like many times before, I enjoy Your benevolence, Father—"pressed down, and shaken together, and running over" (Luke 6:38 KJV). Thank You for giving me more than enough for each day.

> [Jesus said,] "Give, and it will be given to you.
> They [the fruits of your gifts] will pour
> into your lap a good measure—
> pressed down, shaken together, and running over.
> For by your standard of measure
> it will be measured to you in return."
>
> LUKE 6:38 NASB

Apart with You

I steal away awhile to unwind, Lord, apart from the press of my hurried life. Here, in this quiet place, I find peace and tranquility with You. As I seek Your quiet strength, I feel You wipe worry and weariness from me. Things of this world don't matter nearly as much as the precious time we have, communing with one another.

I feel like a child sitting at Your feet. Time stops. I share with You all I've been doing—my failures and victories, fears and hopes. I sense You laugh with me over the amusing things and cry with me when I share my woes.

Here, I draw apart and rest. Here, I gain strength, lest I burn out from responsibilities I shoulder. You offer me spiritual food, the bread of life from Your Bible. Your words are sure and true. I hold them in my heart. Here, I drink from the living fountain of Your cleansing Holy Spirit. You search my heart and redirect my way. We commune as Friend with friend.

I lean back and close my eyes. I see Your face in my mind. What a sweet breakaway this is, physically and spiritually. As I focus on You, my vitality is renewed. My thoughts are set on the ways You lead me. Thank You for welcoming me to draw apart with You.

[Jesus said,]
"Come with me by yourselves to a quiet place
and get some rest."

MARK 6:31 NIV

You Are My Greatest Love

Today is our wedding anniversary, Lord. How I love this dear husband of mine. I can't believe we've been married this long! It's most of our lives. I find myself loving him more each day.

Although we cherish one another, You are still our greatest love. You, heavenly Father and Savior, are the One who dwells in our hearts. Because You are first in our lives, the love we hold for each other grows deeper. Through tests in life, joys, sorrows, and change, we learn to seek You first. This way, we keep getting stronger.

We love You because You first loved us. We lift our praise to You, dear Lord. No greater love do we know. Through this, we acknowledge Your closeness. We feel Your staying power. You, Lord, are the Author of our faith. In You our love began. Through You we find a greater love than humankind can give. It's a love that's always there. Your love is forgiving, unconditional.

This love You give doesn't take away affection from my husband and me. It draws us closer to You and, in turn, closer to one another. Thank You, Lord, for our love for each other—one that will last into eternity.

> *Dear friends, since God so loved us,*
> *we also ought to love one another.*
> *No one has ever seen God;*
> *but if we love one another,*
> *God lives in us and his love is made complete in us.*

1 JOHN 4:11–12 NIV

You Soothe My Mind

I toss and turn in bed. Decisions to be made disturb my sleep. Loved ones cause me worry. I pull back the covers and get up. I put on my robe and slippers and stumble to the living room. I switch on the light and open my Bible. I also open my heart to You, dear Lord.

Here I am, asking for peace of mind. Is there any solace in this sin-filled world? All around me, I see sorrow. Is it possible to escape the things that press in? I want to do Your will, but I need some rest. What of those I care for, Lord? Are they safe? Please take care of them.

Peace I give you, dear one. Focus on Me. Listen while I whisper words of comfort to your soul. Your decisions I direct. As you do My will, I shall reward you. Your loved ones are safely in My care. And the future? I am the King. And I am still on the throne. Do not worry, My child. I take your prayers to heart.

Touch my mind, Lord. Touch my heart. I relinquish everything to You and trust You to meet my needs. I rest now in You. I experience Your comfort as my thoughts stay on You. Thank You for providing me Your peace of heart and mind.

You will keep him in perfect peace,
Whose mind is stayed on You,
Because he trusts in You.

ISAIAH 26:3 NKJV

You Calm My Fears

There are things I face in my life that cause me to be anxious, Father. They are so overwhelming, they cause me to freeze in my tracks. You are my source of strength and my Redeemer. I bring my fears to You now and cast them at Your feet. I trust in You and will not rely on my own perception. In every way, I will depend on You, for I know You go before me.

As you place your faith in Me, My child, I will cause your uprightness to shine like the noonday sun! Be quiet and calm. Do not try to run ahead of Me. Wait patiently for My will to be accomplished, for I am here to defend you and free you from worry. I am your shelter and fort. I am your ever-present Guide through your troubles.

Thank You for being with me, Father. How comforting it is to put my trust in You. Your Spirit radiates infinite hope deep into my heart. Thank You for watching over me and those I love. Even when my faith is minuscule, You are enough, for You are my Lord. You are my strength, the source of my song. Through all these things, You give me joy. Thank You for replacing my fears with faith in You.

> *When I am afraid,*
> *I will trust in you.*
> *In God, whose word I praise,*
> *in God I trust;*
> *I will not be afraid.*
>
> PSALM 56:3–4 NIV

Kitchen-Sink Blessings

Here I am at my kitchen sink, Lord. All morning long I have sought You and felt You near. I'm up to my elbows in dish-soap bubbles. I hear hustle and bustle in the other room. No matter. Right now, I'm enjoying Your presence. I love You so. Refill my hungry soul with Your Holy Spirit.

Ah, yes. I feel Your glorious love surround me. Like rivers of living water, You fill my soul to overflowing. Oh, what joy I experience as You minister to my heart. Your holy presence is almost too much for me to bear. Thank You, Lord, for visiting me at my makeshift altar—my sink—and for surrounding me with love in my prayer room—my kitchen.

Tears of joy drop into my dishwater. Your blessings to me are beyond compare. Thank You for how You are lifting my needs to Your heavenly Father right now on my behalf. Thank You for Your Comforter, the Holy Spirit, who is with me all the time.

The dishes are done. I'm dabbing my eyes. Still, You remain—loving and comforting me. I don't want to leave this spot, Lord. I want to remain here forever. Go with me, I pray, for You don't just dwell in my kitchen; You dwell in my heart.

[Jesus said,] "I will ask the Father
and he will give you another Comforter,
and he will never leave you.
He is the Holy Spirit,
the Spirit who leads into all truth."

JOHN 14:16–17 TLB

A Mother's Prayer

Father, I bring my children and my children's children to You today. Bless and watch over them, I pray. Things are troubling and unsure in this world. Sometimes I shudder at what could possibly happen to my family. Will they live to grow old? Will they love and serve You all the days of their lives?

I know You love my children and grandchildren as much and more than I am capable of doing. Although they are part of me, they belong to You. I believe You prayed for them in the Garden of Gethsemane before You were taken to the cross. They were purchased by You with the price of Your life. As I dedicate them to You, I trust Your promise to keep them in Your care.

Take heart, dear mother. If any of your offspring should soar to the highest heavens or go below the deepest sea, I shall be there with them. I will be with them in the darkest and lightest hours. Nothing can keep Me from loving your children. Each time I hear them pray, I bring their concerns to the throne of My heavenly Father.

Thank You, Father, for answering my prayer. Thank You for Your love that goes beyond time and space.

> *The LORD bless thee, and keep thee:*
> *The LORD make his face shine upon thee,*
> *and be gracious unto thee:*
> *The LORD lift up his countenance upon thee,*
> *and give thee peace.*

NUMBERS 6:24–26 KJV

Mother's Best Gifts

Remember the best gifts You ever gave me as a mother, Lord? Yes, I know You do. Many years ago, our son Bobby Jr. asked his daddy and me to pray with him to have You come into his heart. Bobby's prayer was beautiful music to my ears. Bobby had a quiet, simple faith. He still does.

Several years later, You gave me another wonderful gift. It was when our son Danny was four years old. At the time, Danny was going to Vacation Bible School. A sweet little grandma planted some lessons in his heart that he still mentions today. His childish voice filled our home with songs and Scriptures about You.

Again You gave Your gift, while I tucked Danny in bed. That was when he said he wanted to ask You into his heart. As we knelt by his bedside, he prayed a simple prayer to You. Both times this happened, Lord, I felt as though Your angels rejoiced all around us. This experience was as memorable as when I heard my children's first cries.

Thank You that all of our sons, now grown, love and know You as their personal Savior. Thank You that by Your grace You brought us through the growing years and kept them close to You. Thank You for the best mother's gift ever.

Therefore I remind you to stir up the gift of God
which is in you through the laying on of my hands.
For God has not given us a spirit of fear,
but of power and of love and of a sound mind.

2 TIMOTHY 1:6–7 NKJV

MAY 12

Key to the Unknown

I know not what the future holds, dear Lord, but I'm sure You hold the key. I'm glad You are the One who cares for my days ahead. If they were in my hands, I would probably make a mess of things. How wonderful it is that You are all-knowing. Your insight and wisdom surpass everything else.

Thank You for unlocking the door to each day as it comes my way. I take great comfort and joy in how You step through that door before me. Then You guide me through. I don't have the foresight to make life's decisions without Your counsel. You give me security with each step I take.

When things become a fog and I grope in a mist of confusion, I feel Your sure hand taking hold of mine and leading me. You know my wants and my needs. You understand my greatest concerns. When I become anxious about the future, You turn the key again. Patiently, You unlock the door to faith and help me trust in You.

Thank You, Lord, for holding the answers to the unknown. As I walk this road of life, I look back and understand a little how You have fit things together for my good. My past, my present, and my future, I place in Your capable hands.

> *For I know the thoughts that I think toward you,*
> *says the LORD, thoughts of peace and not of evil,*
> *to give you a future and a hope.*
> *Then you will call upon Me and go and pray to Me,*
> *and I will listen to you.*

JEREMIAH 29:11–12 NKJV

Your Assurance

Thank You, Father God, for giving me Your blessed assurance that I am in Your constant watch—not only me, but everything and everyone I care about. Thank You for helping me to lay my entire life on Your altar. Thank You for helping me remember how much You love me.

In full assurance of Your love, I relinquish my guilt and pain. In full assurance, I know You roll it all away. You remove my bitterness. You comfort me. You cover my tears with Your smile. In the desert scenes of my life, Your hope bursts forth like vibrant cactus flowers blooming after a sudden rain shower.

When my days go as smooth as glass, I praise You for Your assuring love. When the storms of life crash in and billows roar, I still praise You. You are always near—guiding and watching over me. When I'm at my best, I sense Your approval. When I'm at my worst, I experience Your love and forgiveness.

Here with You, I leave it all, my hopes and dreams and wants. Here, I trust Your assuring hands to pick up this struggling life of mine, turn it around, then mold it in the way You know is best. I give my all to You because of the calm assurance You place within me.

"The LORD himself goes before you and will be with you; he will never leave you nor forsake you."

DEUTERONOMY 31:8 NIV

MAY 14

I Come to Your Fountain

Father, occasionally I face so many demands that I don't know which way to turn. I frequently pour everything I have to offer into other people and situations, and I go beyond my abilities. This is one of those times, Lord. I'm so burned out, I don't want to talk with anyone or go anywhere. I need to come away with You.

Here I am in this quiet place. The world goes on around me. But all is calm in my secret spot of worship. No one knows I'm here but my understanding husband. Hear me, O Lord, as I share my heart and mind with You. Thank You for identifying with my every concern. I recognize Your voice speaking to my heart. How I love Your calming words. I open my Bible and ask for guidance. The answers jump off the page and minister to me. I dive into Your spiritual living fountain. You wash away my unwanted attitudes. You soothe my anxious mind. The presence of Your Holy Spirit wraps around me like a comforting blanket. Here, I rest and feel secure. I drink from Your well that never runs dry. You pump new energy and joyfulness into me. You replace my defeated mind-set with Your revitalizing presence.

Thank You for Your spiritual living fountain. Thank You for restoring my soul.

For you are the Fountain of life;
our light is from your Light.

PSALM 36:9 TLB

You Are My Yokefellow

Thank You for this calling You give me, Lord. Although it's a huge undertaking, You furnish the answer to lightening my load. It's simply working hand in hand with You. Your Bible says to take Your yoke upon me, because Your yoke is easy and light. When I first read this, Lord, I wondered how taking on more of a burden could be better. Then You helped me understand.

I read how long ago two people shared a yoke placed upon their shoulders. The yoke helped make them stronger while they carried their load and worked together. Even machinery works this way. Why should this calling from You bring worry when You are offering to help me?

Now I put on Your yoke, Lord, and we work as one. Thank You for taking control and leading me. You are my Yokefellow, my Guide, my Helper. How I enjoy working with You, rather than charging off my own way. Should I tend to stray, please tug me back on the right path.

Thank You for Your gentle commands and sure precepts. I take pleasure in Your being with me. Thank You for how Your hand, the same capable hand that bore creation, still guides and helps me. What joy we share as we work as one!

[Jesus said,] "Come to Me,
all who are weary and heavy-laden,
and I will give you rest.
Take My yoke upon you and learn from Me,
for I am gentle and humble in heart,
and YOU WILL FIND REST FOR YOUR SOULS.
For My yoke is easy and My burden is light."

MATTHEW 11:28–30 NASB

MAY 16

The Great Physician

Father, this illness hit me overnight. Emergency surgery followed. Day and night, I suffer pain with no relief. Will I ever get well? Will I die? The doctors said I should have been better in a couple of days, but that wasn't so. Now more than ever I come to You, the Great Physician.

I know You can accomplish healing in me beyond the capability of any human doctor. Touch me, I pray. Help me rest as much as possible and focus completely on You, for You are my Great Physician.

I feel a soothing balm from Your warm hands working on my aching body. My anxious muscles begin to relax while I concentrate on Your loving ways. When I become discouraged, I trust in You for healing and Your timing in accomplishing it. I give You every fiber of my being. Surely You know me through and through.

How I enjoy Your presence while I recover. What a relief to experience Your mending my wounds. Thank You for placing the words in my mind: *"I will get well."* You tell me when to exercise and when to rest. You urge me to claim victory through Your name.

Thank You for being my Great Physician.

> *O LORD my God,*
> *I cried out to You,*
> *And You healed me.*
>
> PSALM 30:2 NKJV

Your Healing Whisper

My mind is tangled with the cares of the day as I come to You, O Lord. I praise You for Your healing whispers of love and encouragement. In You I find freedom from strife. I wait on Your strengthening presence. In You I find safety, peace of mind. You help me to lay aside my trials. I fix my heart on Your encouraging words of hope.

I come to You and listen to Your teachings. You are so gentle. In You I find quietness and confidence. In You I find strength and inner peace. You heal my emotional scars as You teach me to forgive and let go.

You replace my wounds with wellness. I praise You for working wonderful miracles in me. You are my Shepherd. You are the One who makes me whole—physically, spiritually, and emotionally. Thank You for granting me relief in my days of trouble—for showing me a way through. Thank You for providing me rest and for drying my tears and helping me see things clearly, allowing me to choose Your righteous ways. You are my Lord, my God. Your whispers give me confidence and teach me what is best. My soul finds healing in You, O Lord. How good You are to me.

This is what the Sovereign LORD,
the Holy One of Israel, says:
"In repentance and rest is your salvation,
in quietness and trust is your strength."

ISAIAH 30:15 NIV

Your Restoring Rain

It had been days since rain fell in that little town, Lord. The ground was so dry, cracks jagged through the hard ground. Crops drooped in the scorching sun. Cattle barely had enough to drink. Some of their water was transported by trucks from miles away. Wells on farms dried up. People went to their sinks for a drink, and nothing came out. The air buzzed from heat rays. Many prayed, asking You to bring rain, Lord. They trusted You would supply their needs.

Then a day started with black clouds and loud thunder. One, two, three drops hit the pavement and evaporated immediately. I recall how You sent more rain. It came in a downpour for a while, then lessened to a slow, steady shower. Do you remember how everyone was so excited that they ran outside and just stood in it? Of course You do, Lord. How thankful folks were that You restored water to the wilting crops, people, and animals.

The flowers seemed to stretch toward the sky, trying to soak up every drop. The air smelled fresh and clean from Your cleansing rain. Everything sparkled like brand-new. Just like the way You restore my soul with Your cleansing, purifying showers. Thank You, Lord, for Your faithful, restoring rain.

> For I will give you abundant water
> for your thirst and for your parched fields.
> And I will pour out my Spirit
> and my blessings on your children.
> They shall thrive like watered grass,
> like willows on a river bank.
>
> ISAIAH 44:3–4 TLB

Your Protecting Angels

Lord, thank You for bringing me through a scary time when I worked at a fast-food restaurant. Eating places all around us were being robbed. Each time it happened, the robbers were more violent. Remember how I was working at the counter, Lord? I felt responsible for the young people employed there. Even though plainclothes police were on the streets, I was still concerned. My coworker Sherry and I kept praying for You to watch over us. We also asked You to take care of our friend, Patty, working two restaurants down the street.

Whenever I fretted, Sherry said, "Anita, don't worry. We asked for God to protect us. There are angels all around us and Patty."

One night I felt trouble walk in the door with two men. I took their order, made eye contact, and prayed to You a lot. I felt Your shielding presence. They looked around the restaurant and at each other. Then they took their food and left. I remembered Your promise of protection when we trust in You.

The next night I worked, police sirens screamed by to Patty's restaurant down the street. Patty had been robbed at gunpoint. She wasn't hurt and the robbers were caught.

Thank You for Your protecting angels.

The angel of the LORD encamps around those
who fear him, and delivers them.
O taste and see that the LORD is good!
Happy is the man who takes refuge in him!

PSALM 34:7–8 RSV

MAY 20

You Are My Bulwark

Lord, remember the painting that hung on my grand-mother's wall when I was a child? Its silent message prepared me for future storms in life. The picture appeared to have been painted in the 1920s. A beautiful young woman clung to a large rock while monstrous waves pounded the bulwark. Huge tidal waves tossed around the woman but never pulled her under. She was sheltered in the rift of the rock. Her face showed complete trust as she gazed heavenward.

I asked Grandma what the picture meant. She explained that You were the Rock; and as we trust in You, You would be our bulwark, our buffer during life's storms. As You know, Lord, Grandma is with You now. I miss her and wish I had her painting today. I must have spent hours studying it. Each time I did, You gently etched its lessons in my mind.

When fearsome storms come my way, You often remind me of Grandma's picture and give me the courage to keep clinging to You. No matter what I face, You always protect me with Your powerful hands. No matter how devastating things become, You stalwartly hide me in the rift of Your rock. Thank You for Your protection from evil and harm. Thank You for being my bulwark, my Rock, and my Salvation.

That Rock was [and is] Christ.

1 CORINTHIANS 10:4 NKJV

Your Encouragement

It's the end of an ordinary school day, Father. When it first started out, I was tempted to be impatient. But You reminded me of the time we had together this morning in prayer and how You encouraged me to be gentle, understanding, and steadfast.

I'm glad I listened to Your nudges, especially when a couple of my students were struggling with our reading lesson. Teaching children with special needs requires plenty of patience. Still, I love my little enthusiastic students and wouldn't trade teaching them for anything.

One child had been trying very hard to print letters without having to trace them. Each time he practiced, I praised him. Out of the blue, while reading long *e* sounds together, I heard words of pure joy come from him: "Mrs. D., look! *E!* Mrs. D., *e!*"

What a thrill to look at his paper and see a perfect *e* written, even with the long mark over the top. Thank You for the little accomplishments my students make that encourage them and me. I'm grateful, too, for the flowers a parent brought me at the end of the day. I guess we really are accomplishing something, aren't we, Lord?

Thank You for letting me teach these children. Thank You for the different ways You encourage me.

And it is he who will supply
all your needs from his riches in glory,
because of what Christ Jesus has done for us.

PHILIPPIANS 4:19 TLB

Kneeling at Your Feet

Here I am in Your sanctuary—this holy place of prayer. Not in a church but kneeling on the rug in front of my living room rocking chair. I feel like I'm at Your feet, dear Lord. Like a child, I tell You all that is going on. I share my delights and disappointments with You. How thankful I am that You never tire of listening to me. Here, I sense Your patience while I struggle for the right answers. Here, I draw from wisdom's lessons given by You.

With each passing day and year, I realize more and more how kind You are to me, Lord. You are my wonderful God. When I reach for You, You are here. When my life becomes parched and barren and I thirst for Your presence, You fill me to overflowing from Your stream of living water.

I love listening to Your every word. We have worked through many things in front of this chair, dear Lord. I lift my praise to You. In turn, I feel Your power and splendor. Here, You shower me with Your loving-kindness, better than life itself. Because of Your love for me, I obey and trust in You.

Thank You, Lord, for allowing me to kneel at Your feet. Thank You for being my heavenly Father and dearest Friend.

> *Mary sat on the floor,*
> *listening to Jesus as he talked. . . .*
> *[Jesus said,] "There is really only one thing*
> *worth being concerned about.*
> *Mary has discovered it—*
> *and I won't take it away from her!"*
>
> LUKE 10:39, 42 TLB

A Brand-New Start

Praise You, Father, for Your unwavering love. Your patience with me goes beyond my comprehension. Thank You for how You have forgiven my wrongs and shown me Your steadfast compassion. Even though the sins of our ancestors can go down to the third and fourth generations, I'm grateful for Your making them stop here. This is only possible as I turn my heart and my will completely over to You. Thank You for helping me make a brand-new start.

Each day as I walk with You, I experience Your caring about my every need and concern. Nothing is too great or small for me to bring to You. When I am at my best, I know Your love. When I'm down and not pleasant to be around, You never leave me. Instead, I praise You for remaining close and comforting me. I'm thankful, Lord, that I can be completely open with You about how I feel. I'm amazed at how You never make me feel guilty when I pour out my cares to You.

Thank You for always looking for the best in me and helping me grow in the right ways. I praise You, Father, for giving me a brand-new start.

His compassions fail not.
They are new every morning;
Great is Your faithfulness.
"The LORD is my portion," says my soul,
"Therefore I hope in Him!"

LAMENTATIONS 3:22–24 NKJV

MAY 24

Your Compassion

You are so loving and compassionate, Lord. You are a Father to me. You know me better than I know myself. Your tenderness and mercy follow me each day. Oh, how I enjoy the loving-kindness You show me. I will never forget Your bountiful blessings. I praise You for Your protecting presence.

I'm grateful for the way You go before me along life's path. You make Your ways known to me. As long as I follow Your lead, You help me not to stumble and fall. Day and night, You watch over me. When I'm awake, You are near. When I fall asleep, You surround me with Your presence. When evil or harm threatens, You spread Your wings over my trembling being, like an eagle does over its young. When I become weary and call on You for help, You carry me on Your wings and rejuvenate my soul.

Mere words cannot express my gratefulness for Your endless compassion. You, dear Father, are the One who snatched me from sin's horrible destruction. How wonderful, the way Your presence is here for me all the time. You never tire from watching over and caring for me. Thank You, dear Father. I love You so.

Praise the LORD, O my soul,
and forget not all his benefits. . . .
As a father has compassion on his children,
so the LORD has compassion on those who fear him.

PSALM 103:2, 13 NIV

You Give Me Deep Inner Joy

I climb in my car and turn the key. The moment the motor starts and I back out of our driveway, gratifying praise music on my radio fills my ears. My mind has already been sorting out the things to be done at work today. Some are stressful, Father. Others are good.

I pull into traffic. I hear the next song and feel an anointing of Your Holy Spirit through and around me, so strongly that the air is thick with Your presence. A deep inner joy fills my heart. Plans for the day fall into place. The glorious communion we share overshadows everything.

Things may not always go right today, Father. But You give me a peace and contentment that spill over to everyone around me. Any situation won't be too much for You and me to handle together.

More songs fill my soul. You help me put the things of this world into a heavenly perspective. You make my sensitive feelings calm and change my focus to caring and understanding for those whose paths I cross.

I pull into the parking lot. I'm ready for work, Lord. What satisfaction I feel. You will be with me all through my day. Thank You, Father, for filling my soul with Your joy.

The LORD is my strength and my shield;
My heart trusts in Him, and I am helped;
Therefore my heart exults,
And with my song I shall thank Him.

PSALM 28:7 NASB

Your Holy Spirit Helps Make Things Right

The joy and serenity I receive from You are my source of strength, O Lord. Thank You for stirring up goodness and peace within me through the presence of Your Holy Spirit. In the back of my mind, all day long, I think of You. Scriptures and songs of praise flow through my thoughts and make my heart glad. I thank You for how wonderful You are.

My praise continually lifts to You in silent communion while I fulfill my duties. *"Do this; don't do that,"* I hear You caution. How marvelous You are in the way You care for and lead me. How I rejoice in You, Lord. How happy You make me in all circumstances. You are the awesome God of my salvation. I rejoice when good things happen. Yet even in heartache, You pour into my soul Your comforting balm of peace and joy. When trials come or problems confront me, You help me to remain capable. How amazing, the way You ease and clear my mind.

You, O Holy Spirit, are everything to me. You are the sure One I can fix my mind on. You are the answer to my concerns and needs. Over and over, I marvel at how You work and help make things right.

Trust in the LORD with all your heart,
and do not rely on your own insight.
In all your ways acknowledge him,
and he will make straight your paths.

PROVERBS 3:5–6 RSV

Your Door Is Always Ajar

I had a dream the other night. In my dream, I rose from my bed and walked down the hall to a room I knew You would be in, Father. As I approached, I could see a light streaming from the door that was ajar. I knocked lightly and heard Your welcoming voice say, *"Come in."*

I entered and sat at Your feet. There, we talked for hours. Time didn't matter. I brought up everything weighing on my mind. On and on I went, unloading my cares at Your feet.

"No matter," You said. *"I have plenty of room to take them."*

I continued. I told You about my past and my dreams for the future. I shared my joys and funny things that happened. You laughed, Father! You actually laughed with me. You cried, too. You held me close and dried my tears with the hem of Your robe. I thanked You and rose to my feet. It was time to leave. You smiled and nodded.

"The door is always ajar, dear child," You reminded.

The next morning I felt rested and refreshed. Prayers to You were still on my lips. The warmth of Your love still filled my heart.

I look forward to entering again very soon that door which is always ajar.

[Jesus said,] "Come to me, all you who are
weary and burdened, and I will give you rest.
Take my yoke upon you and learn from me,
for I am gentle and humble in heart,
and you will find rest for your souls.
For my yoke is easy and my burden is light."

MATTHEW 11:28–30 NIV

Until Now

Father, I hear people say they can't be happy unless every circumstance involving them is perfect. Projects have to be flawless. Outings or vacations can't be a happy time unless nothing goes wrong. Only faultless people make ideal friends. Some aren't happy unless they're perfect themselves.

I overhear defeating remarks like, "I can't be content until our bills are paid"; "I get married"; "we have children"; "the kids are grown"; "it rains"; "it stops raining"; "I can get an education"; "I lose or gain weight"; "I get that ideal job"; or "I retire."

Unless? Until? Thank You, Father, for the joy and contentment You give, for how You change "until" to "now." What satisfaction You give me through Your assuring presence during struggles and disappointments, achievements and failures.

Thank You for encouraging me to appreciate my life. You help me to value the rain and rainbows; the pride of hard, bone-tiring, not-so-perfect work; the chance to kiss scraped knees or sit by the bedside of a sick child. Thank You for long walks and talks with loved ones, often used to filter through uncertainties and hurts. I'm grateful for imperfect friendships perfected by love, forgiveness, and acceptance. Thank You for my husband and our love that grows daily. Thank You for Your perfect love that overcomes imperfections and teaches me true happiness starts with "until now."

> *Happy are those who are strong in the Lord,*
> *who want above all else to follow your steps.*
>
> PSALM 84:5 TLB

You Complete Me

It's a workday, Lord. I should be fulfilling my duties. Instead, my chilling body shivers under warm blankets in my recliner. I sip a cup of hot tea. It's comforting, Lord. But not nearly as much as Your being here with me. How I feel Your love and support. How honored I am as You bid me to pray during my time of need.

Even though You are my King, my petitions are never too small (or great) for You to heed. Your grace and power remain within my feeble reach. My burdens are light when I give them to You. You help me to rest and draw from Your strength. My stress, my cares, my pain, I place at Your feet. Your warm, healing hands soothe me. I lean my fevered head upon Your chest. My incomplete, weary soul, I open to You. How wonderful, the way You calm my anxieties and fill the empty, wanting chasm within me.

Time passes. I rest in Your presence. Strengthening Bible verses flow through my mind. I feel You healing and preparing me to return to my duties. Tomorrow I'll go back to work. But for today, I'm grateful for this time with You, Lord. Thank You for making me complete—complete and whole in You.

The LORD is my shepherd;
I shall not want.
He maketh me to lie down in green pastures:
he leadeth me beside the still waters.
He restoreth my soul.

PSALM 23:1–3 KJV

The Hollow of Your Hand

When storms of life toss me about, Lord, like a bobbing cork at sea, and raging billows hide any hint of welcoming shelter, I take heart at being securely planted in the hollow of Your hand. When discouraging dark clouds glower, fearful lightning pierces, and thunderous troubles pound, I find comfort hiding in the hollow of Your strong hand.

When temptation attempts to lure me and seeks to drive me from Your path, I feel Your firm grip. There, I cling to the hollow of Your hand. When endless toil drains my energy to nothing and whirlwind challenges cause my head and emotions to spin out of control, I experience Your presence. You wrap Your steady fingers around mine and hold me in the hollow of Your hand. When I see light at the end of my troubled tunnel and take pleasure in sunshiny days, I rejoice. Still, I nestle in the hollow of Your hand.

When the time comes for life's journey to take a new turn and my earthly existence starts to ebb, I will glance back and praise You for the many times You held me close in the hollow of Your hand. When I walk the valley from death to eternal life, I will have no fear, for You shall be with me, holding me in the hollow of Your hand.

Nevertheless I am continually with You;
You hold me by my right hand.
You will guide me with Your counsel,
And afterward receive me to glory.

PSALM 73:23–24 NKJV

Your Heavenly Presence

Although I love this earthly life You provide for me, dear Lord, I yearn to enter the courtyard of Your heavenly home. There I will get to meet You face-to-face. I wonder how I will even be able to gaze upon Your beauty and holiness. I will only be able to do so through Your love and saving grace. I can't even imagine what it will be like. Oh, how I look forward to being with You, my risen Lord and Savior. You, the Lamb of God, sitting at the right hand of our heavenly Father.

When I someday awaken in heaven, my longing for the things of You will be completely fulfilled. No more will I hunger and thirst for Your awesome presence, for You will be with me all the time, for all eternity. There, You will welcome me and wrap me in Your loving arms. You will take away my pain and sorrow. You will wipe away my tears. You will feed me from Your very own table and give me drink from Your rivers of endless gladness.

In the meantime, I know I have work to do for You. So I will enjoy Your loving presence every day here on earth.

*"For the Lamb in the center of the throne
will be their shepherd,
and will guide them to springs of the water of life;
and God will wipe every tear from their eyes."*

REVELATION 7:17 NASB

I Want to Hear You, Lord

Here I am, Lord. It's early in the morning—a special time. I've set everything else aside. It is reserved only for You and me. I drive out to a park not far from our home. I hike up a short trail and look out over the river. Thank You for Your wonderful presence as I come to You. I can hear the tranquil ring of silence. How peaceful it is. Even the birds are quiet.

Yet during my communion with You in prayer, I want to hear You speaking to my heart, Lord. I sit on a large rock and open my Bible. You are so near. It's as though I am on holy ground. I slip off my shoes in reverence and feel the cool grass beneath my feet. I open my heart to You.

Should the winds of Your Holy Spirit speak to me, I will listen. Like Elijah, I hope it doesn't take an earthquake or a fire for me to hear You! I sense Your presence while I read Your Word, and I hear You gently whisper to my heart.

"Be still, and know I am God," You say.

Speak, Lord, and I shall listen.

> *And after the earthquake, there was a fire,*
> *but the Lord was not in the fire.*
> *And after the fire,*
> *there was the sound of a gentle whisper.*

1 KINGS 19:12 TLB

I Will Meditate on You

The sun creeps a little higher, removing shadows from the trail I hiked up. Dew disappears from the grass around my feet. An energetic robin calls out signals to another. Although its song isn't meant for me, I can almost hear her exhorting, "God loves *you!* God loves *you!*"

During this time with You, my mind wanders to the duties awaiting me. I find myself already organizing each one. I want to keep my heart fixed on You. Please help me, Lord.

As I meditate on You, I want to let everything else go. How quickly the hour is passing. I turn my thoughts to You and pray for You to heed my prayers. Hear my voice this morning, O Lord. I look to You for Your help and guidance. I recognize Your nearness, for I know You, my God, my King. There is no other greater than You.

Cast away all else, My child. All you hear from Me is wise and perfect. Listen to Me speak to your heart. My testimony is sure. My advice will bring wisdom to you and make difficulties become simple. Everything I tell you is right. Obey Me, and you will find rejoicing in your heart.

May my thoughts, my attitudes, my words and actions be pleasing to You, O Lord, my Helper and my Savior.

I will meditate on Your precepts
And regard Your ways.
I shall delight in Your statutes;
I shall not forget Your word.

PSALM 119:15–16 NASB

I Will Wait on You

Lord, there are many things in my life I want to simply jump in and take care of—right now. I hear You advising me. Yet it's still hard to wait for Your timing and direction. Help me to be patient and listen to You.

Teach me to wait on You and receive Your encouragement. Here, I linger in prayer. Here, I seek Your bidding. Prepare me, O Lord, for what lies ahead. Strengthen me. Yes, Lord, I shall wait and obey! Enable my thoughts to become Your thoughts. Let my ways adhere to Yours.

Those who patiently linger and seek Me are greater than the rulers of mighty nations. When you wait, I shall rekindle your strength and wisdom, and carry you on My wings like a baby eagle. So refrain from launching off on your own, dear one. Stay close. Let Me help you to run, and you will not grow weary; to walk, and you will not feel faint. As you do, I will shower My mercy upon you. Each and every day, I will give you hope and certainty. Remain in prayer, and trust in Me.

Lord, here I linger, let go, and place my confidence in You.

> *But they that wait upon the LORD*
> *shall renew their strength;*
> *they shall mount up with wings as eagles;*
> *they shall run, and not be weary;*
> *and they shall walk, and not faint.*

> ISAIAH 40:31 KJV

Your Cleansing Power

Lord, I know there are things in my life that aren't acceptable to You. How I long to please You in every way. I realize I can do so only through the strength of Your Holy Spirit.

I come to You with an open heart. Though my sins are as scarlet, I pray for You to make them white as snow. Though my life is soiled like crimson, please cleanse me. Make me pure as spotless wool.

Walk through every room of my heart, Lord. Take the books, the movies, even my thoughts that are offensive. Here and now, I release them all to You. Help me remove and replace these with what is good, uplifting, and pure. Here and now, I allow You to sweep out the hidden dust bunnies of resentments and jealousies and replace them with Your love and forgiveness.

You give Me joy, dear child, when you open your heart to Me! Listen while I teach you My holy ways and help you walk in My truth. My cleansing power working within you will cause guilt and frustration to be gone. In their place, I will restore to you the delight of My salvation. My Holy Spirit will fill you with true happiness and peace of mind.

My heart I yield to You, Lord, in joyful anticipation.

Create in me a new, clean heart, O God,
filled with clean thoughts and right desires. . . .
Restore to me again the joy of your salvation,
and make me willing to obey you.

PSALM 51:10, 12 TLB

JUNE 5

Rest Awhile

It's the end of another full day. Here I am, sitting by a tree in our backyard. Grant me time with You. I want to relax and enjoy Your encouraging presence, Father.

I've been pushing myself too hard lately. I'm tired at night and when I awaken in the morning. The harder I work, the more I spin my wheels, trying to keep up. I feel like I'm burning out in my service for You. Please help me.

Lord, I come to You to rest awhile. You are my Shepherd. You give me everything I need. I stretch out on the cool, sweet grass. I gaze through the branches of the trees and look to the light blue sky. I sense You watching over me and providing the time-out I so badly need.

Drink in My presence while I restore your weary soul, My child. You will not burn out in serving Me as long as you obey My will. Worry not about meeting the expectations of others. Take, instead, a gentle, humble spirit and rest your soul. Accept My yoke. Allow Me to help you carry your load so your burden will become lighter. I will show you how to eliminate unnecessary things and make your steps purposeful, ordered by Me.

Relax awhile. Just rest.

Ah. Thank You, Father. I'll rest and learn from You.

> [Jesus said,] "Come to me,
> all you who are weary and burdened,
> and I will give you rest."
>
> MATTHEW 11:28 NIV

Your Nourishment

Here I am at Bible study in a friend's home, Lord. Everyone in our group is going through some struggles. You know each one well. Although it's been a day of work, I now sense Your Holy Spirit nourishing and satisfying my spiritual hunger. Help me learn from Your wise Scriptures. Feed my eager soul, I pray. Grant me energy, and help me to be an encourager for my friends.

You are my God, dear Lord. How I treasure the time we have together, receiving Your blessings and love. What wonderful lessons You provide to meet our daily needs. In this little home Bible study, You give us a holy sanctuary.

Recognize My power and glory, My child. Be refreshed and experience My loving-kindness, which is better than life itself. I am the Bread of Life. Dig into the Bible verses of My Word. Feast from My nourishing teachings until you are full. Be encouraged and rejuvenated. Be blessed. Look to tomorrow with enthusiasm, wholeheartedly working as you are doing so for Me.

Believe in Me. Go out. Let My words flow through and out of you so others may also know Me and experience My love.

Thank You for nourishing me to the full with Your life-giving Word.

Then Jesus declared,
"I am the bread of life.
He who comes to me will never go hungry,
and he who believes in me will never be thirsty."

JOHN 6:35 NIV

Quietness and Confidence Are My Strength

Stresses of this world constantly flurry around me. I'm often confronted with discord. Some of these things don't have to do with me directly, Lord, but people come to me for help. I used to dive in and get involved with the problems. Now I'm learning to stop, pray about them, and place my trust in You. Right now, I'm faced with one of those situations. Once again, I bring an anxious concern to You in prayer.

I lay my requests before You, Lord. I rest on the promises of Your Word that You care for me and those I pray for. Then I stand back and watch You work; for through quietness and confidence in You, I find strength and direction. There is no greater problem solver than being able to bring my needs to You in prayer. Because You hear my prayers and care, I trust in You.

Fear not, My child, and be not shaken. Remain calm. Rely on Me. I will keep you in perfect peace when your mind remains on Me. Keep your heart right with Me, and I shall produce fruits of calmness and assurance and peace of mind in you, no matter what circumstances you face. Know that all things are possible with Me.

I will trust in You, Lord, and remain calm. These needs I place in Your care.

> *"You will keep him in perfect peace,*
> *Whose mind is stayed on You,*
> *Because he trusts in You.*
> *Trust in the LORD forever,*
> *For in YAH, the LORD,*
> *is everlasting strength."*

ISAIAH 26:3–4 NKJV

Never Too Busy

Father, I feel my life is jam-packed. The words *new projects, more classes,* and *meetings* make me cringe. Thankfully, my schedule is easier than it used to be.

I think back on the days when our children were growing up. I loved it, Father, but it really kept me hopping. Sometimes we had children in four different schools. Extracurricular activities caused me to often put on my "supermom" cape. Our calendar looked like a little bird had tracked across every date; it was so packed with scheduled events. Later, when I worked two jobs, I came up with every time-saving method I could conjure. Still, in every stage of my life, You make time for me.

It's near the end of another school year with much to do, Father. I feel my time with You slipping. Help me to put You first and never be too busy for You.

Take time to wait on Me each day, My child, and allow Me to show you My ways. I am always here, ready and waiting to meet with you. Follow Me. I can give hours to your days.

Thank You, Father, for never being too busy for me. Here I am. Meeting with You surpasses all else.

Cause me to hear Your lovingkindness in the morning,
For in You do I trust;
Cause me to know the way in which I should walk,
For I lift up my soul to You.

PSALM 143:8 NKJV

I Give My Heart to You

I give my heart to You, Lord God. I trust in You. I allow You to lead me in Your truth. Teach me. No matter where I go or who I am around, I will never be ashamed of being Your child. You are the God of my salvation. You are the One who has loved me since before the beginning of time. You are the One who showers me with tender mercies and kindness all the days of my life. Your love has no beginning or end.

Here, I wholeheartedly come to You. Here, You welcome me and listen to my prayers. How grateful I am for the love You give. With all my might, I will follow Your ways of goodness and uprightness. With all my mind and heart, I will listen while You teach me everlasting wisdom and truthfulness; for Your paths are firm and certain.

Will you always honor Me, My child? Will you always give Me your heart? Turn your face toward Me. In so doing, you gain the secret of how you can obtain true, unconditional, everlasting happiness. Follow Me, and your spirit shall prosper.

Pass on My teachings to your children and your children's children. Trust in Me. No matter what, keep trusting! When you do, you shall be blessed through generations.

Yes, Lord, I shall always follow You. I give You my heart, my all.

To You, O LORD,
I lift up my soul.
O my God, in You I trust.

PSALM 25:1–2 NASB

Changing Brokenness to Beauty

Father, I am broken from the things that have happened in my past. I feel as though my life was shattered in a million irreparable fragments. I am so disconnected that I'm unable to offer You anything of value in my life.

How can You help a lost cause like me, Father? Am I beyond repair?

Come to Me, My dear child. Let Me wrap My comforting arms around you. Allow Me to hug the little girl within you. Here, I hold you close, rocking you as a loving parent does a crying child. I will listen as you pour out all your bad memories. As you tell Me each one, give it to Me and do not take it back. I have broad shoulders. I can carry them all.

Yield to Me while I heal your hurts. Let Me take the fragments of your life and carefully piece them together into a beautiful new pattern. It will be one that glows with enthusiasm and joy and hope. Even life's fractures will sparkle like streaks of gold from My glorious victories. Be healed. Allow Me to replace every part of your new life with a joy that will not be squelched.

Thank You, Father, for turning my brokenness into beauty for You.

The LORD is close to the brokenhearted
and saves those who are crushed in spirit. . . .
Great is our Lord and mighty in power;
his understanding has no limit.

PSALMS 34:18; 147:5 NIV

I Will Let Go and Press Forward

Lord, I think back on my life and have many regrets. Why did I wait so long to follow You? Had I turned to You sooner, I wouldn't have made so many terrible mistakes. I am so sorry, Lord. In the time I have left on this earth, I want to somehow make up for those wasted years. How can I do this?

Teach me to let go of the past and leave it behind me. I realize there is only one way to look. That is forward! I come to You, ready to serve when You bid. Teach me to stretch forward to the things of You that lie ahead. Give me the prize of Your Spirit-filled calling, dear Lord—a call to tell everyone I know about Your unlimited love.

Shove out the negative thoughts of what you left behind, dear one. Think on the good things, for I bestow you with a living hope for the future. I bestow you with an inheritance that shall never perish. Make ready your heart and mind for action. Grow and mature in Me. Walk the same walk alongside Me. Be of the same mind as Me. Exercise self-control. Set your hopes completely on My grace.

Let Me lead, dear one! Press on.

I look forward with great anticipation to a future with You.

One thing I do,
forgetting what lies behind and
straining forward to what lies ahead,
I press on toward the goal for the prize of
the upward call of God in Christ Jesus.

PHILIPPIANS 3:13–14 RSV

I Am Not Alone

Father's Day is one of my favorite times of the year, Lord. I love taking this opportunity to do something special for my husband, my dad, and my father-in-law. Thank You for them and the love they show me. Watch over them each day. Grant them wisdom and strength so they can be useful to You.

I don't know of anything more challenging than being parents and family patriarchs. How can we always set a good example? This is a twenty-four-hour undertaking, Lord. No matter how we try, we aren't able to do it all right. Please help them.

I pray for each of these dads and our grown sons who are parents to seek Your guidance and depend on You. May they trust in You to help solve their problems. May they look to You, Lord Jesus, and Your Father and follow Your example.

My Father in heaven is a Father, too, dear one. He knows exactly how every human parent feels. They are not alone in their struggles. Know for sure I am always with them through every stage of the children's growing years, on into adulthood. I will continue to be there for them down through the generations.

Thank You, Lord, for understanding us as parents. Thank You for helping and leading these ones I love all through their years.

As a father has compassion on his children,
so the LORD has compassion on those who fear him.

PSALM 103:13 NIV

JUNE 13

I Will Be Your Example

I want to live Your example, Lord, yet reflecting You before my family in every area of my life seems impossible. I want my actions to speak louder than anything I say. Show me how to gain their respect by my honoring You—how to treat them fairly so they don't become discouraged or bitter. Remind me to consider their needs. Help me to be honest, rather than resorting to manipulation. How I want to show them Your love.

Do not fear, dear parent. I am with you, even when things go wrong. Let Me reveal to you the way. Choose Me as the Head of your home. Study and memorize My teachings in your Bible. Treasure them in your heart. Place them on your doors and walls. Teach them to your offspring while you go here and there, when you prepare to rest at night, and when you awaken in the morning. Make them a vital part of your everyday life. Love your family unselfishly, as I do you. Show your pride and appreciation for them often. Look at these lively young sprouts around your table and see My blessings!

Thank You, Lord, for helping me live Your example, especially for my family.

> *Write them [the Scriptures] on the doorframes*
> *of your houses and on your gates,*
> *so that your days and the days of*
> *your children may be many.*
>
> DEUTERONOMY 11:20–21 NIV

JUNE 14

My Needs

Lord, I bring a special need to You. This thing I'm asking for may not seem important to others, but it means a lot to me. I know You understand me well, and You recognize my heart. I'm not asking for selfish reasons. I need Your help.

Place a calm assurance within me of Your loving care. No matter how You answer my request, Lord, I will trust in Your wisdom and upright foresight. I know You cherish me more than anyone else does. You created me. You recognize the depths of my heart. I believe You will answer my prayer in view of my concerns and what is best for me.

Do not fret over what will come, My child. Simply trust in Me and do good. Take delight in walking in My ways, and I shall answer the desires of your heart according to what I know is best. Be still. Wait on Me. As you commit everything to Me and trust completely in My wise decisions, I will cause your righteousness to shine like the bright morning sun. Your willingness to obey Me will beam like summer at noontime! Seek first My kingdom and righteousness, and I shall bless you beyond measure.

Above all, Lord, I set my heart on the things of You.

Commit your way to the LORD;
trust in him and he will do this:
He will make your righteousness shine like the dawn,
the justice of your cause like the noonday sun.

PSALM 37:5–6 NIV

JUNE 15

Removing the "Not"

Lord, I'm excited about the wonderful things You do in my life. Each day is a new adventure with You by my side. How awesome it is to sense You nudging me to do this or that for You. Every time You speak to my heart, I feel Your encouraging presence. No matter what is going on in this world, You have a marvelous way of changing the "not" in my life to "can."

When others ask me how to find this joy You give me, I try to tell them. How can I help them see, so they, too, can experience this positive Christian life?

You have already taken the first step in helping them, dear one, by bringing them to Me in prayer. You have answers to your prayers because you ask. Behold, I am knocking at the door of their hearts.

Let the light of your life shine before others so they may see Me in you and give glory to My Father in heaven. In this way, they, too, will seek the joy and positive ways of My salvation.

Thank You, Lord, for how good You are. Thank You for removing the "not" from my life and replacing it with "I can, through You." Surround me with Your presence. Let Your light of positive Christianity shine through me to others.

> [Jesus said,] "Don't hide your light!
> Let it shine for all;
> let your good deeds glow for all to see,
> so that they will praise your heavenly Father."
>
> MATTHEW 5:15–16 TLB

I Think on Your Goodness

How wonderful is the goodness You shower upon me, Lord. There's no way I can begin to know all the blessings You give me. How I adore You.

I think on Your kindness and tuck Your ways deep into the corners of my heart. Each day I wait on You. You make me as sturdy as a cedar planted near the water. My love and trust in You shall not be moved, because I fix my thoughts on You. Let me bear Your spiritual fruit and remain fresh and green like a well-watered orchard all the days of my life.

Your praise is music to My ears, dear child. Continue to think on the love I bestow upon you in the morning and on the faithfulness I show each night. Keep noticing what I do for you by the works of My hands. My actions are more excellent than those of any other. My hopes and dreams for you go beyond your comprehension.

I will continually seek Your mercy, Lord. How can I repay You for all You do for me? It can only be by my love. Through Your goodness, You provide for my needs. Through Your power, You give me victory over temptations and troubles. I want to tell everyone of Your deep compassion. To You I give all glory and praise!

What shall I render to the LORD
For all His benefits toward me?
I shall lift up the cup of salvation
And call upon the name of the LORD.

PSALM 116:12–13 NASB

I Will Let You

Father, I just talked with my friend. You know who she is. When she shares her worries with me regarding her grown child, she weeps. Her son is making some disastrous decisions. I share her sadness. I've known this family since their son was a little boy. If he doesn't turn his heart over to You and change, his actions may cause him to suffer for the rest of his life.

We prayed together and hugged. Again, she gave her grown child to You and placed him in Your care. We know You love him even more than any of us is capable of doing. Along with trusting You, Father, I'm asking for You to calm my friend through Your assurances.

I do care, My child—not only for you, but for your friend and her son. Listen to Me and be comforted; and I will comfort her, as well. You and your friend belong to Me. So does this young man I love so dearly. I will handle this situation in My own way and in My own time. All you need to do during these trials is keep your faith in Me. Trust Me. Obey Me completely. Let go, and let Me do the rest.

I will, Father. Thank You for helping my friend to let go and let You.

> [Jesus said,] "Trust in God;
> trust also in me. . . .
> Do not let your hearts be troubled
> and do not be afraid."
>
> JOHN 14:1, 27 NIV

I Shall Wait on You

Thank You for teaching me to trust You, Lord. When I do, You help my faith to become strong. I praise You for abiding with me all the time. Day after day, You surround me and the loved ones I pray for. Every moment, You protect me from evil and harm. I shall depend on You above all else.

When wrongdoers are up to no good, You replace my fear with faith. I know fretting only causes harm, so I will trust You and obey. No matter what, I praise Your holy name. I continually feed on Your Scriptures and take delight in Your ways.

It is good for you, dear child, to pray that your loved ones will follow Me. Because of your trust in Me, I shall cause the faith within you to grow beyond measure. Yes, I regard the desires of your heart. Fear not. I am honoring your prayers, for those who wait on Me, I bless.

Thank You for keeping Your hand on the ones I pray for and not giving up on them, Lord. Thank You for talking to their hearts, coaxing them to follow You. How I praise You. Those I love are Yours, Lord. I shall wait on You and rest in Your care.

Trust in the LORD with all your heart
And do not lean on your own understanding.
In all your ways acknowledge Him,
And He will make your paths straight.

PROVERBS 3:5–6 NASB

Victory over Defeat

Lord, these things You call me to do are enormous in my eyes. I don't know if I can do well enough to gratify You. What if I fail? I want to obey You. I want You to be pleased with my serving You. Remove my fear of defeat, Lord. I will do my best, then ask for You to take over. Grant me the ability, wisdom, and energy to do this for Your glory.

I look to You, Lord. It is from You that my help comes. You are the One who made heaven and earth. You are the One who hears me and is helping with my needs right now. It isn't by my might or power that these things are accomplished, but by Your Spirit.

What I call you to do may not be accomplished the way you envision or even see as successful; nonetheless, it will be according to My will. When I call you and you obey Me, there is no such thing as defeat. I bless even through failures, so fear not. I am the Lord, your God. I see the bigger picture. Trust in Me. For you, whom I call, are the apple of My eye.

I will follow You, Lord. I will not fear failure or defeat. In You I find victory.

> *And the Spirit of the Lord shall rest upon him,*
> *the Spirit of wisdom, understanding, counsel and might;*
> *the Spirit of knowledge and of the fear of the Lord.*
> *His delight will be obedience to the Lord.*

ISAIAH 11:2–3 TLB

In Danger

Lord, I'm in danger! I must keep my head and not let fear cloud my judgment. Even though I am afraid, I trust in You. Please help me. Watch over me and keep me safe. Be with my loved ones, Lord, and protect them.

Because You are my refuge and strength, I'm learning to cast my fear on You; for You are my help, always present in times of danger and trouble. I know You are with me, so I trust and depend on You. In You, Lord, all things are possible.

Your Bible promises that should the earth shake and crack, or the mountains fall into the sea, or the floodwaters roar and foam, You are here watching over me. Should evil attempt to assault me or dangers cross my path, You are here, surrounding me.

I am your help, My child. I am the One who sustains you. I am the One who delivers you. Each time you call upon Me for protection, I summon My angels to circle and deliver you. I am your shield and fortress. Fear not the terrors by night nor the dangers you may face in a day. I am always with you. I shall never leave or forsake you.

I will trust in You, dear Lord. I will hide beneath Your wings and not be afraid.

God is our refuge and strength,
A very present help in trouble.
Therefore we will not fear.

PSALM 46:1–2 NASB

JUNE 21

Certainty in an Uncertain World

Anxieties press in from every side these days, Father. Children see and hear things they should not. Adults are forced to deal with overwhelming problems because of our sin-sick world. There are wars and rumors of wars, earthquakes and fires, floods and tornadoes. Even nature's balance seems strange.

Our high-technology lifestyle makes our everyday world so complex that the most brilliant people have trouble keeping up. Where does that leave our disabled and elderly? What about our children and grandchildren? What is their future, Father? Where is the certainty of life in this uncertain world?

I am here for those who turn to Me and follow My ways. No matter what is going on in life, it is nothing new. I have always been here for those who belong to Me. As I was with Moses centuries ago, I am still by your side, leading and helping you. Be certain you are My child. I shall also be here for your children, on down through the generations as you trust and obey My precepts. I will by no means leave or disown you. Fear not, dear one. I am your certainty.

My heart is fixed on You, Father. I refuse to be bogged down by uncertainty. Instead, I will follow and trust You.

> *Show me your ways, O LORD,*
> *teach me your paths;*
> *guide me in your truth and teach me,*
> *for you are God my Savior,*
> *and my hope is in you all day long.*
>
> PSALM 25:4–5 NIV

Encouragement from You

Today was just average, Father. But something was missing. My steps felt heavy. Now I'm home and can take time to reflect. I realize I've carried discouragement with me through my whole day. In Your Word, as always, I find my answers.

When I'm discouraged, I can bring You my cares and cast them at Your feet. Tonight I will fix my thoughts on You and Your capable ways. I won't allow myself to fret over life's circumstances. Thank You, my Father, for promising in the Bible to care for me and my concerns. I'm glad I can claim these promises as my own. Thank You for helping me drop this discouragement. I've been lugging it like a shabby, heavy suitcase filled with worries. Thank You for Your warm, hope-filled presence.

Yes, I care for you. You are My child. You carry the name of My Son, Jesus Christ, for you are a Christian. I am always here to help you during good and bad times. Take heart, and do not be discouraged. Take joy in My sustenance and love. Press forward. Keep doing the work I have called you to do. I am with you every step of the way.

Praise You, my Father, for providing me with hope and encouragement. Thank You for giving me just enough for each day.

"Fear not, for I am with you;
Be not dismayed, for I am your God.
I will strengthen you,
Yes, I will help you,
I will uphold you with My righteous right hand."

ISAIAH 41:10 NKJV

You Care

Lord, I have some huge needs. I'm in want not only for my physical well-being, but for relief from relentless amounts of stress I am forced to cope with. I don't see how it is possible for my hardships to be overcome. Everything seems so hopeless.

Does anyone care about what I'm going through? There must be someone. I know You do, Lord. But I ask for Your assurance that You are here, working things out and helping me through all these trials. Please minister to me, I pray. Meet my needs. Encourage my soul. Speak to me, Lord, and shower me with Your care.

I am your refuge, My dear one. I will provide for you each day. Simply trust in Me. I see your heart and hear your cries. I will help you through these troublesome times. In order for Me to do so, you must be determined to seek first My kingdom and My righteousness. See the birds outside your window? I tend them. And I certainly look after you. Give your worries and troubles to Me, for I care for you.

I will trust in You, Lord. Thank You for loving me and watching over for me.

> *The LORD is good,*
> *a refuge in times of trouble.*
> *He cares for those who trust in him.*

> NAHUM 1:7 NIV

A Good Work Begun

Father, Your Bible tells me You began a good work in me before I was born. All my life I've wanted to do right for You. Have You really kept Your hand on me all these years? What is Your plan for me?

I set into motion a fine masterpiece of you even before you were conceived. I still remember your first cry. Oh, what a sweet child you were—such a little one, made in My image. I recognized and loved your tender, caring heart from the time you were young. Through the years, I am guiding you in ways to accomplish My will. Each time you reach out to another and help, I rejoice.

You are the apple of My eye, My child. I love you with an everlasting love. You are My workmanship. I call you to serve Me. As you continue to love and obey Me, I am guiding you. Indeed, I have a purpose for your life.

Let my labor be fruitful through my faith in You, Father. Let my actions be prompted by the love You plant in my heart. Grant me endurance, inspired by the hope I have in You. Continue Your work in me, O God. In You I find fulfillment and purpose.

And I am sure that God who
began the good work within you
will keep right on helping you grow
in his grace until his task within you is
finally finished on that day when
Jesus Christ returns.

PHILIPPIANS 1:6 TLB

You Chose Me

I went to a shower today, Father. It was for an eight-year-old girl named Trisha. Her new parents are my friends. Several children came up for adoption at the same time for my friends to choose from. This doesn't happen very often.

They could have adopted a baby. But when they took one look at Trisha, the couple immediately fell in love with her. They're so excited to have her as their child, Father. They're already talking about the hopes and dreams they have for her as she grows up.

Is that how it was when You chose me? Did you see something special in me right from the beginning? Do You have hopes and dreams for me as I grow in You?

Not only did I choose you, dear child, but I wanted all of humankind to be My own and follow Me. Everyone has been called, but few choose to follow. I saw something special in you from the beginning. I treasured you before you were even interested in Me. You, My child, love Me because I first loved you. Walk, then, in My love; and see the wondrous hopes and dreams I have for you.

Thank You for choosing me, dear Father. I will follow You.

> *[Jesus said,] "You did not choose Me,*
> *but I chose you and appointed you*
> *that you should go and bear fruit,*
> *and that your fruit should remain."*
>
> JOHN 15:16 NKJV

You Are Mercy

A student in our classroom taught me a lesson of mercy and true forgiveness, Lord. She's a sweet, tenderhearted girl. When a boy in our room said mean things about her, she came to me in tears and complained. The three of us talked out the problem. I must admit I was frustrated with the boy's behavior. But she was different. When the boy was ready to ask forgiveness, she gave it in a second and accepted him again as her friend.

How much greater than this little girl's mercy is the kindness You show to me. I first experienced it when You forgave my sins and adopted me as Your own child. Even now in my struggles, You show Your constant compassion.

Sing of My mercy, dear one. Sing of My love forever. Let your friends and family know all about My faithfulness and forgiveness. My love for you stands firm and steadfast. When you err, I forgive you. When you are merciful, I grant you mercy. When you are loving, I shower you with love. When you are generous, I abundantly bless you. When you help the weak in their times of trouble, I am, in turn, always there to help you.

Thank You for Your mercy, Lord. Let me pass it on to others.

Instead, be kind to each other, tenderhearted,
forgiving one another,
just as God has forgiven you
because you belong to Christ.

EPHESIANS 4:32 TLB

I Love Your Ways

The longer I know You, my Savior, the stronger my love for You grows. Your ways have become second nature to me. I think of Your Holy Spirit in my life, and I love everything about You more than ever. Your tenderness and steadiness give me assurance through each day.

When I carefully listen to Your direction and follow Your lead, I feel Your warm approval. When I become careless and open my mouth at the wrong times, I sense You silently cautioning me to stop what I'm doing and to change my attitude. I love You, dear Lord. I love Your being my best Friend, my Confidant, my Counselor, my Lord.

We walk this path of life together, dear child. It is called the way of holiness. It is only for those who willingly come with Me. Copy My deeds. Step in My footprints. Echo My words. Show My compassion. Hold tightly to My hand, lest you slip and lose your spiritual balance. Make My ways your ways. I shall faithfully lead you and never cause you to stray. I am the only Way, the Truth, and Life eternal. No one comes to My Father unless he or she is following Me.

I will place my feet in Your footprints, Lord. I will firmly hold Your hand.

> *Teach me to do Your will,*
> *For You are my God;*
> *Let Your good Spirit lead me on level ground.*

PSALM 143:10 NASB

189

Do You Pray for Me?

Last week was discouraging, Lord. Nothing went right. I was driven to tears and wondered if You were even near. I didn't give up, though. I brought my needs to You, asking for Your guidance. I could only share these troubles with You, Lord. No one else knew how I felt. Out of desperation, I took my hands off everything and asked You to intervene. Before long, I felt total peace. It was as though someone was praying for me. Still, no one else knew of my troubles.

Were You the One praying for me, Lord? Your Bible says Your Holy Spirit makes intercession for us according to God's will. When I had no more words with which to cry out for help and I gave my burdens to You, did You lift them from me anyway? Did You take them to my heavenly Father and plead my cause? This boggles my mind.

Yes, I prayed for you, My child. When you bring your concerns and cares to Me—your Lord—the Holy Spirit hears your prayers and intercedes on your behalf to the heavenly Father with groanings that cannot be uttered by anyone.

How grateful I am for Your praying for me, Lord.

In the same way the Spirit also helps our weakness;
for we do not know how to pray as we should,
but the Spirit Himself intercedes for us
with groanings too deep for words;
and He who searches the hearts knows
what the mind of the Spirit is,
because He intercedes for the saints
according to the will of God.

ROMANS 8:26–27 NASB

I Will Follow You

Lord, I hear You talking to my heart to do something new for You. I'm really struggling with this. As You know, I don't handle change well. I like life planned out in one neatly wrapped package. I want to know what is going to happen from one day, one year to the next—even ten years down the road. But more than what I want, I must accept this calling You give me.

I can't get over how Simon Peter and Andrew dropped their nets without hesitation and went along with You when You said, "Come, follow Me." Grant me the same strength and faith You gave to them. Show me how to adhere to You without wavering.

I will follow You, my Lord. Reveal the great and mighty plans You have for me. Help me put my efforts wholeheartedly into Your service. Here with You, I look straight ahead. I will not long for the past.

Come, child. Dream My dreams. Catch the vision of the things I place before you to accomplish. See the spiritually hungry and how they need to know Me? The harvest of souls is plenty, but willing workers are few. In the same way the heavenly Father has commissioned Me, so am I sending you.

Yes, my Lord, I will follow You.

> *"Come, follow me,"*
> *Jesus said,*
> *"and I will make you fishers of men."*
>
> MATTHEW 4:19 NIV

Will You Remain with Me?

Lord, I hear You calling me to serve You. This is a mountainous undertaking You have given to me. Everywhere I turn, I see the consequences of sin, pain, suffering, and uncertainty. I don't have answers for these people with whom You call me to share Your love. What if I don't do things right? What if I break down under the load? I feel like Joshua just about to cross the Jordan River. Will You remain with me, no matter how difficult things get? Please stay close. Please go before me.

I, the Lord your God, will cross over ahead of you in this undertaking I am giving you, My dear one. Draw from my strength and courage, for your help comes from Me. Fear not. Be not terrified of the destruction caused by the evil one. Do not be discouraged. I am always with you. I am greater than anything you will confront. Be certain that no matter the circumstances, I will never abandon nor turn My back on you. As I once was with Moses and Joshua, so shall I now be with you.

Thank You for being my God. Thank You for holding tightly onto my hand and constantly reminding me not to fear. How grateful I am for Your being here with me. In You I trust and obey.

"Be strong! Be courageous!
Do not be afraid of them!
For the Lord your God will be with you.
He will neither fail you nor forsake you."

DEUTERONOMY 31:6 TLB

Our Growing Family

Here I am on our backyard patio, Lord. The morning sun peeks over the trees, gently warming my face and arms. Folks in our neighborhood are either asleep or quietly leaving for work. I love this peaceful time with You. Our yard reminds me of the things of You.

A fir and a pine tree stretch their branches heavenward. Over twenty years ago our sons, Jonathan and David, and I planted the one-foot fir for David's Cub Scout project. Now it's about forty-five-feet tall! Remember how my parents gave us the pine tree in a little pot, covered with miniature Christmas ornaments, Lord? Our family nurtured and watered both green starts. In time, the trees outgrew our sons. The ice storm we had a few years back broke huge branches and six feet off the top of the pine tree. It looked like an emerald giant lying in our yard. I put sealer on the broken parts and prayed for its survival. The tree still lives. A burl now appears in place of the missing branch. Noble scars and gnarls along the trunk remind me of the storms You have helped our family survive.

Thank You for showering our family with Your faithfulness and care through the years, Lord. Thank You for continuing to send blessings to our future generations and forever.

I will sing of the mercies of the LORD forever;
With my mouth will I make known Your faithfulness
to all generations.

PSALM 89:1 NKJV

Rose of Sharon

Look at the roses climbing along our fence, Lord. Their loveliness causes me to think of You, the Rose of Sharon, the Lily of the Valley, the Bright and Morning Star. The center bush is called Joseph's Coat. It brings to mind the faithfulness, humility, and forgiveness Joseph showed through all kinds of trials. Help me to be like that. Another rosebush has red blooms. When I pick them and inhale their soothing fragrance, I think of when You were tortured and crushed in spirit. Still, You never ceased to love. I get pricked once in a while while tending these roses. When I do, I'm reminded of the crown of thorns pressed on Your brow and the price You paid for me.

Our yellow roses cause me to recall Your endless joy and peace. In spite of hard rains and hot sun causing the blossoms to fade, they still bloom a good share of the year. Thank You for being with me in all kinds of weather.

When Bob buys me lilies, I plant them alongside the house where they're sheltered. I often think of Your purity when their fragrant trumpets open into full bloom.

I sometimes slip out here when I can't sleep and look up at the morning stars. They may fade someday. But You, my Morning Star, are always here with me.

I am the rose of Sharon,
And the lily of the valleys.
Like a lily among thorns.

Song of Solomon 2:1–2 nkjv

The Silly Squirrels

Here come the silly squirrels, Lord. They are such cute little pests. I'll toss out a few nuts for them. See how their bushy tails twitch? Their black eyes gleam like tiny pieces of coal. They quickly glance around the yard, alert to potential danger. Two more nuts are devoured. These critters must be hungry. But look how they hurriedly bury the rest. Although they are cute, I wish they would stay out of our flowerpots!

Do squirrels even remember where they bury things, Lord? No matter how many nuts they get, they just keep finding spots to hide them. It's almost like they are greedy.

They remind me of the story of the rich fool in Luke 12. Regardless of how great the crops the rich man produced, they never seemed to be enough. Rather than sharing with others, he kept building bigger barns to store his yield. I wonder if he even paid attention to what he had or where he hid everything.

Help me to appreciate the blessings You give me, Lord. My grandmother taught me to give a tenth of my crops and everything I have to those around me. Remind me to do so. Today I'll pick some roses and take them to my friend who needs encouragement.

Thank You, Lord, for all You give me.

> [Jesus said,] "Give, and it will be given to you.
> A good measure, pressed down,
> shaken together and running over,
> will be poured into your lap.
> For with the measure you use,
> it will be measured to you."
>
> LUKE 6:38 NIV

Treasured Times

What a special day this is, Lord. We are celebrating our nation's independence. Thank You for those who helped form our country. I'm grateful for the many who, through the years, died so we can remain free. Bless us, I pray, that we may continue to be one nation under God.

Help us treasure our freedom and never take it for granted. Thank You for the opportunity You gave us to worship You when You died on the cross for our sins. No matter where we live, male or female, bond or free, You give us liberty of heart to come to You in prayer. Thank You for being our Lord and Savior. Bless our brothers and sisters around the world as they, too, worship You, our Lord, our God.

At the end of this special day, my husband and I go to the front yard. There, our neighbors and their family and friends are shooting off fireworks. We gaze into the darkness, awestruck at the dramatic display. Bob and I sit in our lawn chairs, holding hands, occasionally jumping up to spray water on our roof with the hose!

We finally go inside. We hear the patriotic songs on television. Again, we take hands and thank You for these treasured times and for our freedom.

[Jesus said,] "The Spirit of the Lord is upon me;
he has appointed me to preach Good News to the poor;
he has sent me to heal the brokenhearted
and to announce that captives shall be
released and the blind shall see,
that the downtrodden shall be freed from their oppressors,
and that God is ready to give blessings
to all who come to him."

LUKE 4:18–19 TLB

JULY 5

The Swing Set

It's so quiet this morning, Lord. Fireworks went off last night until dawn. I wonder if I'm the only one awake. A gray haze of smoke shrouds everything. I walk through the yard, picking up bits of fireworks litter. Now it's time to settle down for my talk with You.

A swing set stands silently in our backyard as though it awaits our grandchildren and friends to come play on its bars and swings. Remember when our children were growing up, Lord? We decided we wanted a swing set. We shopped for the best—made with galvanized steel. Bob and our older sons spent hours carefully anchoring it to a strong layer of concrete in the ground. I repainted it recently. It's over twenty years old now, but it still stands strong. The groundwork made the difference.

Although there are flaws, our nation was also built on a solid foundation. It, too, still stands. More importantly is the firm foundation You help me build my life upon. It's a foundation of You, my Christ, my solid Rock. You are my cherished Cornerstone. Thank You that each time storms and sleet and hail pound against me or the earth shakes, You help me cling to You and Your sure foundation.

> *The LORD is my rock, my fortress and my deliverer;*
> *my God is my rock, in whom I take refuge.*
> *He is my shield and the horn of my salvation,*
> *my stronghold.*
> *I call to the LORD, who is worthy of praise.*

PSALM 18:2–3 NIV

Catching Up

Lord, thank You for my mother- and father-in-law's visit. They live far away. It's been a long time since we've been able to see them. Although they are in their eighties, Dad is a spiritual tower of strength, and Mom is filled with morsels of wisdom to share. We certainly had a lot of catching up to do.

From early morning until late at night, we talked and talked—and talked some more. Love and care constantly flowed between us. Thank You, Lord, for how they both love and serve You. The time came too soon for them to leave. We will look forward to when we can be together again.

That's the way it is with You and me, Lord. We get together. I talk and You listen. Then You remind me to pause and listen while You do the talking. How I wish everything would stand still as we share with one another. You always understand how I feel. Whenever I tell You what's on my heart, You never alienate Yourself from me.

Amid the hurry-scurry of each day, I often find myself looking forward to later, when we get together and catch up. Thank You, Lord, for always having time for me.

"Blessed is the man who listens to me,
watching daily at my doors,
waiting at my doorway.
For whoever finds me finds life
and receives favor from the LORD."

PROVERBS 8:34–35 NIV

JULY 7

Just Plain Fun

Lord, thank You for my dad. Poppy and I get together, laugh a lot, and just plain have fun. As you know, sometimes we go to the ocean and stay in the trailer for a few days. During the day, we drive around and see the sights or walk along the beach. At night, I open the windows to hear the ocean roar and the frogs sing in "croaky" harmony. We light the propane lamp and drag out the ten-thousand game. We play and laugh until we feel like our eyes droop.

The other day my dad came to our house. Bob, Poppy, and I enjoyed a wonderful salmon barbecue. What a great cook Bob is. After we finished eating and cleared the table, Poppy broke out the ten thousand game. Once again, our afternoon was filled with laughter and fun.

I know I work too hard, Lord. I place goals before myself and am determined to meet them. Sometimes I pile work onto myself that isn't necessary. My family is always gently reminding me of this and trying to get me to relax more.

Thank You for my dad and how much he means to me. Thank You for reminding me to take time from responsibilities and just plain have fun.

A cheerful heart is a good medicine,
but a downcast spirit dries up the bones.

PROVERBS 17:22 RSV

My All-the-Time Friend

Lord, I want to tell you about my friend, Sharon. I realize You already know her. She's very special. Sharon's more than a regular friend. She's my all-the-time friend. I'm still amazed at how we have been close buddies since I was seven and she was eight years old. After we graduated from high school, we went our separate ways. Still, You had a way of causing our paths to cross.

Now we are part of the same church. Sharon loves the Lord with all her heart. We're not only friends; we are sisters in Your family. Like the Bible says about the church: One rejoices when the other is happy and weeps when the other is sad. I can depend on my all-the-time friend anytime—day or night. I don't have to beg her to care or to be there. She just is.

I'm grateful for Your friendship, Lord. I know when I ask in Your name and in Your will, I can trust You to answer. When I knock and seek Your advice, You are near, ready to guide me.

How blessed I am to enjoy all-the-time friendships with You and Your family. Help me to be an all-the-time friend.

[Jesus said,] "So I say to you:
Ask and it will be given to you;
seek and you will find;
knock and the door will be opened to you.
For everyone who asks receives;
he who seeks finds; and to him who knocks,
the door will be opened."

LUKE 11:9–10 NIV

My Good Samaritan

I spent some difficult years working a second job at a fast-food restaurant. Those were tough times, Lord. My co-workers and I often went home bone tired. Working there brought out the best and the worst in us.

One dear young lady named Sherry became my friend. Sometimes we drove each other crazy, Lord. How amazing, the way You put two people so completely different together and caused a lasting friendship to develop.

She never minced words. How she saw it was how she said it. Her greatest character trait was and still is honesty. Sherry has always been a good listener. She cares and tries to help others whenever she can. I'll never forget, Lord, how she helped me. I drove a rattletrap car. Even though it wasn't much, I was thankful for it. One day my car was stolen. I didn't know what to do. Bob and I came up with some money to buy another. We couldn't find anything reliable in our price range. But Sherry did.

Sadly, Sherry's grandmother could no longer drive. So the two of them decided to sell her little silver Toyota to me for half its value. Thank You, Lord, for Sherry and her grandmother. They both were true good Samaritans.

> [Jesus said,] "Which of these three do you think
> was a neighbor to the man who fell
> into the hands of robbers?"
> The expert in the law replied,
> "The one who had mercy on him."
> Jesus told him, "Go and do likewise."
>
> LUKE 10:36–37 NIV

Watercolor Flower

Lord, I saw my former student, Jerry, today. I was reminded of the lesson in school I learned from him one year. For days he had been asking if we could paint watercolor flowers. Each time he asked, I put him off. He shrugged his shoulders and walked away. We were busy with the basic academics, Lord. We didn't have enough time for art that week. Along with our daily studious routine, we were training the children to run in the Special Olympics.

One afternoon during Special Olympics practice, we had a relay race. The kids divided into two teams. My student was at the end of one line. He would be the one to finish the race. It was exciting, Lord. Then came his turn. Halfway through, he stopped. I pleaded for him to finish. Instead, he bent down, picked a flower from the grass, walked toward me, and handed the flower to me. His big brown eyes and warm smile melted my heart. All I could do was hug him and rub his curly black hair.

Thank You for helping Jerry not to give up and for teaching me to listen and care. Thank You for making time to hear my prayer and for helping me when I come to You.

By the way, Lord, the next day we made time to paint watercolor flowers.

[Jesus said,] "Don't you think that
God will surely give justice
to his people who plead with him
day and night? Yes!"

LUKE 18:7–8 TLB

Patchwork Relationship

There was a time, Father, when I thought the way to please You was to learn the fruits of Your Holy Spirit, patch them onto my life, and fervently practice each one to perfection: love, joy, peace, patience, gentleness. That shouldn't be too hard. However, in spite of how much I attempted this, it resulted in disaster and disappointment.

I remember my first attempt in repairing our two-year-old son Bobby's corduroy pants. How proud I was putting cute little patches on the knees and saving a little money. I found the bright red remnants for practically nothing at the fabric shop. I was very pleased. I measured and carefully sewed them on. Bobby's little pants looked so nice—that is, until I washed them.

I was shocked the way the patches had shrunk and pulled away from the pant legs. This is when Your lesson in Matthew 9 made sense. I couldn't conjure up replicas of the fruits of Your Spirit. Instead, I had to turn from my old ways and allow You to make me new.

Remind me, Father, never to settle for a patchwork relationship with You. I want our bond to remain strong each day and allow You to keep me clean, pure, and true.

> *Therefore, if anyone is in Christ,*
> *he is a new creation;*
> *old things have passed away;*
> *behold, all things have become new.*

> 2 CORINTHIANS 5:17 NKJV

The Lost Purse

This morning I planned to run some errands with my dad, Lord. I had arranged to meet at his place at a certain time. When I was ready to go, I couldn't find my purse. The search began. The more I looked, the more frustrated I became. I about tore the place apart trying to find it. This was scary, because everything important I need seems to be in my purse.

I couldn't drive without a driver's license. It was time to meet my dad, and there I stood. I took a big breath and prayed for Your help. Then I called my dad and told him about my dilemma. Bob, Dad, and I had been to Bible study at a friend's home the night before. Dad asked me if I had left it there. I thought back. Sure enough, that's where it was. Thank You for my dad. He picked me up in his car; we got my purse, then went on with our errands.

I'm certain I'm more important to You than a lost purse or coin, Lord. Once I was lost spiritually. You and Your angels must have rejoiced when I finally gave my heart to You. Thank You for keeping me in Your sight and for always caring for me.

[Jesus said,] "She calls her friends. . .and says,
'Rejoice with me; I have found my lost coin.'
In the same way, I tell you,
there is rejoicing in the presence of the angels of God
over one sinner who repents."

LUKE 15:9–10 NIV

You Found Me

When Danny was two years old, Father, he and our dog Pretzel were inseparable. Wherever one was, I could find the other. Since we lived in an apartment just off a busy street, I kept an extra close watch on our children. I thought there could be only one way to escape, but I was mistaken. Danny disappeared almost before my eyes.

With our four-year-old Bobby in tow, my neighbor and I frantically began searching for Danny. I knew he hadn't gone toward the busy street, so we headed in the direction of the fence behind the apartments. There we found a hole under the fence just big enough for Danny to follow the dog through.

In a matter of minutes, we tracked Danny down to the block behind the apartments. I promptly took his hand and led him and Pretzel safely home.

Once, I followed the wrong leaders in my life, Father, and got myself into some wrong situations. I'm grateful for the way You reached out to me like the lost sheep in Luke 15 and brought me safely to Your fold. Thank You for loving me and bringing me to You. No more do I want to stray from Your care. Now I want to remain safely close to You.

> *[Jesus said,] "When he has found [the lost sheep],*
> *he lays it on his shoulders, rejoicing.*
> *And when he comes home,*
> *he calls together his friends and his neighbors,*
> *saying to them,*
> *'Rejoice with me,*
> *for I have found my sheep which was lost!' "*

LUKE 15:5–6 NASB

Help Me Pray and Forgive

I was shocked and brokenhearted, Lord, when I discovered what terrible things someone had done to one I love. I wondered how anyone could be so unkind. I hated this wrongdoer. Even the thought of this awful person made me cringe. I wanted to do something to make things right, but I could not see a way. Then I came to You in prayer and asked for Your help and guidance.

You showed me the story of the unmerciful servant in Matthew 18. You helped me understand that even though the offender wasn't sorry, I still had to forgive and leave it all in Your capable and just hands. If I had refused to forgive, that awful hatred would have consumed me like deadly spiritual cancer.

Although I had no forgiveness within me, I asked You to help. Still, You requested more of me, Lord. You told me to pray for the one who had mistreated my loved one. I knelt before You, releasing my loved one and my anger to You. I didn't ask for You to bless this wrongdoer, but I pleaded for that person to repent and come to You.

Continue to speak to that person's heart to turn from a sinful life. Along with this, keep my heart soft and pliable. Help me always to be willing to pray and forgive.

[Jesus said,] "But I say to you,
love your enemies and pray for those who persecute you,
so that you may be sons [and daughters]
of your Father who is in heaven."

MATTHEW 5:44–45 NASB

The Butterfly Process

When our children were young, we witnessed some astounding miracles of nature. Once, we discovered a small green caterpillar creeping up a leaf on a tree. Remember how excited the kids were when we gathered the little green critter with the branch it was attached to, then carefully placed it in a widemouthed jar, Lord? We poked holes in the lid and kept it on our porch, sprinkling water in the jar each day.

The boys anxiously waited. In a few days, we watched it busily spin its cocoon. No one told it what to do. You must have had a hand in that.

We remained close during that time. The lifeless gray cocoon began to crack, exposing a tightly folded butterfly. I still thrill when I remember lifting the branch from the jar, butterfly attached. The wet, exhausted creature slowly worked its wings until it was ready to fly.

When I first met You, Lord, my life didn't seem to matter much. I was aimless. I was going nowhere. Then I died to my wasted past. You took over and slowly started making changes in me. You wrapped me in Your tender care and gave me a brand-new life. Somehow You made something beautiful through Your power and love.

Thank You for the butterfly process You brought about within me.

> *It is God himself who has made us what we are*
> *and given us new lives from Christ Jesus;*
> *and long ages ago he planned that*
> *we should spend these lives in helping others.*

EPHESIANS 2:10 TLB

Azure Blue Reminder

Thank You, dear Lord, for the many times You provide Bob and me with simple stress relievers. I still treasure that afternoon when You gave us an azure blue reminder of Your miracles and blessings.

We were driving home from a town ten miles away. I suggested we take the "stress reliever" way home—a quiet road along the river. It was a cool, cloudy day, the kind of weather birds love. We had our windows rolled down so we could hear the chirps as we drove along.

When we rounded one bend, Lord, Your sun rays broke through the clouds and caused the leaves in the trees to glisten. I can still visualize our next glorious sight. An azure blue heron stood by the roadside only a few feet ahead. Its four-foot-tall body stood aloof with absolute elegance. We watched as it spread its wings and flew effortlessly over the river. Amazingly, it glided parallel to our car window for several minutes. I was so excited, Bob was afraid I would run the car off the road! The blue heron eventually veered off and downward, most likely after a fish.

Our stress was gone, our day complete. Thank You for Your surprise azure reminder of Your blessings and incredible creations.

The birds of the air nest by the waters;
they sing among the branches.

PSALM 104:12 NIV

Mustard-Seed Faith

I have a friend who has the most prolific mustard-seed faith I have ever seen. My friend used to be homeless. Things were not going right in his life. He was a long way away from me, so there was little I could do to help except pray.

Although life was very difficult for him, my friend did not give up. He held a tremendous faith in You, and he put his faith into action. He didn't just stand still and feel sorry for himself. Instead, my friend worked very hard, hand in hand with You, to get himself back on his feet. He moved his mountain one scoop at a time.

Now he is happily married to a wonderful lady, has a good job, and is in the early stages of a growing business he now owns. He and his wife are about to buy their first home. How wonderful the way they love You and are active in their church. Thank You, Lord, for helping my friend help himself. Thank You for watching over and still caring for him and his wife.

I am proud of them, Lord, and all they are accomplishing. I'm grateful and honored to have both as my friends—my friends with prolific, bountiful mustard-seed faith.

> [Jesus] replied, "Because you have so little faith.
> I tell you the truth,
> if you have faith as small as a mustard seed,
> you can say to this mountain,
> 'Move from here to there' and it will move.
> Nothing will be impossible for you."

MATTHEW 17:20 NIV

The Splinter

I recall facing a challenge many years ago, Lord, when our six-year-old neighbor, Ginger, came to our house with a huge splinter in the bottom of her foot. It must have been about three inches long. She looked up at me with tear-filled eyes and asked if I could take it out.

Her mother had tried but wasn't able to remove it. Ginger's family was large and seldom went to doctors. Although I was afraid to work on it, I said a prayer and started in. It must have been You who gave me the wisdom and strength I needed.

Tweezers didn't budge it. Finally, I asked her if she could trust me to work it out with some small, needle-nose pliers. Ginger sniffled, looked hopeful, and relented.

I quickly sterilized the utensil and prayed for help. Tears pooling in my eyes, I managed to grab the end of the splinter and pull hard. It came out. I helped Ginger hobble home. Her mother soaked the injured foot in a soothing salt solution for a long time. Thankfully, it healed nicely.

I appreciate Your helping Ginger to trust me. Thank You for granting me the strength I needed for Ginger and aiding me with other difficult tasks I've faced through the years.

And He said to me,
"My grace is sufficient for you,
for My strength is made perfect in weakness."

2 CORINTHIANS 12:9 NKJV

Another Splinter

This was a frustrating day, Lord. After dealing with problems and those around me doing things incorrectly, I became impatient and had a not-so-loving attitude. I ignored the words of caution You whispered to my heart. Instead, I plowed full-steam ahead, not considering who was in my path. Why was I so inconsiderate?

Before long, I turned everything into discord and disaster. Hurt feelings and retaliation resulted. I guess my way wasn't so good, after all. I'm embarrassed and ashamed. Please forgive my impatience and holier-than-thou attitude.

My unkind actions must have saddened You. As with Ginger's splinter, here I am giving You a monstrous plank to remove from my life and a mess to help me straighten out.

Grant me the humility I need to ask for forgiveness. I know I have plenty of faults. It certainly isn't hard to find them, especially for You. Who am I to set someone else straight, when I'm kneeling here pleading for Your mercy and pardon? Help me to focus on the work You are doing with me so I can help rather than hinder.

When I'm faced with unpleasant circumstances with others, remind me to pray for and love them. And please tell me often, Lord, to leave the faultfinding to You.

[Jesus said,] "Don't criticize. . . .
Should you say, 'Friend,
let me help you get that speck out of your eye,'
when you can't even see because of the board in your own?
Hypocrite! First get rid of the board.
Then you can see to help your brother [or sister]."

MATTHEW 7:1, 4–5 TLB

from Nitpicking to Mending

A group I knew used to meet and work on handcraft projects for missions. I enjoyed being with them, Lord, except for one thing. Several took every opportunity to criticize a leader in the church. The ladies decided since this person was a leader, she should have no flaws. Whenever the leader was around, bad attitudes were displayed. The criticizers rolled their eyes, exchanged knowing glances, and made cutting remarks.

I really prayed to You about these hurtful actions, Lord. Time came to attend the next get-together. I had to drag myself there. I was pleasantly surprised that a missionary came. Before long, however, the nitpicking began.

The missionary broke into the conversation. She had been knitting a beautiful afghan. She started tearing it apart because of a couple of "small" mistakes in the center. Bits and pieces fell everywhere. The other ladies looked shocked. The missionary told the others she thought they wanted perfection. She explained how that's what they were doing to the church leader's life. They were tearing her apart!

Thank You, Lord, for the beautiful example of how to change a situation without criticism. The group learned instead how to rebuild and mend the lives of others. Help me change, Lord, and be willing to stand up for right.

Love is very patient and kind,
never jealous or envious, never boastful or proud,
never haughty or selfish or rude. . . .
It. . .will hardly even notice when others do it wrong.

1 CORINTHIANS 13:4–5 TLB

Changing Weeds to Flowers

Thank You for all of our neighbors, Lord. We are a little community in a bustling city. We watch out and care for each other. This evening I was visiting with Thomas, our next-door neighbor, while he was tending his and his wife's flower garden. Thomas and Claudia's garden displays a flamboyant arrangement of all kinds of flowers. Thomas pointed out some plants he couldn't identify. To my surprise and his, a mixture of wildflowers had graced the garden, blending their colors with the domestic ones. It is beautiful to behold. Some folks call these plants weeds. We see them lining freeways and roads, but the blooms are lovely and add brightness to passing traffic. Thank You for my friends and neighbors, Lord. They are like the flowers.

Now and then I meet people who are considered not so lovely. When I do, I'm learning to be less judgmental at our first meeting. If they are unpleasant, help me pray for each one, rather than wanting to avoid them. Help me to look for the good in people like Thomas does his wildflowers. Show me how to care and how to lead these ones to You. As You work in my life and theirs, I delight in watching each of Your beloved ones change from weeds to wildflowers.

> *For, "All men [and women] are like grass,*
> *and all their glory is like the flowers of the field;*
> *the grass withers and the flowers fall,*
> *but the word of the Lord stands forever."*
>
> 1 PETER 1:24–25 NIV

Hidden Treasures

While visiting in Montana, I came upon some pyrite stones, better known as fool's gold. I purchased them, Lord, and brought them back to share with my grandchildren and my students in my church school class. The kids love how they sparkle.

Plans are being made to take some of the young people at church into the hills, where they will try their hand at panning for gold. I wonder what hidden treasures they will find, Lord.

The fool's gold I came upon is without value. But these grandchildren of mine and my students at church are our priceless future. They are bright and curious. Their eyes sparkle with enthusiasm when they learn new things. I look at them and see hidden talents emerging. Use their abilities for You, Lord.

What do You have planned for them? I pray for You to prepare their futures and protect them. Through each of their growing years, sift away things of no value that might weigh them down. Turn these ones I love around in Your hand, Lord, and develop the amazing hidden treasures they have to offer. Help these youngsters learn to use their talents for You. Watch over them, and keep them close to You each day.

Let them do good, that they be rich in good works,
ready to give, willing to share,
storing up for themselves a good foundation
for the time to come,
that they may lay hold on eternal life.

1 TIMOTHY 6:18–19 NKJV

Homemade Bread

Everything had been going wrong for me lately, Lord. I felt like I was traveling the wrong way on a one-way street or hitting all the red traffic lights. Life's obstacles kept blocking my way. The more things didn't go right, the more frustrated I became. And the more I spun my wheels, trying to catch up, the more I put off finding time with You, Lord. Order began leaving my days. I became irritable. I wondered if You cared about me.

About that time, our church was having a bake sale. I decided to make homemade bread. That shouldn't take long. People would love it. I waited impatiently for the dough to rise. I wanted to bake it early. Then I remembered what happened the last time I tried that. The loaf came out heavy, rock hard, and not done in the middle.

It was then You helped me see I had my priorities wrong. I wanted everything microwave style—right now! I hadn't allowed time for You to minister to me. I wasn't spiritually done in the middle. Thank You for reminding me to put You first and seek Your direction. Thank You for kneading life back into me and filling me with You—so I could be done in the middle.

> *Then Jesus declared,*
> *"I am the bread of life.*
> *He who comes to me will never go hungry,*
> *and he who believes in me will never be thirsty."*
>
> JOHN 6:35 NIV

The Peach Tree

Lord, this is our little dwarf peach tree. It has produced so many peaches, we propped the lower branches with boards so they wouldn't break. I always pruned, watered, and sprayed for leaf curl. The peaches were big, sweet, and juicy—until this year.

In early spring, I sprayed. But its leaves began to curl. I sprayed again. Still, the tree got worse. Leaves fell. Its branches looked lifeless. Only a few blossoms appeared.

My friend, Grace, looked at the tree and knew immediately what was wrong. It was diseased with a fungus. If we didn't do something, the tree would die. Its condition would spread through the entire yard. We faithfully pruned away dead limbs and fed the tree. I took a sample to a garden store and obtained a better spray to kill the disease.

I was once like that sick tree, Lord. I neglected feeding on Your Word and drinking from Your living water. My life was spiritually sick and dying inside until I turned to You for help. It was painful while You pruned useless, bad ways from me, yet You removed my spiritual disease. You fed and watered me from Your Word. Like the peach tree, I started doing better. Thank You for how my life is renewed now and that I'm able to produce abundant spiritual fruit through You.

[Jesus said,] "I am the vine, you are the branches.
He who abides in Me, and I in him,
bears much fruit;
for without Me you can do nothing."

JOHN 15:5 NKJV

Sheets on the Clothesline

It's midafternoon, Father. I just finished some housework and laundry. Now I'm sitting on the backyard patio, taking a break and enjoying time with You. Sheets hang on the clothesline. They're so white, they sparkle and reflect the sun.

Remember when our children were babies, Father? Back then I didn't use disposable diapers much, except when we took trips. Instead, the diapers were made of cotton. Almost every morning I took pride in getting them white by washing once, soaking in a borax solution, rinsing again, then hanging them on the clothesline. The diapers could be seen flapping in the breeze a mile down the road from our old farmhouse. They, too, sparkled like new and reflected the sun. I felt it was something that symbolized my love for my babies. Although the new system is nice, I still like the cotton.

Father God, I want my life to be like that for You. I love You so much. I ask for You to wash me each day and cause me to become as white as snow. Make me pure so there is nothing offensive to You; then rinse me once again with Your restoring, living water. Each day as You search and cleanse my heart, I pray others can recognize my love for You and that I'll be able to reflect Your Son, Jesus Christ.

> [Jesus said,] "Don't hide your light!
> Let it shine for all;
> let your good deeds glow for all to see,
> so that they will praise your heavenly Father."

MATTHEW 5:15–16 TLB

One Little Song

Thank You, Father, for the little grandma who taught our four-year-old son, Danny, in daily Vacation Bible School. Little did she realize one song and one Bible verse would be so important to him and the rest of the family.

Danny came home from Bible school singing the timeless message: "Jesus is with me through every day and night. I will not be afraid but will sleep safely in His care." His modified Bible verse (Isaiah 12:2) is one I still repeat: "When I am afraid, I will trust in God."

The song captured our family. Before long, Father, we sang it while doing chores, going to the store, and especially at bedtime. We continued singing it through the years, and I taught it to our younger children.

Remember when Dan was sixteen, Father? He was terribly ill with a ruptured appendix and intestine. You were certainly there with us. For a while, Dan was too sick to be aware of anything going on. When he got better and looked around his hospital room, Dan read a plaque on the wall. His voice lowered to a whisper. "Look, Mom." Comforting words soothed our minds and hearts: *"Behold, God is my salvation; I will trust, and not be afraid"* (Isaiah 12:2 KJV).

Thank You, Father, for Your promises that ring true all through our lives.

"See, God has come to save me!
I will trust and not be afraid,
for the Lord is my strength and song;
he is my salvation."

ISAIAH 12:2 TLB

Use My Talents

Father, since I was a little girl, I've loved to sing. My child-hood friend Sharon and I sang everywhere we went. She crooned the melody and I learned to harmonize. Even now, we often sit together in church and sing praises to You.

After high school, I moved away from home and met my new pastor's wife, Shirley. Thank You for how Shirley and her husband, Buzz, coached our thriving youth group for future church leadership. Shirley taught me to sing solos. I was scared at first, but with prayer and practice I caught on. Singing became my joy.

While our children were growing up, I had water-stained music from practicing songs while washing dishes. (I still do sometimes.) Some sad experiences came later, though, that crushed my spirit. During that time, I refused to sing in church, Father. I had nothing to sing about. This went on for about a year. It must have saddened You.

I made it through those times. Thank You for helping me rebuild my life and for having someone ask me to begin singing again. It was like starting over. I realized I had almost lost my talent. With Your help, I caught on once more.

Thank You, Father, for the talents You provide me. No matter what happens, help me to always keep using them for You.

*Sing a new song to the Lord
telling about his mighty deeds!
For he has won a mighty victory
by his power and holiness.*

PSALM 98:1 TLB

The Whole Family of God

Yesterday in church, we experienced something so awesome, Lord. Different people had carefully prepared the worship service. And You put the service together. Our worship team, consisting of a teenager, a young mother, and a couple of grandmas, led lively songs of praise. An eighty-year-old man played the piano. Bob played the guitar; a young mother, the drums. The congregation joined in with a few shakers and tambourines. Our sixth graders took the offering.

Later in the service, a middle-aged man led hymns while his wife played piano; then she gave a children's moment. An eighty-year-old lady sang a special song about heaven. Testimonies came from all ages. Then Bob and I sang another special song: "The Longer I Serve Him, the Sweeter He Grows."

How did all that happen, Lord? Through this, You helped us realize that when it comes to Your family, You are no respecter of persons or age. I hope I can still sing when I'm eighty, keep up with exciting things, and give glory to You. I look forward to the children who take part now becoming leaders in Your church when they are grown.

Thank You for our whole family of God, who enjoys sharing Your love.

Just as there are many parts to our bodies,
so it is with Christ's body.
We are all parts of it,
and it takes every one of us to make it [the church] complete,
for we each have different work to do.
So we belong to each other,
and each needs all the others.

ROMANS 12:4–5 TLB

JULY 29

Birds on a Telephone Wire

Good morning, Lord. I step outside to get the newspaper. The air is unusually crisp. Clouds glide across the darkened sky, driven by chilling winds from the north. After experiencing several recent hot days, I shiver. I'm anxious to get back inside. This kind of weather has invaded my comfort zone.

Irritating screeches from the telephone wires above the driveway pierce the silence. I glance up and see crows lined up in a straight, ebony row. The birds act as though they prefer snuggling together, seeking comfort from one another.

I'm kind of like that, Lord. I enjoy the company of the strong Christians I know. It reminds me of the birds on the telephone wire. It's good to enjoy the strength that comes from our friendships. Still, I know You want me to step out of my comfort zone and allow those who don't know You to become part of my life.

I slip on my sweatshirt and walking shoes and step back out the door. The wind whips my hair. The air clears my lungs and mind. Walk with me, Lord. Talk to my heart about who I can share Your love with today.

When I feel uncomfortable, I'm thankful for Your presence being with me.

> *[Jesus said,] "But you will receive power when*
> *the Holy Spirit has come upon you;*
> *and you shall be My witnesses both in Jerusalem,*
> *and in all Judea and Samaria,*
> *and even to the remotest part of the earth."*

ACTS 1:8 NASB

I Will Keep On

Lord, when I visited my uncle Russell this summer, I was pleased at how well he's doing. You know that Russell will be ninety years old in September. He is still very active. He mows and waters five yards for people in the area. In the winter he gets his small-sized snowplow out and clears their driveways. Most of the folks he helps are younger than he is! Along with this, he feeds and cares for farm animals.

During his off hours, Russell goes to a nearby nursing home where my aunt Dorothy stays. Along with enjoying her company, he takes some of the older ladies from the home to the stores and beauty shop. Some of their goings-on and conversations are amusing to him. Most of these ladies are also younger than my uncle.

Russell and I have discussed, quite a bit, what keeps him going. It's simply that he keeps on keeping on. Help me to do that, too, Lord. Whatever task You place before me, help me not to give up. Remind me to think young, to grasp life, and to enjoy every morsel of it. Even when I'm so tired and can hardly put one foot before the other, I want to do for others. Help me, Lord, to keep on keeping on.

And let us not get tired of doing what is right,
for after a while we will reap a harvest of blessing
if we don't get discouraged and give up.

GALATIANS 6:9 TLB

Eternal Legacy

Here I am, Lord, on my knees. My little spade in hand, I work weeds out of the moist soil to make more room for the flowers. I've spent countless hours out here in the flower garden. I remember planting different things and watching them grow from tiny sprouts into beautiful, colorful displays. Good memories come from this garden, Lord—the kids at play and bouquets given to family, neighbors, and friends.

I work my way through the rows. My spade hits something hard. I pull the object from the dirt and find an old bone—probably buried by a beloved dog we had. I've dug them up before. Funny—I miss that dog so much, I just drop the bone back in the ground and cover it. I guess he had a way of leaving his treasures for us.

I lean back on my heels and think of all the heirlooms we plan to pass to our children and grandchildren someday. Like this bone, they will rust and waste away, Lord. There's only one legacy I can leave that will matter. That's to plant in the hearts of those around me the message of Your love.

Help me share a growing heritage in You with everyone who will listen.

> *For the LORD is good and his love endures forever;*
> *his faithfulness continues through all generations.*

PSALM 100:5 NIV

to Share You

Popcorn Christian

I want to share You with everyone around me, dear Father. Sometimes I become fearful of saying the wrong things or being rejected, but I do much better now than I used to. When I was in elementary school, the opportunity would come to give testimonies of Your love in church. I longed to but felt as though glue held me to my seat.

When I grew old enough to be in the youth group, I would stand up, blurt out, "Jesus loves me," and sit down. Our youth leader had a perfect description of people like me. He called us popcorn Christians. He said we popped up, turned white, and sat down. My testimony wasn't too great; but it was the beginning of my learning to share.

The more I walk with You, Father, the more fantastic things I have to tell. Now I long to let others know of Your wonderful, life-giving love. Even still, there are times when I'm hesitant. That's when I take a deep breath and ask You if You want me to share. Much to my relief, You guide me. Your answer may be "yes"; "wait for the right time"; or "keep silent and pray."

Thank You for each time You lead and help me, through Your powerful holy presence, to tell others about You.

The Lord God has given me his words of wisdom
so that I may know what I should say to all these weary ones.
Morning by morning he wakens me
and opens my understanding to his will.

ISAIAH 50:4 TLB

Bubbling Over

Everywhere my friend Riker goes, Lord, he bubbles over with enthusiasm and love for You. I don't know how he does it. He isn't afraid to speak the words needed to be said at the time. When he talks, it's easy to listen, because he has something worthwhile to share. He's like a magnet when it comes to people following him.

He isn't very old, Lord, but his abilities go beyond his years. I see purpose and enthusiastic talent in him. Thank You for the fact that he loves You. Thank You for giving him the ability to lead. Use his gifts, I pray, to be a blessing for You throughout his life.

I wish I could be that way, Lord. I simply keep putting one foot in front of the other and sharing Your love every way I can. I get excited about all You do for me, but in a quieter way. I realize You made me the way I am, and You use me in the ways You choose.

Thank You for blessing Riker and me with abilities to tell others about You. Help us to be obedient in the things You lead us to do. All You do for my friend and me fills us with joy and causes us to tell others of Your great and powerful love.

The words of a man's [or woman's] mouth are deep waters,
but the fountain of wisdom is a bubbling brook.

PROVERBS 18:4 NIV

Teddy-Bear Comfort

My junior-age students from church are gone to camp now, Lord. Please be with them. Help them learn to draw closer to You. For some, this is their first time. Comfort them so they won't be afraid. Guide their counselors as they enjoy and lead these kids.

I still remember when our son Jonathan went to church camp for the first time. He looked a little scared, Lord. Praying together before we left the car helped a lot. By the end of the week, he grew to appreciate his cabin counselor.

Remember how the campers gathered in the cabin with their counselor that first afternoon, Lord? Most likely, they weren't willing to admit how anxious and homesick they were. Each young camper perched on his bunk while the counselor explained that he felt just as uneasy about leaving home as they did. He told them there was one thing he had to bring with him. Then he pulled a teddy bear from his duffel bag— and another and another. . . . As he talked, the counselor tossed teddy bears to each of the campers.

Lord, help me be aware of those who are anxious. Help me pass on to them Your teddy-bear comfort and love with my words and deeds.

Therefore encourage one another
and build each other up,
just as in fact you are doing.

1 THESSALONIANS 5:11 NIV

AUGUST 4

Joy-filled Daisies

Here I am, Lord, standing with You by our flower garden.
This morning I tended the daisies. Some of the blossoms
are drying now, so I snipped them and scattered most of
the seeds from the dried blooms over the moist soil. Next
spring they will produce more daisies. I took the remaining
seeds inside and placed them in an envelope.

I recall how years ago my friend Joi and I were visiting
while she took care of the daisies in her yard. I watched her
snip the dead blossoms, break them open, and scatter the
seeds over the soil. That day she snipped a few for me. Thank
You for how she spread her joy to my garden and my life.

Although she has moved hundreds of miles away now,
Joi still has a way of spreading cheer and happiness to every
person with whom she comes in contact. Thank You that I
am one of them. Thank You for the unlimited delight You
give me.

How can I pass Your happiness to others today, Lord?
To start with, I'll write a few notes of encouragement. One
of them will be to my friend Joi. I'll tuck in a tiny card with
a poem filled with hope and brightness. And, Lord, I think
I'll slip in some small envelopes of daisy seeds.

> But let all who take refuge in you be glad;
> let them ever sing for joy.
> Spread your protection over them,
> that those who love your name may rejoice in you.

PSALM 5:11 NIV

Stir Your Spirit within Me

Good morning, Lord. Yesterday Bob and I met our son and daughter-in-law, Jonathan and Cynthia, at a hotel partway between our homes. I couldn't help awakening early today. The swimming pool beckoned to me. No one else is in it. Am I the only one crazy enough to swim this early, Lord?

I settle into the sauna. Ah, how good it feels. Hot water swirls around me. It soothes and loosens my stiff muscles. Steam fills my nostrils. Now, Lord, to the pool. One lap after another I swim. My breath quickens. My muscles tingle and come alive. My sleepy, foggy mind clears. Vigor fills my being. Thank You for this time alone with You, Lord.

I finish my laps. My pulse slows. The water becomes quiet. Ever so gently, I stir the blue water and watch the circle widen and glisten in the morning sun. I slowly climb out of the pool and go to a nearby table. The circles are still expanding. Soft waves slap against the sides of the pool.

Lord, like these ripples, stir Your Holy Spirit within me. Let the warmth of Your love bless our family and those around us today. Use us for Your glory. Let Your waves spread and spread and spread. . . . In Your name, I pray. Amen.

"At that time the Spirit of the Lord
will come mightily upon you,
and you will prophesy with them
and you will feel and act like a different person.
From that time on your decisions should be
based on whatever seems best under the circumstances,
for the Lord will guide you."

1 SAMUEL 10:6–7 TLB

Windows of the Soul

Thank You for my friend Skyler. Although he is only eleven years old, I see something special about him. He has a way of understanding how a person feels about things without even needing to ask. He observes, listens a lot, and cares.

The other day his sister had a problem. No one seemed to be aware of her dilemma except Skyler. He immediately understood what she was going through without her saying a word, and he jumped right in and came to her aid.

It amazes me, Lord, how Skyler notices things most of us overlook. He seems to look beyond the trivial and peer into the windows of our souls. His tenderheartedness causes him to care deeply for others. He's also learning to ask You to help. Thank You for Skyler. Encourage him and others to use their abilities and sensitive ways as a blessing for You.

Teach me to look beyond trivial things and see the needs of people. Grant me Your discernment, dear Lord, so I can understand those around me better. Help me be mindful of their needs. Remind me to show love to them in practical ways. Remind me not to intrude but to be there— to care and help when needed. Most of all, let me lead them to You, their Lord and Savior.

> *Lord, deal with me in lovingkindness,*
> *and teach me, your servant, to obey;*
> *for I am your servant;*
> *therefore give me common sense*
> *to apply your rules to everything I do.*

PSALM 119:124–125 TLB

According to Your Convenience

Father, I am thrilled about the way You are working in Bill's and Kari's lives. Kari told me their family went for a drive in the neighborhood where Bill grew up. Of course, Bill couldn't resist going by the house where he lived as a child. But, Father, he also decided to go up to the front door and ask if he could see the house!

Kari told me how this really tested her patience. The children were getting restless, ready to go home. She wanted to get out of the car and ask if they could leave, when You spoke to her heart and urged her to be patient. Instead, she and the children spent the time playing word games.

Much later, Bill returned to the car. On the way home, Bill explained how he had arrived at the door just as the owner of the home was planning to take his life. Thank You, Father, for leading Bill and Kari. Through this, the homeowner changed his decision. With Bill's assistance, the man decided to recommit his life to You, call his pastor for help, and return to the church he had once attended.

Thank You for Bill and Kari's willingness to follow Your lead. Remind me also to do so—according to Your convenience.

And so I solemnly urge you before God. . .
to preach the Word of God urgently at all times,
whenever you get the chance, in season and out,
when it is convenient and when it is not.

2 TIMOTHY 4:1–2 TLB

AUGUST 8

The Adventure

It appeared to be a routine bus trip from my uncle's home in Montana. I was ready to curl up in the seat and do some writing. But You had different plans, Lord.

In Missoula, I noticed a young man, about twenty, board the bus. He sat down across the aisle from me. He seemed quiet, unassuming, with a long chestnut brown ponytail. He opened his pack and pulled out a book. I went back to my writing.

Idle chatter floated around us. I didn't feel like talking. The young man was polite to others but not much for words. I wondered where he was going. But I still kept writing.

After miles of traveling, I felt You tugging at my heart to strike up a conversation with the youth. It didn't make sense to me. He was still reading. I shrugged off Your nudge.

Several more miles down the road, I set my tablet aside. I knew I had to obey You, so I started a conversation. As You know, his name was Brady. He'd been seeking adventure and fortune in Missoula. Things away from home hadn't gone very well for him. Now he was traveling to Ellensburg, Washington, to see his parents and grandparents. I sensed he had some important decisions to make while traveling home.

Thank You, Lord, for reminding me to stop and care.

We are the ones who strayed away like sheep!
We, who left God's paths to follow our own.

ISAIAH 53:6 TLB

The Regrets

I remember the drone of bus wheels as I listened to Brady's story. He didn't go into detail, but it was obvious life on his own hadn't been easy. I could see the toll it had taken both spiritually and economically. I noticed a tenderness about him, Lord. Could it have come from how he'd been raised?

He had a Christian family in Ellensburg waiting for him. His eyes lit up when he talked about his mother and father and his grandfather. Perhaps his stay would be longer than a weekend.

I'm glad You urged me to say a silent prayer before pursuing the conversation. I could feel Your Holy Spirit blessing it.

Thank You for leading me to tell Brady a little about myself—how I, too, had struggled during my youth. I was determined to go my own way. Then You helped me. Thank You for giving me the freedom to talk about my husband, my family, and my love for them, and how I pray for my grown children and grandchildren daily. Thank You for Brady's open heart. Thank You, Lord, for putting me in the right place at the right time and nudging me to listen and share.

If anyone has slipped away from God
and no longer trusts the Lord,
and someone helps him understand the Truth again,
that person who brings him back to God
will have saved a wandering soul.

JAMES 5:19–20 TLB

The Long Journey Home

Your Holy Spirit continued to work silently as Brady went back to reading his book and I returned to my writing. A few minutes later, Brady glanced up. He looked at me with a shy smile. I laid down my writing, ready to listen again.

I enjoyed hearing him tell me about his mother and father. For years they had farmed an area outside of town. Brady's grandfather worked some land nearby. Not only did his parents do farmwork, but they also were involved in a jail ministry. His father and mother had a wonderful way of blessing everyone they came in contact with. Remember how Brady beamed at the mere mention of his parents and grandfather?

His grandfather taught a church school class for teens. For teenagers? I marveled at the thought. Brady went on to describe how his grandfather's telling of Bible stories had the kids, including Brady, sitting on the edge of their seats.

I'm glad I asked Brady what his plans were when he returned home. He wanted to be a paramedic. Step-by-step, he was also drawing closer to You. Thank You again, Lord, for giving me the courage and guidance to talk with this young man.

> *"I [the prodigal son] will set out
> and go back to my father."*
>
> LUKE 15:18 NIV

Welcome Home

When night fell, everyone struggled to get some rest. Humming from the bus mixed with silent songs of praise swirling in my dozing mind: *"Thou art worthy, O Lord, to receive glory and honor and praise"* and *"Come home, it's suppertime."*

Red-orange morning sun rays slivered through the windows. I awakened to the bus driver announcing a stop. I reached in my bag and pulled out a book that You and I had labored on so long: *When I'm on My Knees.* I hastily wrote in it and handed it to Brady as a gift for his mother. He thanked me warmly and put it in his bag.

On our way again, I noticed Brady's look of anticipation. He pointed out the knoll near his parents' farm. "Only a few more miles," he announced.

What a wonderful feeling, Lord, to spot the couple huddled together in the morning sun. When Brady said good-bye and leaped from the bus, absolute joy welled inside of me. Do You remember seeing the way he ran across the lot with his arms stretched wide? How bags and arms wrapped around the three of them? I know You do, Lord, because he belongs to You.

I could almost hear them say, "Welcome home, Son." In the same way, You had once welcomed me.

[Jesus said,] "And he arose and came to his father.
But when he was still a great way off,
his father saw him and had compassion,
and ran and fell on his neck and kissed him."

LUKE 15:20 NKJV

AUGUST 12

Money in a Coffee Can

I want to tell You about Homer, Lord. Ever since I met him, Homer lived a simple life in a small, modest home in the same little town for over fifty years. He knew most everyone. He faithfully went to church, loved singing and praying with the congregation, and especially enjoyed the young people. Although he was older, Homer tried to relate to the kids.

Rumors were that he secretly had a lot of money. Still, no one except You and one other person really knew what he did with it. I wondered if he hid the money in coffee cans, buried somewhere, or sewed it into the linings of his clothing.

Then, at the age of ninety-eight, he went home to be with You, Lord. Almost everyone in town came to Homer's funeral. At the end of the service, the pastor shared how Homer had anonymously donated huge amounts of money to the church youth center, the children's church camp scholarship fund, and many other endeavors for youth. Since his wife was gone and he had no children, the church youth became Homer's "favorite kids." He didn't want anyone to know about his giving.

Thank You for Homer, Lord. Help me never to hide my gifts like money in a coffee can but to willingly use them to help win souls.

> *"And remember the words of the Lord Jesus,*
> *that He said,*
> *'It is more blessed to give than to receive.' "*
>
> ACTS 20:35 NKJV

Potpourri Presence

Lord Jesus, the heat of stress is coming at me from all sides. Difficult decisions need to be made quickly. There are insurmountable problems, pressures that are almost too much to bear, and endless bickering. Those around me who don't know You are looking to me as a Christian example. I'm turning to You right now, Lord, so all of this won't bring out the worst in me. Please help me, I pray.

I realize stress and anxiety aren't something new. You must have experienced a tremendous amount of strain while You were here on earth. The Bible tells how You were ridiculed, lied about, pressured, beaten, and finally crucified. I am awed at how You continued to love others, no matter who they were or what they did.

When You were crushed, Lord Jesus, You brought forth a pure Spirit, sweet as a rose. Fill and surround me with Your presence, Lord. Help me change this pressure into a Spirit-filled potpourri presence so others will recognize You in me and want to know You as their Savior.

Thank You, Lord, for helping us. Thank You, too, for the person who asked me later how I remained kind and calm. Speak to her heart while I tell her how it all comes from You.

So if you are suffering according to God's will,
keep on doing what is right
and trust yourself to the God who made you,
for he will never fail you.

1 PETER 4:19 TLB

I Want to Catch Your Vision

Lord God, I see people all around me suffering from sin's devastating blows. Some struggles are brought on by their own rebellious, uncaring actions. Others are suffering because they don't know You as their personal Savior—yet. But there are Christians who are grief-stricken by what sin is doing to those they love.

Surely You love each person far more than I am ever capable of doing, Lord. I want to catch Your vision. How can I reach these lost and struggling souls for You? I realize I will never be able to perceive all of this through Your eyes. If I did, I wouldn't be able to take it in. With my limited human comprehension, I struggle to acknowledge sad news reports and painful firsthand experiences and observations.

I'm only one person in this vast world. Please show me what I can do to help others accept You. Let me weep with them. Comfort them, I pray. Let me lead them to You. May Your Holy Spirit take over and bring them into Your loving arms. Help them accept You. Then I will celebrate with the angels. Let them be filled with joy, and I shall rejoice with them.

Thank You for a glimpse of Your vision, Lord God. I open my eyes and my heart to Your vision.

> *"I will pour out my Spirit upon all of you!*
> *Your sons and daughters will prophesy;*
> *your old men will dream dreams,*
> *and your young men see visions.*
> *And I will pour out my Spirit even on your slaves,*
> *men and women alike."*

JOEL 2:28–29 TLB

Vision of Gold

I'm looking out our kitchen window, washing lunch dishes. What lovely blessings You give me. Afternoon sun kisses the flowers and trees in our backyard—*and* the golden dandelions. It's also kissing the freckles on my redheaded Liza's nose. She's here visiting with her "Gamp" and me. What a joy she is.

Look how the yellow weeds are popping up everywhere, Lord. I can never completely get rid of them. It's funny, though, how they have become my favorite flower. It's because of the happiness I've felt each time a child brings a handful to me, accompanied by a big grin and an "I love you." Of course, I tell these little ones to pick all they want!

Look at Liza, Lord. She's in her own little world. She loftily lifts a granddaddy dandelion toward the sky, blows long and smoothly into its seedy chamber, and turns the air into a fairyland. How can I complain and interrupt her pleasure? Before long, we'll have a whole new harvest of the sturdy yellow flowers.

Like the dandelions, I visualize souls galore out there waiting to be harvested for You. I don't even have to search for them. They are everywhere I go. Please grant me the perseverance, strength, and power of Your Holy Spirit to lead them to You.

[Jesus said,]
"The harvest is plentiful but the workers are few."

MATTHEW 9:37 NIV

Seeds of Salvation

Thank You for giving me a portion of Your vision, Lord. I can see myself as Your servant scattering Your seeds of salvation everywhere I go. Fast. Slow. Steady. Constant. I'm actually planting Your upcoming Church! The Body of Christ. Like the dandelion seeds, some will germinate and grow; others will not.

In the same way flower seeds land on fertile soil, I pray those who hear about Your love and salvation will listen and accept You as their Savior. Remind me not to abandon them after they accept You but to nurture these souls with Your spiritual food and living water. Grant me faithfulness and time to pray with them, to search the verses in Your Bible together. In the process, let me grow along with those I care for.

Help me to believe in the ones I reach for You as they embark on their new walk with You, Lord. When they take their spiritual baby steps, stumble, and fall, grant me patience as You and I stoop down together and help them up, again and again.

I will never give up telling people about You. Even when they refuse or put off receiving You, I'll pray for them. Lord Jesus, I will keep scattering Your life-giving seeds of salvation to every available soul throughout the rest of my life.

[Jesus said,] "The farmer sows the word. . . .
[Some,] like seed sown on good soil,
hear the word, accept it, and produce a crop—
thirty, sixty or even a hundred times what was sown."

MARK 4:14, 20 NIV

239

A Matter of Life or Death

When You and I went walking on the ocean beach this morning, I had a wonderful time worshiping and praising You, Lord. It was only seven o'clock. No one else was in sight. Just You and me. Mist rose from the wet sand. The sun silently broke through low, passing clouds.

While I walked with You along the seashore, I came upon some sand dollars. Most were broken, but a few remained whole. I picked one up. I realized from the movement on the underside that it was still alive. I wanted to keep it, Lord, but I decided to spare its life. I carefully placed it in a small puddle near an approaching wave.

I thought of how much effort we often put in to saving a beached whale or an injured animal. "It's a matter of life or death," we say. I love animals and want to care for their safety. What about the souls of humankind? Isn't this is a matter of life or death? Eternal life or death? Everything in Your creation is a treasured gift. Yet more important is the spiritual eternal life offered to those we encounter every day.

As regular as changing tides, time is ticking away for people to accept You. Help me to bring as many perishing souls to You as I possibly can.

[Jesus said,]
"For the Son of man [Jesus] came to seek
and to save the lost."

LUKE 19:10 RSV

Closing the Deal

It's becoming a little easier to tell those I come in contact with each day about You, Lord. The more I'm around people, the more I hope and pray they recognize me as a Christian. Grant me opportunities to share Your love with them, I pray, and make me alert to the openings when they come.

The frightening part in leading someone to You is helping them take that final step of accepting You as their personal Savior. In a salesperson's words, it's the stage of "closing the deal."

Help me be keenly aware of this time when it comes, Lord. Remind me to take a deep breath, send up an arrow prayer for help from You, then invite this one to give his or her life to You. I'm so glad that this is when I can rely on You and allow Your Holy Spirit to step in, work, and change lives. I can lead people to You, but I am unable to save souls. Only You can do this, Lord.

Thank You for helping me lead each person to that final step of accepting You and for "closing the deal." I praise You for Your awesome power. Thank You for saving each precious one and making them Your own.

> *But as many as received him,*
> *to them gave he power to become the sons of God,*
> *even to them that believe on his name.*
>
> JOHN 1:12 KJV

Producing Soul Winners

Father, I visualized Your leading me to be a soul winner, but I never dreamed You were tugging at my heart to go a step further—to produce soul winners for You.

I get excited each time I think of the church school students You have placed in my care. Some, through regular Bible lessons, have gone on to follow Your call to become teachers, preachers, and active Christian leaders in all walks of life.

It thrills me to teach my students how to lead their friends to You. Step-by-step, we mark the verses in our Bibles: Everyone has sinned (Romans 3:23). Payment for sin is death and destruction (Romans 6:23). You sacrificed Your Son for us (John 3:16). The only way to You, Father, is through Your Son, Jesus Christ (John 14:6). Jesus died for our sins (1 Corinthians 15:3). When we believe in Jesus, we are saved (Acts 16:31). Whoever asks Jesus into his or her heart receives the right to become Your son or daughter (John 1:12). If we confess our sins, You are faithful and just to forgive us and cleanse us from all wrong (1 John 1:9).

Thank You for teaching me these steps, Father. Thank You for helping me produce soul winners for You.

[Jesus said,]
"But the good soil represents honest, good-hearted people.
They listen to God's words and cling to them
and steadily spread them to others who also soon believe."

LUKE 8:15 TLB

Shirttail Relationship

Lord, I want to talk with You about my friends at work. I've been telling them about You and how You help me. One is a good person. She has gone to church all her life and was raised in a Christian home. Still, she says she never remembers asking You into her heart. She believes since she has Christian parents, she's automatically a Christian. It's like she's riding on her parents' relationship with You.

Another friend told me his church teaches You aren't God's Son—that You are called by different names. He says going to any church will still get him to heaven.

I'm concerned about them, Lord. I read in Your Bible that *You* are the Way to salvation. Chapters 3 and 6 of Romans explain how everyone has sinned and how the consequence of sin is spiritual death. It goes on to say that the gift of salvation and everlasting spiritual life is through You, Jesus Christ.

I don't want to argue with them. Help me be a good example for You. Help me tell them how wonderful You are, without being overbearing.

Talk to their hearts, I pray. Give them a hunger and thirst for You. Keep after and help them, the way You helped me.

> *"Jesus [is] the Messiah. . . .*
> *There is salvation in no one else!*
> *Under all heaven there is no other name*
> *for men to call upon to save them."*

ACTS 4:11–12 TLB

Open Wide the Door

Father, I'm thrilled at how You are using me to reach others for You. A lot is being accomplished. Souls are being saved in our church. Spiritual growth is happening in baby Christians. It's all so wonderful the way You are blessing, but I'm getting so caught up in the needs of others that I'm neglecting my own needs. My busy schedule causes me to charge ahead, cram as much as possible in each waking hour, and help everyone along the way. I'm even stealing needed sleep to do more and more. I feel myself slipping, Father.

Once again, my life is turning into mass confusion. I'm making sure everyone else is all right. Somehow I simply forget about myself, especially the time I need with You.

So I'm here again, Lord. Forgive me for being so careless. I'm opening wide my door to You. Please come in and dine with me so we can feed on the wise and strengthening words in Your Bible. Help me bring my lifestyle back into balance within Your will. How happy I am to come and enjoy Your fellowship. Once more, You give me strength so I can pass on Your love to others.

[Jesus said,]
"I will come in and fellowship with him [or her]
and he [or she] with me."

REVELATION 3:20 TLB

Is Anyone Home?

I come to You today, Lord, asking You to help a new friend of mine. She's going through a lot, and I'm concerned about her. She has made tremendous progress in her life, but she has a long way to go.

Once, she was homeless, on alcohol and drugs. Back then, everything must have seemed impossible. Then she started attending church. You knocked on her heart's door and she answered. Step-by-step she began making huge changes in her life.

How I thank and praise You for helping her get off drugs and alcohol. I'm so grateful for the way You have provided her with work and a little apartment she can call home.

However, I can see the battle isn't over. I know she suffers terribly from depression. At times I can't reach her by phone or by knocking on her door. I wonder if she is even home.

I really love her. I won't give up, Lord. I'll continue calling and caring the same way You faithfully do for me when I'm feeling down. I know she loves You. When she's down, please keep her heart's door open to You. Ease her pain and heal her, Lord. Thank You for telling her You love her, even when she can't hear me.

[Jesus said,]
"Look! I have been standing at the door
and I am constantly knocking."

REVELATION 3:20 TLB

When Sin Holds On

Father God, I'm asking for Your help for another friend. She often tells me her troubles. When she talks, I listen. I share with her how You can make a difference in her life. So many times she has come close to accepting You, then shut fast her heart's door and turned away. It's as though sin has a terrible grip on her.

I can't pull her away from sin's lure. Am I getting anywhere in talking with her about You, Father? Are my words falling on ears that refuse to hear? I won't stop trying to reach her. Will she be lost from You for eternity? Please don't let it be so. I know there is power in my prayers. Your Bible says the same power that raised Your Son, Jesus Christ, from the dead and delivered me from sin is available in my words and prayers today.

Hear my prayers. Guide what I say. Talk to her, Father God. You can get through to her when no one else can. You have the power to save her. Break the chains of sin's bondage and set her spiritually free, in the name of Your Son, Jesus Christ.

Thank You for loving her. Thank You for speaking to her heart and beginning the process of her gaining victory over sin's hold—victory in You!

Greater is he that is in you,
than he that is in the world.

1 JOHN 4:4 KJV

Accepting Your Love

I bring this dear soul to You, Father. She loves You with all her heart, but she feels she doesn't deserve Your love. My friend tells me no matter how hard she tries, she doesn't do things right. It's two steps forward and one step back for her. She's discouraged and wants to give up. Sometimes she tells me she wonders if life is even worth living.

Grant me wisdom as I listen to her tell about her anxieties and needs, and I, in turn, share Your love with her. Help this dear person to realize You didn't sacrifice Your Son for any of us because we are deserving. Jesus died and rose again because You love us and want to free us from all that guilt, regret, and pain.

Peel the layers of hatred and shame from her soul. Help her to accept Your forgiveness and love. Soothe her emotional and spiritual wounds with the balm of Your Holy Spirit. Heal her hurts, Father. Replace them with hope and purpose for the future. Shower Your love upon her from Your cleansing fountain. Fill her with Your life-giving, victorious Holy Spirit. Not once. But again, and again, and again.

May you be able to feel and understand,
as all God's children should, how long, how wide,
how deep, and how high his love really is;
and to experience this love for yourselves,
though it is so great that you will never see
the end of it or fully know or understand it.
And so at last you will be filled up with God himself.

EPHESIANS 3:18–19 TLB

Those Who Are Closest

Today I feel Your nudge to share You with someone close. How, Lord? This person understands me well. I think she knows me almost better than I know myself. We've talked about You before. But every time I bring up Your name, she brushes me off.

She's experiencing some big changes in her life, Lord. I'm really concerned about her. Poor choices in her past have caught up with her. Now she doesn't see any way out. I don't have the answers. But You do.

We're to meet for lunch. Create an opening so we can really communicate about what Your love can do. You've cared so much for me, Lord. If it wasn't for Your being my Savior, my life would be in shambles. Instead, You have gently loved and guided me every step of the way.

Remind me not to intrude on her privacy but simply impart to her what You do for me. Remove my fear. Replace that fear with Your love, power, and discernment. Guide me in knowing when to talk, what to say, and when to stop talking and listen—and pray.

Have You already been speaking to her heart, Lord? You must be, since You are leading me to share Your love now. Well, here goes. Help me, please. Let's go talk with her—together.

Listen to my cry for help,
my King and my God,
for to you I pray.
In the morning, O LORD, you hear my voice;
in the morning I lay my requests before you
and wait in expectation.

PSALM 5:2–3 NIV

Tested

Lord, I can't think of anytime when my Christian example was tested more than while our children were in their teenage years. At times, when I tried sharing You with them in words or actions, they challenged and questioned me. Before I knew it, I was defending myself. My greatest encouragement came from You and Christian friends who had survived the teenage breaking-away years.

My children knew my strengths, faults, and weaknesses. Perhaps they simply wanted to see if what I stood for in loving You was genuine. Sadly, my endeavor to share You with them sometimes resorted to manipulation. How I regret not trusting You more when I prayed for them. You were working in their lives. My responsibility? To stay true to You, to love them without wavering, and to believe in them. When they bounced back and forth in their careless ways, You wanted me to be a steadfast, consistent example they could look to. I learned to share You with them by actions and a strong prayer life, rather than with mere spoken words.

Now I glance back, Lord, and marvel at whatever I did right. Thank You for answering many prayers. I thank You again and again for Your grace and how each of my grown children loves You.

> *Be anxious for nothing,*
> *but in everything by prayer and supplication,*
> *with thanksgiving, let your requests be made known to God;*
> *and the peace of God, which surpasses all understanding,*
> *will guard your hearts and minds through Christ Jesus.*

PHILIPPIANS 4:6–7 NKJV

Let Me Reflect Your Son

It's late at night, Father. An exciting event is happening, one that will be recorded in history. Look to the southeast with me. See what looks like a bright star? Next to the moon, it's the most brilliant object in the sky. Astronomers tell us it's the planet Mars. According to their studies, 2003 is the first time Mars has come this close to Earth for up to sixty thousand years. It is supposed to be within thirty-five million miles from us.

I stand gazing toward the night sky, amazed I can witness such a miraculous event. It won't be seen again until the year 2287. What power, what magnitude is wrapped up in this brilliant display! More so is the energy and light it reflects from the sun.

Thank You for creating this, Father. Greater than Mars, the moon or sun is how You blessed us with Your only begotten Son, Jesus. He *is* the Light of the World. In Him there is no darkness at all (1 John 1:5 NIV). He is the Light of all lights.

Let me reflect Your Son—a light and message grander than anything else in Your creation. Let me share Your message of eternal life that's here with us every hour, every day. Let me tell all who will listen about Your constant, abiding presence and love.

[Jesus said,] Let your light so shine before men,
that they may see your good works,
and glorify your Father which is in heaven.

MATTHEW 5:16 KJV

AUGUST 28

A New Song

This day started like any other. Work. Errands. What makes it special, Lord, is how You planted a new song in my heart. It's one I've been hearing on the radio recently. Its melody and words connect to my heart and mind. The song offers praise and glory to You, Lord. Not only from believers right here, but from those who love You all over the country, clear around the world.

The song whirred through my brain in soothing repetition the entire morning. By afternoon, I found myself humming it quietly during my work. Those nearby just looked at me and smiled. Some asked what I was humming. I shared the words of the song and Your love for us.

It remained with me at the gas station, the bank, and the grocery store. More smiles came—and some questions. One lady approached while I waited to pay for my milk and tomatoes and shared how she recognized the tune. She recited the words aloud, accompanying them with a big smile.

She spoke in front of everyone of how she loves You and how You are the King of Kings, Lord of Lords. She affirmed how over all the heavens and earth You truly do reign. Thank You, Lord, for the blessings from sharing a new song.

> *He has given me a new song to sing,*
> *of praises to our God.*
> *Now many will hear of the*
> *glorious things he did for me,*
> *and stand in awe before the Lord,*
> *and put their trust in him.*

PSALM 40:3 TLB

The Best about Bible Study

It began like any other Bible study, Lord. We were just a small group of people gathering to study Your Word and pray. Then something amazing happened. Your Spirit began to stir in each one of our lives. Ears perked up from what we were learning. Eyes bugged with excitement as we found out how we could apply these lessons to the everyday events in our lives. Prayers were (and are still) being answered.

As You know, most of the time Bob leads the study. Occasionally Kristina takes a turn. Kristina aptly described what was taking place. "Hey! Something is really happening here." Our group began to focus not only on our own needs, but on the needs of those around us. The drive to share Your wonderful love with others is so intense, no one is surprised when we meet and hear of the weekly, even daily, miracles taking place for those we pray for. Through this process, I thank You for how discouraged, listless attitudes are being transformed into vibrant, enthusiastic outlooks on life.

Thank You for our Bible study group. I'm grateful for the way You teach us to help one another. As we grow in You, Lord, I pray we will share Your love with more and more people every day.

But we Christians have no veil over our faces;
we can be mirrors that brightly reflect the glory of the Lord.
And as the Spirit of the Lord works within us,
we become more and more like him.

2 CORINTHIANS 3:18 TLB

Bring My Country Back to You

What was our country like spiritually when it was first founded, Lord? Was it as fine and noble as the historians depict? Or did our forefathers also have their share of struggling with right and wrong? I read how humankind in this country repeatedly made serious errors. They fell away from You for a time, then experienced Your holy presence and great spiritual awakenings. Thank You for brave Christian leaders who went wherever You led them and obeyed Your will. Thank You, too, for those who rocked cradles and molded young lives into becoming those leaders.

What of our churches, Lord? Thank You for their starting schools, hospitals, and organizations to help the orphaned and needy. Help us to continue doing good and hold on to the Christian principles our nation was founded upon. Help us as a Christian body in our country to love and care for one another and turn our back on sin, backbiting, and inner destruction.

Perhaps I can't be as great as those Christian leaders of old, Lord, but I can rock the cradle, teach the children and adults, and bring dear ones to Your throne of grace. Help me fast and pray through the night for one more lost soul to come to You.

So here I am, Lord, asking, pleading. Please bring our country back to You.

> *Turn us around and bring us back to you again!*
> *That is our only hope!*
> *Give us back the joys we used to have!*

LAMENTATIONS 5:21 TLB

Prayers around the World

I just watched the world news, Lord. New technology makes us seem closer together than ever before. Bad news: Wars. Earthquakes. Tornadoes. Floods. Good news: People making peace. People helping people. New beginnings. Worldwide missions. Revivals. Sacrifices for others. Kindnesses shown. I treasure those good reports, Lord. When I hear bad news, I feel called to help however possible.

Lord, help when tragedy strikes. Be with leaders everywhere. Rally them to follow You. Watch over Your ministers, missionaries, and Christian workers. Grant each one protection, strength, wisdom, and plenty of love. Clothe them with Your holy armor. Let all people know Your love. Show me ways I can make a difference. Lord, I realize there are Christians all around the world who love and serve You. They are praying fervently for each other. Some pray for us! Thank You for them.

Help us as Your followers to join our prayers. Turn hearts to You. For those in bondage or free, You paid the price to truly free our souls. Help our hurting world call on You and obey Your will. Heal us. Restore us. Grant us the peace of heart that comes only from You.

[Jesus said,] "I am not praying for these alone
but also for the future believers who will come to me
because of the testimony of these.
My prayer for all of them is that they will be of one heart
and mind, just as you and I are, Father—
that just as you are in me and I am in you,
so they will be in us,
and the world will believe you sent me."

JOHN 17:20–21 TLB

Why Me?

If I could to see You face-to-face right now, Lord, I would have many questions to ask. When I try to answer them myself, I feel like I'm looking at everything through dark-colored glasses after coming in from the sunny outdoors. Nothing is very clear.

I can't see You, Lord, but Your presence is here with me. Assist me as You and I search the Scriptures together. Please grant me insight, comfort, and assurance.

I want to know "why me?" Why was I one of the lucky ones to be saved when so many others are lost from You for eternity? The greatest day of my life was when I asked You into my heart and You became my Savior. You actually adopted me as Your child, Lord. How blessed and fortunate I feel.

Did I ask You to be my Savior first, or did You first knock at my heart's door? Did You choose me? What of the others? Your Bible says that You loved the entire world so much that anyone who believes in You will become Your own and will gain everlasting life.

My child, anyone who comes to Me with a humble, repentant heart shall be saved and become part of the kingdom of heaven.

Thank You, Lord, for calling us all.

> *[Jesus said,]*
> *"Whoever believes in Him should not perish*
> *but have eternal life."*
>
> JOHN 3:15 NKJV

Do You Accept Me as Your Own?

I love You with all of my heart, soul, and mind, Father. I love You more than all else. I know You love me. But why do I not feel worthy of Your recognition? Do You really accept me as Your child? Is it because You created me, and I belong to You?

I cherish my children. I still remember their first cries. I fell in love with them while they were still in my womb. What a thrill when each little body stirred within me. And, oh, when I saw them! In my eyes, my babies were the most beautiful children in the world. I love them because they are mine, not because they had to earn my love.

Do You remember my first cry, Father? Do You perceive everything about me? Did You know and plan me before time—before I was even conceived? It was You who knit me in my mother's womb, wasn't it? Do You love and care for me just the way I am? Is it so, that I can trust in Your love and acceptance because You are my heavenly Father?

I love you, My child, with an everlasting love. You belong to Me.

How I praise and thank You. Though I'm undeserving of Your love, I can be sure I am Your own.

See how very much our heavenly Father loves us,
for he allows us to be called his children—
think of it—and we really are!

1 JOHN 3:1 TLB

Why Do Our Loved Ones Die?

When my loved ones pass away, I feel a huge chasm within me. Why must they be struck by tragedy, sickness, or aging, and leave me? Some actively serve You to the day they die. Why don't You keep them well and healthy? Why do they have to die? Is there any good that comes from this, Lord? I don't understand, but You do, so I will trust You.

Occasionally I wish I could talk with different loved ones, especially my grandmother. Grandma and I were very close. Yet when I have a question I would ask now, I already know what she would say.

The lessons of Your faithfulness and hope for the future that my loved ones passed down have become timeless and still live in me! It's as if the torch of You wisdom and love was given to me so I may carry it to future generations. Help me be worthy to do so, Lord.

Show me how to keep alive Your blessed truths—to tell them to my children, grandchildren, and great-grandchildren. Let each generation learn from them, even those not yet born.

Thank You, Lord, for Your comfort. Thank You for keeping alive in me the priceless wisdom You gave my loved ones. Thank You for how Your same Holy Spirit that led them now leads me.

Tell to the coming generation the glorious deeds of the LORD,
and his might, and the wonders which he has wrought. . .
that the next generation might know them,
the children yet unborn,
and arise and tell them to their children,
so that they should set their hope in God.

PSALM 78:4, 6–7 RSV

Why Do Christians Divorce?

Another friend is in the midst of divorce, Lord. She's brokenhearted and grief-stricken. "Why is this happening?" she asks.

I'm asking why, as well. I thought Christians shouldn't have to go through these things. Our lives are supposed to be in perfect accordance with Your will. Still, I see more and more dear ones who love You suffer from divorce's heartbreaking blow. Some people tell me it's like part of their life is being torn away or like experiencing surgery with a dull teaspoon. How very sad and devastating.

Could this be happening more because of the terrible spiritual struggles and tension we face each day, Lord? Could it be that we as Christians are allowing ourselves to slip away from a close walk with You?

But, Lord! Some truly follow You and still suffer because of their mates' actions. How I pray for hearts to change and marriages to be restored. I pray for a new spiritual awakening to begin within us. Help us fend off the unnecessary stress and pressure we often allow in our lives that threaten to pull us apart. Replace it with Your unconditional love and peace.

Remind me to avoid taking sides for my friends but to simply love, encourage, and care for others. Bless and comfort these dear ones, Lord, and keep them close to You.

For the LORD has called you like a wife [or husband]
forsaken and grieved in spirit,
like a wife [or husband] of youth when she [or he] is cast off,
says your God. . . . But with everlasting love I will have
compassion on you, says the LORD, your Redeemer.

ISAIAH 54:6, 8 RSV

SEPTEMBER 5

Why Was I Born in These Times?

Everything is push button or flick of a switch these days, Lord. I enjoy the conveniences and technology we have at our fingertips. Yet I long for years gone by. While growing up, I heard stories of how "life was simpler back then." Lots of land. Nature everywhere to enjoy. Fewer restrictions. Certainly less traffic. I feel as though I've been placed in the wrong era. Why was I born during these times?

Do You have a purpose for my being here now? The Bible says You chose me when You planned creation, and my days are written in Your Book of Life. I'm amazed how You determined exactly when and where I would live.

You must have me placed here for a reason. In 2 Corinthians 6, You tell me now is the time You show me Your favor. Now is the time of my salvation—for me to worship and serve You. Thank You for giving me the right to choose. Because of Your love for me and mine for You, dear Lord, I choose to follow You anytime, anywhere. Thank You for promising me a future especially for me, filled with hope and joy.

I guess I'm not misplaced in time after all, Lord. In fact, I feel assured that You want me right where I am right now to glorify You.

For I know the plans I have for you, says the Lord.
They are plans for good and not for evil,
to give you a future and a hope.
In those days when you pray, I will listen.

JEREMIAH 29:11–12 TLB

Is My Life Significant to You?

Father, all around me I see people accomplishing great things for You and humankind. Many folks are better-looking, smarter, more educated, and wealthier than I am. The "wealthier" part doesn't bother me, but I feel limited in what I can do to serve You in other areas.

Is my life significant to You, Father? Does it matter to You that I struggle with these insecurities? Though I have little to give You, I love You and want to serve You with every part of my being. Perhaps I'm selling myself short. Increase my faith, I pray, and help me.

My dear one, take delight in the way I made you. For it is I who gave you your looks, your talents. You are My beautiful creation, brimming with gifts I love for you to share. I rejoice over you with singing. You are My child of great value, My treasured possession. I love to do good for you. I will inspire you as I plant you in this place, here and now, to serve Me.

Everything you say and do is important to Me, like ripples in a pond, affecting others around you. Trust Me. I am able to accomplish more with your life than you can ever imagine.

Thank You, Father. How worthy You are of my love and service.

May our Lord Jesus Christ himself and God our Father,
who loved us and by his grace gave us
eternal encouragement and good hope,
encourage your hearts and strengthen you
in every good deed and word.

2 THESSALONIANS 2:16–17 NIV

Why Were We Given a Choice?

Lord, there are a lot of noble attitudes and actions coming from people in this world that bring happiness and peace. Others, however, are causing much pain and stress because of the indifference and hatred they demonstrate. If it saddens me, it must cause You tremendous pain. How can You stand us when we are so selfish and arrogant? Why were we given a choice of how we want to live?

Your love is greater than what I can comprehend. You look beyond our faults and see the possibilities of who we can become for You. Does my choosing to love and follow You mean more than if I were some kind of robot, ordered to do this or that? I think it does. Lord, forgive me when I falter and become self-centered or uncaring. Thank You for not giving up on me. Thank You for helping me to get back on course with You.

I wish sin would just go away. But as long as I'm forced to contend with it, I will. With all power given me from You, I shall do everything I can to make a difference. I love You, Lord. It is You I choose to live for.

> *"And if you be unwilling to serve the LORD,*
> *choose this day whom you will serve. . .*
> *but as for me and my house,*
> *we will serve the LORD."*

JOSHUA 24:15 RSV

Why Is Satan Allowed So Much Power?

I cringe in fear at the evil happening around me. The Bible describes Satan as a prowling, roaring lion, searching for someone to devour. I want to avoid this tempter at all costs, Lord. Dreadful happenings cause us to lock our doors. Wherever we go, we are defensive. Trust in others is gradually being squeezed from our lives because of evil's destructive blows. How can we win over Satan's terrible force? Why is he allowed so much power?

Does it have to be this way? Christians who love and serve You aren't under his rule. You, Lord, are far greater than Satan's forces. What awesome strength and victory come at the mere mention of Your name! People are delivered from self-destructive sin, healed from sickness, and even brought back from the dead because of fervent prayers to You. You don't give us a spirit of fear but one of adoration of You, of power over evil, and a sturdy soul.

Can it be that Satan has no more power than what we give him? I cling to You, Lord. You provide victory over Satan. I will have no part of him. You are my God, my Overcomer. Help me share You with everyone around me so they can experience freedom from sin and a triumphant life.

You are of God, little children,
and have overcome them [those who tempt you],
because He who is in you is greater than he
who is in the world.

1 JOHN 4:4 NKJV

SEPTEMBER 9

How Can I Forgive and Get Past My Hurts?

How many things from my past have caused me pain, Lord? They are more than I can number. Some were so bad, they pushed me to the limit of endurance. Had it not been for You, dear Lord, I don't think I would have survived them. Thank You for bringing me through.

Even though I've attempted to leave these dreadful things behind and forgive those who have hurt me, memories return and haunt me. Now and again, the pain is overwhelming. Tears well and spill over. How can I forgive and get past all of this, Lord? Please help me.

Come into My open arms, dear one. Don't be afraid to cry. Then give it all to Me. Each time you do, the burden will get lighter; the pain will lessen. I will help you forgive, even those who aren't sorry. I will help you not dredge up the past. It wasn't right. But I, the Great Physician, am here now. Touch the hem of My garment, and allow Me to remove your pain and make you whole.

Lean on Me. Draw from My strength. Press forward. See My blessings for you.

Thank You, Lord, for helping me to forgive and let go. I look forward to a restored life in You.

Surely He has borne our griefs
And carried our sorrows. . . .
The chastisement for our peace was upon Him,
And by His stripes we are healed.

ISAIAH 53:4–5 NKJV

How Could You Leave Heaven for Me?

Before You came here, Lord, You had everything. A throne. No sin, sadness, or pain. How could You leave heaven and Your Father's side to come to a world You knew would hate You? Why did You save me and make me Your child? I don't deserve it.

How sorry I am for causing You sorrow through my wasted years and actions before asking You into my life. No matter what good I do, I can never make it up. I love You, Lord. I'm grateful for Your love and forgiveness.

You left heaven, knowing what would happen. Still, Your love for me and all humankind caused You to come. You left royalty to be born in a stable. You accepted ridicule and torture. And You died for me. Why, Lord?

You are My own, dear one. I came so you can know and rely on My love. I came here to overcome sin. Not because you deserve Me, but because I love you with an everlasting love. My desire is to lavish My love upon you and give you a life filled with inner peace and joy. Accept it. Treasure it, and live for Me.

Thank You, Lord, for leaving heaven and saving me. Your gracious love truly is sufficient. Let my soul magnify You in all I say and do.

And He said to me,
"My grace is sufficient for you,
for My strength is made perfect in weakness."

2 Corinthians 12:9 NKJV

SEPTEMBER 11

How Do You Feel about Evil?

Many times, malicious, terrifying actions bring devastation beyond description. I run to You like a child, and I cry out, "Look, Father! See what they did?"

I hate the way wickedness tricks lost people. How do You feel about evil and wrongdoers? What about Your Son? Did You abandon Him when He bore my sins?

The Bible says to flee from evil. It declares that sin causes ruined lives and eternal death. I believe You despise evil, Father. But the people? You constantly plead for everyone to receive You.

I can't comprehend what happened when Your Son died. I do know Jesus took my sin and anguish upon His shoulders. Rejected by many, He paid the price. Your power provided escape from sin for all. You didn't interfere, Father. Still, You were there when the temple's veil tore from top to bottom, when the earth shook, the rocks split, and the tombs broke open and the dead came alive. You were there when the sick became well. You were there when the centurion exclaimed, *"Truly this was the Son of God!"* And You were there, Father, when Your Son victoriously rose from the grave!

Victories over wrongs still happen. Through them, You bring forth loving, caring people. Love conquers all. Truly You are my righteous Father. Truly Jesus *is* the Son of God!

> *Hold fast that which is good.*
> *Abstain from all appearance of evil.*
>
> 1 THESSALONIANS 5:21–22 KJV

Why Can't People Show More Love?

Lord, thank You for those in my life who love me. They give me joy. They make me laugh. They fill me with enthusiasm and pump life into me. But there is one who doesn't seem to have any love to give. No matter how hard I try to please or show kindness, this person shows little response. I usually go away feeling empty. How very sad. Not for me but for the one who lacks the ability to show love.

You must know other people who experience this, Lord. Do they have relatives or friends who put on such a stiff, rough exterior that no one can penetrate it with warmth and sincere thoughtfulness? What causes them to be so cold? When some are no longer alive, there is nothing we can do but leave it with You. Others are still here, however, never experiencing what real love is all about.

Please find a way to break through their uncaring veneer, I pray. No matter the cause, saturate and soften their calloused hearts with Your never-failing tenderness. Give them a glimpse of what real love is all about.

Remind me to pray each time I see the unlovable person I care about. Give them Your unfailing love through me.

Love never fails.

1 CORINTHIANS 13:8 NKJV

SEPTEMBER 13

What Brings You Joy?

You are my dearest Friend, Lord. I love taking walks with You and enjoying Your creation. I appreciate talking with You and sharing my joys, my concerns, and my secrets. When I'm upset, I come to You—my hiding place and my comfort. You are my refuge and strength. You help me with problems. I have no other friend like You, Lord.

I don't want to neglect our times together. When I do, emptiness grows inside me, and I miss out on Your direction. This must sadden You. Please keep me close.

What brings You joy, Lord? Show me Your ways.

Come to Me once again, dear child. Give Me your worship and praise. Open your soul and share your life with Me. Oh, how I delight in you, when your days are filled with righteousness that shines like the dawn. I love it when the joy of your salvation glows like a blazing torch. Keep doing good, for this is My will. It pleases Me. Continue showing your love to Me and to others. As you do, My joy remains in you and your joy is made full in Me.

I praise You, O Lord. With all my might, I love You and want to share Your love with others. Teach me Your ways so the joy we share is made complete.

> *[Jesus said,]*
> *"I have told you this so that my joy may be in you*
> *and that your joy may be complete.*
> *My command is this:*
> *Love each other as I have loved you."*

> John 15:11–12 niv

Why Are Answers to Problems Hard to Find?

It's happening again, Lord. Strife twists around me like a hurricane and presses in on every side. Thin skin. Quick tempers. Hurt feelings. Will we survive? Why am I called on to be the peacemaker? Why must I be caught in the middle? Why are answers to problems so hard to find? I can't do this on my own.

Perhaps I get caught up in what others say and forget to rely on You. Teach me to wait on You. When things escalate, let me seek Your face. Help me avoid yielding to pressure, and help me stand for right. When others look to me, I look to You, my source of wisdom. Show me when to help and when to step back. I'm relying on You, Lord, instead of my own understanding. Direct me now, I pray. Renew my strength, for my hope comes from You.

Come to Me, weary one. Allow Me to give you rest and direction. Place your shoulders under My yoke. Submit to My lead. I will make your burden light. Be patient. Answers take time, sometimes years. Trust Me. I will work it out in My way.

I can't solve these problems, Lord. But You can. I trust You to provide the right answers.

Wait on the LORD;
Be of good courage,
And He shall strengthen your heart;
Wait, I say, on the LORD!

PSALM 27:14 NKJV

Why Do Children Have to Suffer?

Father, thank You for the children You place around me. Their energy and enthusiasm has an incredible way of becoming contagious. Their transparent personalities are priceless. When a child describes a happening through elaborate gestures and a missing-toothed lisp, it melts my heart.

Thank You, Lord, for allowing me to teach children who have disabilities. I love being with them. At our first meeting, I mostly notice the child's disability. Soon I look beyond it and get to know that little boy or girl.

But, Lord, what some youngsters are forced to deal with breaks my heart. Occasionally, adults cause problems. Sadly, some are inflicted on little children. Other times, things just happen. Why do children have to suffer? Why don't You make it right?

Thankfully, some manage to get well. Others miraculously overcome obstacles every day. Through these children, lives are tendered and blessed. I know mine is. I have no answers, Lord. But You do. In heaven, You'll show me the whole picture. Children I've taught will be there with bodies and minds made whole. I hope they will know me.

I know You treasure these young ones in a special corner of Your heart, Lord. Surely Your guardian angels are near. Thank You for loving and caring for children who suffer. Thank You for bringing each one into my life for me to love.

[Jesus said,]
"Therefore, whoever humbles himself like this child
is the greatest in the kingdom of heaven.
And whoever welcomes a little child like this
in my name welcomes me."

MATTHEW 18:4–5 NIV

Why Do Some Christians Become Martyrs?

Lord, tonight the news told of another missionary taken captive, tortured, and killed. It's happening to Christians worldwide, in all walks of life. Thankfully, some are released from captivity. Others, however, die. Even teenagers are being gunned down for taking a stand for You.

Why, Lord? Why must many Christians suffer as martyrs? What good comes from such dreadful, violent acts? Let their suffering not be in vain. You were pierced and crushed, were smitten and afflicted, and died as a criminal. Your punishment brought us peace and eternal life. Countless times, tragedies cause others to step forward and zealously carry on with Your love and forgiveness. Ultimately, more people than ever find eternal life with joy and peace.

Would I be willing to suffer or die for You, Lord? Even a little criticism causes me to draw back. The Bible says my life belongs to You. You help me overcome the sins of this world in all kinds of circumstances—life or death, the present or the future. Help me to willingly take up whatever cross is given to me, to relinquish anything You ask. May I never be ashamed of taking a firm stand for You and what is right.

Thank You, Lord, for Christians who are martyred for following You. May their sacrifices be rewarded through Your victory.

*[Jesus said,] "Blessed are you when they revile and persecute you, and say all kinds of evil against you falsely for My sake.
Rejoice and be exceedingly glad, for great is your reward in heaven, for so they persecuted the prophets who were before you."*

MATTHEW 5:11–12 NKJV

Are You Pleased with Me?

What will it be like when I meet You face-to-face, Lord? Some of my friends say they will stand in awe and praise You. But I feel unworthy. Will I be on my knees, with my head bent low? Do I deserve to appear before You?

Are You pleased with me? I love You with all my heart. Yet I have only a grain-sized faith. At times I mess up and get discouraged. Will I pass the tests of life? You are my rescuer, my only hope.

Your shortcomings are already forgiven, dear child. Your repentant heart causes Me to remember them no more. They are removed as far as the east is from the west. My grace has made you whole. You are cleansed and given a new life in My name. Once, your sins were like scarlet. Now you are made sparkling clean, as white as snow.

Keep loving Me, dear one, and obey My precepts. Seek Me first and My righteousness. Whenever you fail, I will help you start over. When you come before My throne, I will greet you with open arms. I will wipe away your tears and strife. I will lead you to My springs of living water, where you shall experience boundless joy forever.

Oh, what awesome grace I feel when You are pleased with me.

[Jesus said,]
"But seek first the kingdom of God
and His righteousness."

MATTHEW 6:33 NKJV

How Can You Use Me?

I want to be valuable to You, Lord. Every day, You shower Your blessings on me. How can You use me to glorify You?

The Bible says Your first and greatest commandment is for me to love You with all my heart, soul, and mind. The second commandment is like it: to love my neighbor as much as I do myself. Is this the utmost way You can use me? By my showing love?

Some people are easy to love. But others are difficult to even like! Yet You say if I don't have Your love, my words and actions matter for nothing. I can't do this by my own strength. Please help me, Lord. Show me in Your Bible how to do this.

I also read how this love You want me to give is of You. It says when Your Spirit fills my life, You grant me a pure, unselfish love that puts off childish ways. Your love is patient and kind and doesn't demand its own way. During my daily frustrations, help me remember Your love isn't touchy or irritable. Help me not to hold grudges but to be willing to forgive. Teach me to look for the best in others and not be so quick to criticize.

Use me, Lord. Help me have a loving spirit in all I say and do.

Jesus replied:
"Love the Lord your God with all your heart
and with all your soul and with all your mind. . . .
Love your neighbor as yourself."

Matthew 22:37–38 niv

SEPTEMBER 19

Do Things Happen for a Reason?

Remember that night, Lord, when I was working my second job? It was three thirty in the morning, the end of my shift. When Tammy and I walked to our cars, mine wouldn't start. I was so tired, Lord. Thank You for Tammy staying and helping me get it started. It took about ten minutes, but it seemed like forever. We drove toward home in the same direction. As we approached an intersection, police cars were everywhere. We had to take a detour to get home. We learned later that ten minutes before we arrived, a double murder had occurred, and the fugitive escaped on foot. Because my car stalled, we were kept safe.

Many experiences cause me to feel countless things happen for a reason. Do You allow some events to occur in order to accomplish something else? Do You use difficult experiences to help me be tried and refined so I might grow stronger and shine like gold? Do some mishaps occur so others can be blessed?

You promise that You will never leave me or forsake me. In Philippians 1, the Bible says when trouble comes, You give help through the prayers of others and Your Holy Spirit. Somehow You cause things to work together for good.

Thank You for watching over me, Lord, for being my refuge and strength.

> *I am going to keep on being glad,*
> *for I know that as you pray for me,*
> *and as the Holy Spirit helps me,*
> *this is all going to turn out for my good.*

> PHILIPPIANS 1:19 TLB

What Is Heaven Like?

Father, I enjoy my life here on earth. I treasure my family, friends, and being able to worship You in church. And, oh, the blessings of camp meetings! It's like a little bit of heaven here on earth.

Thinking about heaven makes me homesick inside. Was my soul with You before I was born? What is heaven like? Will I really get to see You, Father? Will I know my loved ones who go there before me? Will my husband still be my husband? Or will we be one in Your body of Christ?

Like Mary, may I sit at Your feet with no concern for time? I want to enjoy Your presence and praise You for eternity. I want to bring You my questions, and I will trust You to help me with each one.

Your Bible tells me I'll get to shed this earthly body. There will be no sin, sickness, or pain, no sadness or mourning. No longer will I need to fend off worry or strife. Best of all, I will see Your glorious Triune—God the Father, Son, and Holy Spirit. I will get to meet You face-to-face.

When I kneel before You in heaven, I imagine Your Son bending down, taking my hand, and saying, *"I paid the price for you to come here. Welcome home."*

"Behold. . .
God Himself will be with them and be their God.
And God will wipe away every tear from their eyes;
there shall be no more death, nor sorrow, nor crying.
There shall be no more pain,
for the former things have passed away."

REVELATION 21:3–4 NKJV

How Can I Listen to You Better?

Here I am, Lord. I managed to find some quiet time with You. What a great pleasure it is, sharing with You all that's going on in my life. Thank You for listening and caring. I'm finished talking now. I know I have more time to spend with You, Lord, but I've told You everything that's going on with me. Waiting responsibilities flood my mind. How will I manage to complete everything?

As I ponder closing my Bible and going about my duties, I feel You coaxing me to remain. Could it be that You want me to listen to You now, Lord? Teach me to open my heart and mind to You and hear what You have to show me. Help me lay aside the clutter of wants and mundane tasks. Cause these thoughts to dim. Redirect my focus toward the things of You. Help me meditate on Your ways. What would You have me do for You? Caution and direct me.

How I adore You, Lord, as You talk to my heart. When You answer my prayers with "no" or "wait awhile," I will still trust You. Search my heart. Weave Your will and mine together as one. Here I am, ready to listen and stay my mind on You.

Trust in the LORD with all your heart,
and do not rely on your own insight.
In all your ways acknowledge him,
and he will make straight your paths.

PROVERBS 3:5–6 RSV

How Can My Faith Grow Stronger?

Father, I'm frustrated. I bring this seemingly impossible situation to You again, asking for Your help. Still, nothing gets better. I don't understand. Why are things not going right? Is my faith too small?

I know You care for me. I'm glad I can bring You my anxieties and questions. Thank You for being patient with me. Yet I wonder if questioning "why?" may at times be pleading for my will instead of Yours. When I do, am I expressing my lack of faith in Your ability to handle things best? Do I think I can do better than You, the Lord God, the Creator of all?

Like exercising my body, help me to exercise my faith by trusting Your will. The more I put my faith in You, the stronger it will grow. I wonder if I should change my question more often from "why?" to "how?" How would You have me pray? How would You use me in word and deed?

I think I'm catching on, Father. I'm realizing that rather than placing my trust in Your answering yes to my prayers, I must wholeheartedly place that faith in Your will and purpose for my life.

Thank You, Father, for helping me to actively trust You by learning to ask "how?" more often than "why?"

Commit your way to the LORD;
trust in him and he will do this:
He will make your righteousness shine like the dawn,
the justice of your cause like the noonday sun.

PSALM 37:5–6 NIV

How Can I Help Others Know How Wonderful You Are?

Lord, I want others to realize how alive, wonderful, and personal You are. I try to explain it, but I often can't get the message across. How can I help them understand? Show me the way, Lord, so I can reach these people for You.

Mere words don't seem to be enough. How can people get to know You through me? Help me become a vibrant reflection of You. Let all I do and say be living proof of what pleases You. Help me to relax and simply allow You to use me however You wish. Anoint me with Your powerful Holy Spirit. Let me magnify Your name and show how marvelous and great You are. As I let my light shine out to the lives of others, I ask for Your Spirit to speak to their hearts. Whisper Your words of love to them.

Remind me to hold them up in prayer every day. Help me to commit each one of these souls to You and trust You to work in each of their hearts. Grant me patience to have confidence in Your timing. You know best how to reach them. Let me never give up on them and Your wondrous grace.

Thank You for revealing how glorious and awesome You are.

> *But this precious treasure—*
> *this light and power that now shine within us—*
> *is held in a perishable container,*
> *that is, in our weak bodies.*
> *Everyone can see that the glorious power within*
> *must be from God and is not our own.*

2 CORINTHIANS 4:7 TLB

How Can I Serve You Better?

I often find myself busy doing different things to serve You, Lord. Some are simple tasks like cleaning the church and helping with fund-raising activities. I also like to teach the children and sing with the worship team. What really gives me pleasure is showing kindness to someone else. These things aren't hard, Lord, but I feel there is more You want from me. Please show me what it is. How can I serve You better?

Perhaps it's learning how to be more thoughtful toward others. Often the area I have the most trouble with is in demonstrating a give-and-take attitude with my friends and coworkers. Much of the time, I feel You urging me to relinquish my wants and desires to please the wishes of another. When I do, Lord, I feel good about this. However, when it comes to taking on people's burdens caused by their making poor choices, I struggle.

Show me how to love others as myself. When they experience sadness from doing wrong, help me to be there for them. Let me show patience and gentle perseverance for right as I help these people work things out with You. Remind me to avoid a holier-than-thou attitude.

Teach me to serve by loving as You did, Lord. Teach me to love without fail.

Bear one another's burdens,
and so fulfill the law of Christ.

GALATIANS 6:2 NKJV

SEPTEMBER 25

Did They Miss the Boat?

Lord, I have friends who are Your faithful servants. One enjoys serving You by what she's doing. Still, she sees needs around her and wonders if she has missed her calling. Another friend of mine is experiencing a change in Your calling. Waiting on what You have planned next is difficult. Like many of us, both wonder if they missed the boat for some reason or if they are really where You want them. Please help them, Lord.

I don't recognize what Your will is for their lives. But I'm thankful You know. Without a doubt, You have a purpose for them and for others searching for Your calling. Your Bible says we are to go preach the gospel to every nation. How we do this is in Your hands, Lord.

Perhaps it's by walking with You each day and spreading Your good news to everyone we can. Could it be that time, rank, and place don't matter nearly as much as having a willing, obedient heart?

Put these dear servants in the right spot at the right time, where You want them to be. Strengthen their confidence in Your timing and leading. Bless them, I pray. Thank You already for Your plans in their lives, Lord. To You be the glory.

Show me Your ways, O LORD;
Teach me Your paths.
Lead me in Your truth and teach me,
For You are the God of my salvation;
On You I wait all the day.

PSALM 25:4–5 NKJV

Is It Wrong to Look Back?

I recall when Bob told me You were calling him to the ministry, Lord. We were only twenty years old and had been married about three months. Remember our cozy little white cottage? It was nestled among fir trees near the river. The only way to get to the house was by use of a footbridge. We could sit on our patio and cast a fishing line in the water if we liked. Both sets of parents lived only a few miles from us, and we saw them often.

Although I was excited about Your calling and willing to obey, I had no idea of the changes we would face. We packed all our belongings in the back of my parents' pickup truck and left for college. We moved into an old two-story apartment in the busy city of Portland, Oregon. Oh, how I missed that peaceful little house, Lord. I longed for it.

That's when I asked You if it was wrong to look back. You made it very clear to me that it was all right to have good memories, but I should not long for things of the past. Thank You for the many times You remind me to focus on You, to press forward with hopeful anticipation and be worthy of Your calling.

But one thing I do:
Forgetting what is behind
and straining toward what is ahead,
I press on toward the goal to win the prize
for which God has called me
heavenward in Christ Jesus.

PHILIPPIANS 3:13–14 NIV

How Does the Universe Work Together So Perfectly?

Thank You, Lord, for the long relaxing walk along a riverside trail Bob and I were able to take yesterday. Crisp, multicolored leaves hanging over the river's edge swung lazily in an early autumn breeze. They picked up reflections of the sun's rays glimmering on the water. As we walked, I could feel my body and mind relax.

That evening, we sat on the patio with bottles of ice water and watched the sun silently slip below the horizon. Like clockwork, stars gradually popped out in precise locations. Is there any other life up there? I wonder.

What a mystery this vast creation is. How does everything in this universe work together so perfectly? Even with storms, floods, and extreme season changes, You bring nature into balance.

I'm amazed how scientists, through their discoveries, are recognizing historical accuracy in biblical events. However, numerous questions remain unanswered.

You, O God, spoke and ordered everything into existence. Your comprehension goes far beyond the grasp of our finite minds. Our plans and purposes are often obscured and thwarted, but Your plans stand firm forever. Even more awe-inspiring is the way You change our hearts and give us new lives in You.

Thank You for Your order of creation, Lord. Help us care for it. Thank You for including me in Your vast creation plan.

Let all the earth fear the LORD; Let all the inhabitants of the world stand in awe of Him. For He spoke, and it was done; He commanded, and it stood fast.

PSALM 33:8–9 NASB

How Can I Find Real Victory and Joy?

Lord, there are so many negative and discouraging things happening around and to me. I'm tired. My patience is worn thin. I'm discouraged because nothing seems to be going right. My hectic lifestyle has left me used up and exhausted.

Today, someone came up to me and asked how I was. My response was, "All right, under the circumstances." At that very moment, I felt You speaking to my heart. I was allowing myself to play a supportive role in the pessimistic attitude that causes me so much grief. Forgive me, Lord. How can I find real victory and joy in all circumstances?

I realize I've been focusing on everything that's wrong. Your Bible says You want me to think on whatever is honest, righteous, pure, good, upright, beneficial, and praiseworthy. When I'm tempted to become depressed, help me shove out the negative thoughts and meditate instead on You.

Thank You, Lord, for providing me the victory over bad habits in words or deeds. Help me not to tolerate any of them in my life. Thank You for letting me feast on Your Scriptures. Cleanse my soul and fill me anew with Your holy presence. Thank You for granting me the victory and joy that come from You.

Now may the God of hope fill you with
all joy and peace in believing,
so that you will abound in hope
by the power of the Holy Spirit.

ROMANS 15:13 NASB

How Can I Get "Religion" Out of Christianity?

Lord Jesus, I bring a dedicated Christian friend to You in prayer. She has worshiped in the same church for years and has always been a faithful helper. Everyone in the congregation has been caring, but now something is changing.

Church members are being scrutinized. Leaders are making up long lists of rules for church members to adhere to. Rigid church bylaws and politics have slowly overridden a church once filled with humility, love, and compassion. Money and status have become extremely important. Sermon quotes have become "don't" and "shame on you."

What's happening, Lord? Are they getting caught up in unnecessary man-made rules? This controlling, negative spirit is not of You. Please help this dear congregation, Lord.

How can we get this imposing man-made "religion" out of Christianity? It reminds me of the Sadducees and Pharisees, with their long, pious prayers, their public displays of giving, and their unbearable, strict rules.

Lord Jesus, You teach us the first and greatest commandment is to love You with all our hearts, souls, and minds, and the second is to love our neighbors as ourselves. Thank You for showing us that when we love You, *really love You,* we have no problem keeping Your commands. Remind us, Lord Jesus, to love and care for one another as You love and care for us.

Jesus replied [to His accusers]:
" 'Love the Lord your God with all your heart
and with all your soul and with all your mind.' . . .
And the second is like it: 'Love your neighbor as yourself.' "

MATTHEW 22:37, 39 NIV

Will My Good Deeds Be Recognized in Heaven?

Lord, I just finished putting in another full day of cleaning the church. I stand back now and admire how much better it looks and smells. I feel so pleased. I hope You are happy with this work I did for You.

I want to be of service to You in whatever way You ask. Each time I serve, it gives me a warm feeling deep inside. Will my good deeds be recognized by You when I get to heaven? When I was a little girl, I was told they would be rewarded with a crown. Each act would be an added star. Is this true, Lord? It doesn't matter, because I'm still glad to serve You.

I read how James and John asked if they could sit on each side of You in heaven. It certainly didn't take long for the other disciples to get upset about their request, Lord. You told them the important thing was for them to be willing to do as You had done.

I see in Your Bible that I will receive a crown—a crown of gladness and everlasting joy! Suddenly, my insignificant service pales in light of Your grace given to me. Thank You, Lord, for the best crown ever—that of Your eternal joy.

And the ransomed of the LORD will return.
They will enter Zion with singing;
everlasting joy will crown their heads.
Gladness and joy will overtake them,
and sorrow and sighing will flee away.

ISAIAH 35:10 NIV

My Example

Lord Jesus, two little words I often hear You tell me are ringing in my ears: *"Trust Me."* It's easy to say I'm going to trust You. When I'm pressed to put my words into action, it's a whole different story. Trust? Be confident? Rely? Wait? This is difficult for me.

I'm a doer, Lord. This isn't always good, especially when I should be waiting on You. I want everything done yesterday—microwave style. If I could do things instantly, I would be all for doing so. Relying on You shouldn't be impossible. When I lack trust, I'm not wholeheartedly submitting. I can't do this on my own, Lord. Help me, I pray. Teach me how to walk in Your footsteps.

Did You really want to come to this earth as a baby? You certainly didn't receive the comforts of a king. What about Your growing years, when others didn't understand how You felt, or Your preparing to die on the cross? You must have longed to be with Your Father. Still, He had a plan for You to fulfill, and You trusted in Him.

I'm only a Christian who wants to love and serve You. I'm not very strong on my own. I can only trust You through Your help and example. Please show me how.

> *Trust in the Lord God always,*
> *for in the Lord Jehovah is your everlasting strength.*

ISAIAH 26:4 TLB

The Best Belt Ever

Lord, several years ago my son Jonathan was active in sword fighting. Once while I visited him, he demonstrated his skill for me. It took Jonathan quite awhile to put on his suit of armor. How tall and handsome he looked as he tramped out into his backyard and stood before me! Ever so slowly he went through multiple maneuvers. He even tried to teach me some of them. The movements were great. I was also impressed by his armor. Each piece had a purpose.

I read in the Bible about putting on Your spiritual armor. One piece of armor used during Bible times was a belt. It was tight and confining. It helped hold other pieces of armor in place. Perhaps that's why the belt in the armor of God is called the belt of truth.

Place Your belt of truth on me, Lord. Help me recognize what is true. Give me the courage to be honest in all I say and do. In doing so, I feel my faith in You grow as You guide me along the right path. I can see this is the best "belt" ever to put on. Thank You for helping me trust You through Your belt of truth.

Jesus said, "If you hold to my teaching,
you are really my disciples.
Then you will know the truth,
and the truth will set you free."

JOHN 8:31–32 NIV

OCTOBER 3

Sticking to the Truth

I met someone who says he loves You, Lord. He has quite a magnetic personality. Whenever I see him, he's surrounded by a captive audience, clinging to his every word. At first I admired his charming ways and wished I could be like him and win more souls for You. Then I realized some of the things he was saying didn't match up with what I read in Your Word. He was rather like a wolf in sheep's clothing. The more I watched, the more I saw him living a life not pleasing to You in the things he did and said.

The next time I went to Bible study, I brought up some things he said. It didn't take long for our group to search our Bibles and discover this man's words were taken out of context. They were twisted and false. Thank You, Lord, for helping me to be cautious. Appearing to be a "super" Christian isn't the answer. Instead, I realize You simply want me to live my life for You and stick to the truth of Your Word.

Thank You for guiding me to take my questions to those who know Your Bible and to ask for their assistance. Thank You again for helping me recognize the truth.

We should no longer be children,
tossed to and fro and carried about with
every wind of doctrine,
by the trickery of men. . . .
Grow up in all things into Him
who is the head—Christ.

EPHESIANS 4:14–15 NKJV

What's Broken?

I have a close friend, Father, who overflows with love and compassion for those around her, especially her family. She has a way of understanding how others feel. When someone hurts emotionally, she takes time to care, listen, and offer appropriate suggestions. Her greatest strength is honesty. She "tells it like it is." When friends or family face medical problems, she guides them to doctors who can give them truthful answers, instead of the runaround. Thank You for her being the thoughtful, attentive person she is.

This reminds me of years ago when there was something emotionally and spiritually wrong with me. I felt lost until I learned to come to You and give You my trust. The first step in my healing was to listen to You identify the things that were defective in my life. You helped me recognize what was broken so I could become a whole person in You.

It was painful for me to face up to these things, but I was determined to listen to the truths You gave me. Like peeling an onion, one layer at a time, the brokenness in my life wasn't pleasant to deal with. The more I trusted You, the more confident I became in Your love, and the more my broken life began to heal.

Examine me, O LORD, and try me;
Test my mind and my heart.

PSALM 26:2 NASB

OCTOBER 5

Guard of My Heart

Over and over I give You my pain and shortcomings. Each time I do, Father, You show me answers in Your Word of healing and assurance, of love and protection. I find myself often turning to Ephesians where it tells about Your spiritual armor and the way it helps me. First, I read about Your belt of truth. Then I learn about Your breastplate of righteousness.

I recall how the breastplate used by soldiers in Bible times was made of overlaid pieces, which didn't allow even the smallest weapon to penetrate. It protected the heart of the soldier. In the same way, I discover how Your breastplate of righteousness protects my heart from the harmful evil one. I know I have to keep listening to Your guidance and make sure I allow no careless cracks to form. I must stay close to You in order to get through the spiritual and emotional battles I face. I trust You to fight them on my behalf.

Somehow, step-by-step You help me realize I don't need to struggle with wrong. You are doing that for me. Your righteous Spirit cleanses and heals my hurts and eases my mind. Thank You, Father, for how You are the guardian of my heart, keeping me safely in Your care.

And the peace of God,
which surpasses all comprehension,
will guard your hearts and
your minds in Christ Jesus.

PHILIPPIANS 4:7 NASB

Your Blueprint

Father, things seem off center in my life right now. I can't put my finger on it, but there's no harmony inside me. Like so many times before, I must back off from the needless distractions and take a good look at the things I need to learn of You. Teach me so my heart is right with Your will.

When You put my broken pieces back together years ago, Father, You began the rebuilding process in me. It was like You rolled out Your blueprint for my life and showed me what You wanted me to do—one step at a time, one day at a time. What a wonderful experience it was as I allowed You to go through every area of my existence and do some serious spiritual remodeling. The more You did, the more I saw things You wanted me to accomplish.

I sense that's what You are teaching me to do now. Show me through Your Word the designs You have for me. Pull me back to Your plan. Let me be the temple where You dwell. Fill me with Your peace and joy, satisfaction and love.

Thank You for giving me a blueprint to keep me on center with You.

For I know the plans I have for you, says the Lord.
They are plans for good and not for evil,
to give you a future and a hope.

JEREMIAH 29:11 TLB

OCTOBER 7

A Firm Foot-Tread

Father, recently several people in our church went shopping for a friend who is serving overseas in the armed forces. One person knew what to buy and provided a list of needed supplies. I headed to a nearby store. Thank You for helping me find several things at great discount prices. The items I wanted most to buy for him were a couple pairs of comfortable socks. When I get tired and my feet hurt, I hurt all over. I thought of discomforts he might be going through. I slipped a note inside the socks telling our friend I was praying for his foot-tread to be firm and sure. I imagined him preparing for his day by putting on thick, comfortable socks and lacing up his boots.

In Bible times, soldiers prepared their feet for protection and surety in step by wearing the right shoes. I read that some were even fitted with nails or spikes. Thank You for preparing me for the spiritual battles I face by giving me another piece of Your spiritual armor—the shoes of the gospel of peace. Your gospel, Your good news in the Bible, gives me peace of heart and mind. No matter what comes my way each day, I can trust You wholeheartedly to give me a firm foot-tread with You.

Stand therefore. . .
having shod your feet with
the preparation of the gospel of peace.

EPHESIANS 6:14–15 NKJV

The Grain of Sand

Thank You for teaching me how to follow Your ways. Learning is one thing, Father. Yet the more I walk with You, the more my trust in You grows. When I face obstacles and discomforts, I'm thankful for Your presence.

Remember a few months ago when I went to the ocean to work on this book, Father? Something unpleasant was gnawing at my soul. I couldn't put my finger on it. I shoved the thought to the back of my mind and went to work writing, but it never went away.

That day when I took a break and strolled along the ocean shore, I thought the fresh, salty air would clear my mind. Before I realized it, I started limping. Something was making my toe feel raw. When I stopped and took off my shoe, I found a grain of sand near a bright red toe. Such a little thing, but it caused much discomfort. After I dipped my foot into some salt water, cleansed it, dried it with my jacket, and replaced my sock and shoe, it no longer hurt.

You brought to my mind that my soul was harboring a grain of resentment toward someone. Thank You for washing my unforgiving attitude away, helping me trust You with the situation, and once again making me spiritually whole.

That is what the Scriptures
are talking about when they say,
"How beautiful are the feet of those who preach
the Gospel of peace with God
and bring glad tidings of good things."

ROMANS 10:15 TLB

OCTOBER 9

Help Me Do My Part

Along with learning to believe in You by seeking Your truth and righteousness, Father, I'm discovering my next step in trusting You: I must work with You. Under the umbrella of Your will, I'm learning to do my part in helping make things better in my life. This is putting my trust in You into action.

As You know, Father, my back gives me trouble off and on. My doctor and chiropractor tell me the best thing to do for myself is walk and get plenty of exercise. Whenever I twist a muscle and cause myself physical pain, I know I need to trust the advice of those in the medical field and do as they say.

I read in Your Word that I must also exercise spiritually, take action, and do what's right by following Your lead for me. I'm running a race for You, Father. Thank You for strengthening me spiritually, emotionally, mentally, and physically as we go through each day together.

When I'm confronted with temptations and worries of things that can tangle me up or weigh me down, I ask You to help me avoid them. Instead, I will keep my focus on You, Father, and do my part. Thank You for showing me how.

> *Let us throw off everything that hinders*
> *and the sin that so easily entangles,*
> *and let us run with perseverance*
> *the race marked out for us.*
> *Let us fix our eyes on Jesus,*
> *the author and perfecter of our faith.*

HEBREWS 12:1–2 NIV

Persevere with Promises

Thank You, dear Father, for never leaving me alone. No matter where I am or what circumstances I face, I'm confident You are with me—helping, guiding me every step of the way. Each time opposition comes, prompt me to face it without fear and trust You to work things out.

Some frustrating situations happen around me. But others occur within my heart. When I'm a part of the problem, help me be open to You and willing to change. Soften my stubborn will and make me pliable, I pray, so You can use me in whatever ways You see best. In doing this, I'm learning more how to trust You.

When answers don't come easily and problems aren't solved as quickly as I would like, I turn to Your Word for guidance and assurance from You. As I read Your promises, they seem to jump off the pages of my Bible like they were put there especially for me. Thank You for them, Father.

Grant me the presence of mind to recall and stand on the promises You give me. In so doing, You help keep my steps sure and right.

For God has said,
"I will never, never fail you nor forsake you."

HEBREWS 13:5 TLB

OCTOBER 11

Beyond My Ability

More than anything, I am learning to trust You, Father. One of the pieces of spiritual armor I read about is Your shield of faith. It is all-encompassing. It has a way of covering and shielding me on every side.

I read in Bible history how some shields were made of wood, beveled like a large, shallow dishpan. The rim, often brass, held heavy thicknesses of hide in place. Soldiers frequently anointed the hide with oil, most likely to keep it from cracking. The oil made the shield slick so flaming arrows would glance off it. A soldier slipped his arm through the strap in back to hold it in place. He could swing it in any direction to protect all parts of his body.

Like fiery arrows in Bible times, I, too, am attacked by Satan's harmful ways, Father. I don't have the capacity to fight these things. I praise You for going beyond my ability during these spiritual battles. I believe You even help hold my shield of faith. Thank You for extinguishing the evil one's fiery darts, protecting me on every side. I'm so glad I can rely on Your power rather than my own. I put all my trust—all my faith—in You.

David shouted in reply,
"You come to me with a sword and a spear,
but I come to you in the name of the Lord
of the armies of heaven and of Israel—
the very God whom you have defied.
Today the Lord will conquer you!"

1 SAMUEL 17:45–46 TLB

Pushing Out the Toxins

Father, I'm still enjoying the overflow of blessings You recently gave me at a women's retreat. My whole body relaxed as I pulled into the campground parking lot. I stepped out of my car. Your presence could be felt everywhere.

I attended a workshop given by my friend Sandy, a massage therapist. She described how massaging physical injuries helps reduce swelling, rids the area of toxins, and increases the healing process. Then she explained how God does the same thing with the injuries and toxins of our souls.

After she spoke, Sandy invited people to come to her for help with minor pains. My knee was hurting from an old injury, so I did. Sandy rubbed an ointment on her hands and gently massaged my knee, gradually working deeper into the pain-filled muscles. In a few minutes, I felt better. She also showed me how to massage it myself.

Later that day You tended my soul. You reached inside and found unpleasant things that were causing me spiritual pain. You filled me through and through with the healing balm of Your Holy Spirit. Thank You for working on the hurts in my soul. Thank You for going deeper and deeper until the toxins in my heart and mind were forced out and replaced with Your cleansing, healing love.

Search me, O God, and know my heart;
test me and know my anxious thoughts.
See if there is any offensive way in me,
and lead me in the way everlasting.

PSALM 139:23–24 NIV

OCTOBER 13

My Loved Ones

Father, in this quiet time, I bring my loved ones to You in prayer. Remembering the countless miracles You have performed for each person causes my faith to increase. I used to agonize over their spiritual welfare and needs. How patient You were in teaching me that You are the One who handles the problems. I didn't have to worry but simply trust.

Not long ago in an empty church sanctuary, I found a way to release every individual I love to Your care. Although those I love mean more to me than life itself, I knew I had to trust You to answer my prayers as You saw fit. Holding on to them and not giving them to You was wrong.

After pouring out my concerns to You, Father, I slipped up to the altar with paper and pencil in hand. I wrote each of their names on a sheet of paper and committed them to You. After I finished, I thanked You for watching over them. Then I erased their names from the paper and left the blank sheet on the altar.

Here I am again, Father, with paper and pencil and a heart filled with faith. Here I am again, handing over my loved ones to You.

For the LORD is good and his love endures forever;
his faithfulness continues through all generations.

PSALM 100:5 NIV

Working Circumstances for Good

I feel as though I'm waiting forever, Lord, for You to answer this prayer. I don't understand why it's taking so long. Forgive me for wanting my problems solved microwave style—here and now. Teach me to wait and be patient. Help me relax and leave everything in Your capable hands.

Thank You for helping me realize You have a far better picture of timing than I do. Now I put my faith in You and in the way You are handling things. You, dear Lord, know what is best and when it should be done.

You promise that everything works for good when I put my trust in You and Your purpose. I come to You in hope and faith, believing. You, dear Lord, are my comfort and shield. Because Your love rests upon me, my heart rejoices, and I trust completely in You.

As I bring this prayer to You, I don't know how things will work out. But You do. I thank and praise You for Your answers to come. I know You are already working on behalf of these concerns. You are my Lord, my God. All the circumstances, all the timing, I place in Your hands.

These troubles and sufferings of ours are, after all,
quite small and won't last very long.
Yet this short time of distress will result in God's
richest blessing upon us forever and ever!

2 CORINTHIANS 4:17 TLB

OCTOBER 15

Hope for the Future

How grateful I am for another piece of Your spiritual armor, Lord. It is Your helmet of salvation. By Your grace, I am saved from sin and hopelessness. Because of Your unfailing love for me and my love for You, I am and always will be Your child.

I read again in Bible times how soldiers wore helmets made of brass or thick leather that guarded their heads from deadly blows during battle. Thank You for the helmet of salvation You provide me that guards my thoughts and my soul.

Because of You, dear Lord, I have no worries for the future. I know You care for me as loving parents do their child. Because of You, I have hope for the future on this earth and a wonderful, eternal life to look forward to in heaven with You.

Thank You for guarding my thoughts and helping me focus on the things that are beneficial and constructive. Each day as I go about my activities, I pray You will give me a positive, healthy outlook. As You do, I will reflect Your ways to those around me.

Thank You, Lord, for Your hope. Thank You for Your helmet of salvation.

> *The LORD delights in those who fear him,*
> *who put their hope in his unfailing love.*

> PSALM 147:11 NIV

"Humbility"

Our son told me an amusing story of how one of our grandchildren gave his brother a firm lecture on not being a know-it-all. The words poured out loud and clear: "You need to learn more humbility."

At first I laughed, Father. However, the more I thought about what he said, the more it made sense. I wonder how many times in our society we catch ourselves trying to impress others with what we know or can do. Whenever I display these arrogant attitudes, You have a way of popping my proud bubble and bringing me back to reality. It really hit home when I read Proverbs 11:2 (NKJV): *"When pride comes, then comes shame; but with the humble is wisdom."*

I met someone not long ago, Father, who left a positive impression on me. He is well known in educational circles and has numerous initials behind his name. What impressed me more than his status was his humble way. He's a person who says little about his accomplishments. Instead, he and his wife radiate Your love by helping children in need.

I want to learn as much as possible, Father, but I don't want to be wise in my own eyes. Teach me "humbility," I pray. Help me be a useful tool for You.

Do not be wise in your own eyes;
fear the LORD and shun evil.
This will bring health to your body
and nourishment to your bones.

PROVERBS 3:7–8 NIV

It's Your Money

Father, the last couple of years have been difficult for people all around the world. Many have lost their jobs, their homes, and large shares of their savings in retirement or stock. Through tragedies, other people have even lost lives of loved ones.

I have a friend who took a huge cut in pay. I know she was concerned about how to adjust financially, but she seemed quite calm about it. She told me that in light of what others were going through, her problems were small. She said You gently reminded her to watch out for the unnecessary wants. There were many belongings she could do without. She simply exercised frugality and concentrated on the essentials until things got better.

The wonderful part was how You helped her to be faithful in giving You her tithe and trusting You to meet her needs. She feels her money belongs to You, Father. I loved hearing her tell how a few days after she wrote the check and put it in the offering, an unexpected turn of events caused her to have enough to pay her bills. She even had money left over.

Thank You, Father, for my friend's willing spirit in trusting You. Thank You for providing for her needs. In You, she is truly rich.

> [Jesus said,] "For if you give, you will get!
> Your gift will return to you in full
> and overflowing measure, pressed down,
> shaken together to make room for more, and running over.
> Whatever measure you use to give—large or small—
> will be used to measure what is given back to you."

LUKE 6:38 TLB

Trusting Your Word

The final piece of Your spiritual armor I learn about is the sword of the Spirit—which is Your Word, the Bible. I read that the swords the soldiers used during Bible times were short daggers with two edges. Other weapons they possessed were battle-axes, spears, and bows. The most treasured, apparently, was the sword.

When I worked a second job at a fast-food restaurant, You helped me fight spiritual battles on a daily basis by claiming Your powerful Word. When I was tired and didn't think I could work another hour, You brought to mind, *"The joy of the LORD is your strength"* (Nehemiah 8:10 NKJV). When I was tempted to be careless in word or action, You helped me recall, *"Love the LORD your God with all your heart, with all your soul, with all your strength, and with all your mind"* (Luke 10:27 NKJV). When my patience was tried, I remembered, *"Love your neighbor as yourself"* (Luke 10:27 NIV). When dangerous people appeared, I whispered, *"The angel of the LORD encamps all around those who fear Him, and delivers them"* (Psalm 34:7 NKJV). When I walked through dark hours of discouragement, You remind me, *"Your word is a lamp to my feet and a light to my path"* (Psalm 119:105 NKJV).

Thank You, Father, for Your protecting Word.

For the word of God is living and active.
Sharper than any double-edged sword. . .

HEBREWS 4:12 NIV

The Battle Is Yours

How grateful I am that whatever situation I'm in, Lord, You are here with me. Thank You for going before me, standing behind and beside me, and covering me with Your protective presence.

When I face danger, You are my guardian. When I'm a victim of false accusations and gossip, You are my defender. When the tempter is hammering at my heart's door, You deflect his fiery darts. When I'm ill, You fight for me to regain my health. When my loved ones go through various trials, You, dear Lord, surround them with Your love and protection.

There are instances when I get anxious and would like to take things into my own hands. I impatiently want to solve the problems my way, in my timing. Please give me a firm warning to stop at this point and trust You.

The Bible says these conflicts I face aren't fought with swords or spears. They aren't against flesh and blood. They are between Your goodness and the spiritual forces of evil, the rulers of darkness. As I trust in You, my battles become Yours. I don't need to fight them or even worry about them. Thank You, Father, for loving and taking care of me and fighting my battles.

> *"Thus says the LORD to you,*
> *'Fear not, and be not dismayed at*
> *this great multitude;*
> *for the battle is not yours but God's.'"*

2 CHRONICLES 20:15 RSV

A Light to My Path

Working my night job was scary at times, Father. The news warned us to carefully check for people hiding in our back-seats and under cars before getting in. Because I got off work late at night and the parking lot wasn't well lit, I was cautious.

My friend, Wendy, bought me an umbrella with a flash-light as part of its handle for my birthday. I used it to watch out for predators with either two or four legs. Remember the skunk that sat under the driver's side of the car one night, eating a chicken sandwich? I wondered if it would ever leave so I could go home. My flashlight also removed harmless shadows and exposed things not frightening at all. Thank You, Father, for how this gift still helps me.

I think of Your Bible, Your Word. It lights my path when I'm forced to combat darkness during uncertain times. When I'm afraid, I'm grateful I can shed Your light on things and see them clearly. Then my fear leaves. I know You are with me, guiding all the way. I treasure and respect the les-sons in Your Word, for they keep me from being tripped up by wrong decisions. Thank You, Father, for the light of Your Word.

Your words are a flashlight to light the path ahead of me, and keep me from stumbling.
I've said it once and I'll say it again and again:
I will obey these wonderful laws of yours.

PSALM 119:105 TLB

OCTOBER 21

Depending on You

Father, I have a friend I bring to You in prayer. She has always worked hard to make ends meet financially. Although she doesn't have a lot of material belongings, it's plain to see she's comfortable and happy. She's a kind person, Father. More times than I can count, I've watched her care for others. Sometimes she uses her last dollar to do so.

Now she's feeling as though she's a failure because she doesn't do as well financially as those around her. What really frightens me is how she has made some new acquaintances. They are encouraging her to invest everything she has in a get-rich-quick scheme. These people are proud and pushy, Father. Their ways don't seem right. Please guide my friend. Help her obey and depend on You above all else. Grant her the wisdom and courage she needs. If the people trying to influence her are doing right, forgive me for being suspicious. If they are dishonest, expose them before it's too late.

I don't understand this situation, but You do. I trust You to work this out in Your way, Father. Thank You for hearing my prayers for my friend. Thank You that I can depend on You to answer as You see best.

> *Blessed is that man who makes the LORD his trust,*
> *And does not respect the proud,*
> *nor such as turn aside to lies.*

> PSALM 40:4 NKJV

Faith's Reward

Lord, I'm grateful for how You spoke to my friend's heart and helped her to make wise choices. She listened to Your guidance and turned down the tempting offer to invest in a get-rich-quick scheme. I praise You that the very next morning after she firmly stood her ground and said no, she read in the paper that these people were cheating innocent folks out of their entire livelihood.

How good and kind You are, dear Lord! Thank You for blessing her for the many times she has reached out and helped others. Thank You for rewarding those who are faithful and trust in You. Not only did my friend escape a bad situation, she received an increase in pay from her employer. The following weekend, someone in our church gave her some beautiful furniture they no longer needed. Your ways are so marvelous!

Help my friend and me to learn and remember from this experience, Lord. Keep teaching us humility and thoughtfulness, I pray. Grant us strength to put our trust in You, rather than depending on riches or proud, dishonest people. Thank You, Lord, for giving us material and spiritual riches beyond what we need as we obey and depend on You.

Many, O LORD my God, are Your wonderful works
Which You have done;
And Your thoughts toward us
Cannot be recounted to You in order;
If I would declare and speak of them,
They are more than can be numbered.

PSALM 40:5 NKJV

OCTOBER 23

Bless Our Church

Father, our church is struggling. I bring it to You in prayer and ask You to help and direct us. Grant us a spiritual awakening. Let Your cleansing Holy Spirit rest upon our congregation and its leaders. Show us more and more how to depend on Your guidance and provision. Help us focus on Your marvelous goodness, rather than on discouragement and worry.

There are so many broken people in our congregation. Some situations seem impossible to overcome. Give us the faith to commit these things to You, Father. Teach us ways we can be overcomers in Your name.

Surround our church leaders with Your love and wisdom and power. Light a torch in each of our hearts. Give us a vision of what we can do for You. Grant us enough faith to depend on Your help as we walk this spiritual pilgrimage. Help us reach those around us with Your love.

Father, I commit my church leaders and congregation to Your care. This is Your church. May everything we do and say be pleasing to You. I thank and praise You for the blessings and answers to come. How grateful I am for Your love and care. Thank You for blessing our church.

So this is what the Sovereign LORD says:
"See, I lay a stone in Zion, a tested stone,
a precious cornerstone for a sure foundation;
the one who trusts will never be dismayed."

ISAIAH 28:16 NIV

307

The Broken Helping the Broken

A wonderful worship service just ended, Father. We've had so many hallowed times with You lately. It's like You opened the church roof up and poured Your spiritual blessings all over us. And our pastor, Father—his sermons are filled with so much power. Praying for him and our other church leaders really does pay off.

I stand back and watch different people in the fellowship room visit and enjoy refreshments together. There's a hope on many faces I haven't seen before. The amazing thing is how people are sitting down with each other, just caring and listening. I can't get over how Your Holy Spirit is weaving in and out among these dear folks, using them to help and encourage each other. Broken people are helping other broken people. We are so busy reaching out and telling those around us about Your love that we have forgotten our own cares.

Thank You, Father, for the revival that has begun in our hearts. Thank You for giving us hope. Thank You for helping us to depend on and trust in You to help us with our needs. Thank You for showing us how to love and trust each other. I praise You for the way You are showing broken people how to reach out and help each other.

When others are happy, be happy with them.
If they are sad, share their sorrow.
Work happily together. Don't try to act big.
Don't try to get into the good graces of important people,
but enjoy the company of ordinary folks.
And don't think you know it all!

ROMANS 12:15–16 TLB

Making My Teaspoon a Shovel

Father, I've faced some huge mountains in my life. Some, through faith in You, I overcame. There was one, though, where no amount of faith I mustered or lengthy, pleading prayers I uttered made a bit of difference. That obtrusive mountain loomed before me, almost laughing in my face.

I was frightened and confused, Father. I wondered why I couldn't get it out of my life. I recall crying out to You through clenched teeth, "Why me, Lord?" I struggled, trying to move my mountain a teaspoonful at a time.

The challenges I faced tested my faith to the limit. Finally, I changed my plea to "Not my will, but Yours, Lord." That's when I handed my puny teaspoon over to You and stepped back. You knew a better way to move my mountain.

You taught me to trust You more and yield to whatever outcome You willed for me. My anxiety disappeared. My soul felt at peace. I watched in amazement while You worked. The mountain never moved, Father. What moved was my mountain of distrusting Your will. Thank You for how You made my little teaspoon into a hefty shovel. Before I knew it, You and I had tunneled through. In the process, You gave me wisdom more valuable than nuggets of gold.

So Jesus said to them, "Because of your unbelief;
for assuredly, I say to you,
if you have faith as a mustard seed,
you will say to this mountain,
'Move from here to there,' and it will move;
and nothing will be impossible for you."

MATTHEW 17:20 NKJV

All the Time, No Matter What

Father, I want to thank You for my husband's relentless never-give-up attitude. Bob has an amazing way of seeing the cup half full rather than half empty. He has dreams for his congregation. He has ideas that sometimes cause others to laugh. I used to chuckle at some of his dreams, too. However, I've learned to hold my tongue, because so many things he has visualized and prayed about have come to pass.

Thank You for his example of trusting You all the time in all kinds of circumstances. Thank You for filling his heart to the brim with Your faithful Holy Spirit and for giving him a never-give-up love for others.

How I praise You for honoring the prayers we constantly lift to You on behalf of those around us. We don't always have the answers. Tests and challenges don't dictate Your plans for the future. You are in charge. When we bring our concerns to You, dear Father, You never, never fail us. You are the Way, the Truth, and the Life. Thank You for helping us to keep trusting You to lead us along Your paths. I praise You for being near to us all the time, in all circumstances, anywhere.

Trust in him at all times, O people;
pour out your hearts to him,
for God is our refuge.

PSALM 62:8 NIV

OCTOBER 27

Behind It All

Thank You, dear Lord, for handling the hurt feelings, the heartbreak, the frightening events and temptations I'm forced to contend with every day of my life. Nothing is too difficult when I turn it over to You. Along with Your coming to my rescue when I ask, I realize there are times You spring into action before I know what's happening.

During these trials, one of my greatest temptations is to lash out at those who treat me unkindly—especially when I'm accused of something I didn't do. The test is to remain calm when I have done something with a good heart and am accused of having the wrong motives. These things really hurt, Lord. I feel the hair on the back of my neck rise with my self-righteous attitude. After all, those wrongs were supposed to be made right. That's when You get me to listen and help me realize I don't have to be "right" when I feel I'm right.

Thank You for reminding me that my anger shouldn't be focused at people who do wrong. Instead, I can be angry at sin and all the heartache it brings. Thank You for helping me to put this behind me so I can move forward in Your will.

For we are not fighting against people made of flesh and blood, but against persons without bodies— the evil rulers of the unseen world, those mighty satanic beings and great evil princes of darkness who rule this world; and against huge numbers of wicked spirits in the spirit world. So use every piece of God's armor to resist the enemy whenever he attacks, and when it is all over, you will still be standing up.

EPHESIANS 6:12–13 TLB

Getting Rid of the Grime

Father, occasionally when I'm forced see what causes the struggles in this world, I'm reminded of when Bob and I decided to cover our kitchen floor with a hardwood-appearing laminated material. We decided to pay a company to do it for us. Then we found out that they don't do floors. This astounded us. The contractor explained how they would come in and lay down the material. First we would have to remove the current flooring and anything beneath it. Otherwise the floor wouldn't turn out right.

Thank You for friends who spent hours helping us scrape and chisel about six layers of glued-on, nailed-on old tile and linoleum, clear to the bare boards. We were grateful there was no rotten wood needing to be replaced.

Then we worked on the squeaks, Father. I slowly stepped across the boards. Whenever a board squeaked, Bob securely drilled in a screw. Hours later we were finished—with not one squeak. The company came in and did their job. The floor looks beautiful now.

Thank You for peeling away my faults so I can please You, Father. Thank You for anchoring my life to You and eliminating the irritating squeaks in my heart.

This certain hope of being saved is
a strong and trustworthy anchor for our souls,
connecting us with God himself behind
the sacred curtains of heaven.

HEBREWS 6:19 TLB

OCTOBER 29

The Upside of Life

Father, I want to thank You for my friend, Cathy. She is one of the most positive persons I know. She has a way of looking at everything in her life in an "upside" way. Instead of constantly complaining and criticizing, Cathy sees the good in situations. She makes it a way of life to build up people around her, rather than tearing them down. What she does causes me to recognize the good in others, as well.

As You know, Father, Cathy's upside attitude is even more amazing because she is paralyzed from the waist down. She refuses to sit around feeling sorry for herself. Instead, she trusts You to use her whenever and wherever possible. She spends her days working as a school librarian and a pastor's wife. Her main goal is to bless those around her any way she can.

Father, I trust You and give You my hurts right now. Change my turned-down mouth into a smile, and flip-flop my negative attitude to a positive, upside lifestyle to glorify You and bless those around me.

I trust You to change my admonition to admiration, my dishonor to honor, my complaining to thanksgiving. Let everything I do and say be encouraging. Thank You, Father, for giving me an upside life.

Finally, brethren [and sisters],
whatever is true, whatever is honorable,
whatever is just, whatever is pure,
whatever is lovely, whatever is gracious,
if there is any excellence,
if there is anything worthy of praise,
think about these things.

PHILIPPIANS 4:8 RSV

In the Pits

Praise You, Father, for the way I can trust You when I'm in the pits. Not the pits of despair and discouragement, but the pits in the race I'm running for You. Each time I take a curve, I find You waiting for me, ready to fine-tune my life so I can be an effective Christian.

Here I am again, Father, ready for You to search my heart, my mind, my emotions, even my physical stamina. I wait patiently as You work within me, cleansing, taking apart and rebuilding things that need to be fixed. Unlike the races I've watched with my husband and boys, the tune-ups aren't quick with a pat on the back and I'm on my way. There is no set time with Your work. Several areas You are rebuilding in my life can be done quickly. Others, however, are slow and sometimes painful.

Cleanse me, Father. Remake and remold the broken areas in my life. Refuel me with Your Holy Spirit so I can run this race You place before me and come out victoriously in Your name.

I yield to You, Father. Here in the pits, I trust You and am confident in Your love as You tune me according to Your will.

Oh, how kind our Lord was,
for he showed me how to trust him and
become full of the love of Christ Jesus.

1 TIMOTHY 1:14 TLB

OCTOBER 31

Stand firm—Victoriously!

What incredible victories I experience, Lord, when I put on Your armor. Each time I do, I draw closer to You. As I draw closer to You, my trust in You grows. Thank You for leading me step-by-step and teaching me Your wise and certain truth and righteousness. Thank You for allowing me to experience Your wonderful peace. I praise You for assuring me of Your saving grace and the hope You give me for the future. The more I walk with You, the more my faith in You steadily grows. Thank You for Your Word and how its verses guide me through every hour of every day. Now, during this challenge I face, I depend on You again.

I praise You, Lord, for how You help me stand firm, fully trusting in You, no matter what the circumstance. Nothing is impossible when I depend on You to work things out in Your timing and in the way You know best. Thank You for the spiritual triumphs You give me. They come only from You. When victories happen, keep my mind free from self-pride. When I face possible defeat, let it not darken my heart. With You, dear Lord, there is no such thing as defeat. You see the whole picture. You are triumphant. You are the victor over all.

Therefore, take up the full armor of God,
so that you will be able to resist in the evil day,
and having done everything, to stand firm.

EPHESIANS 6:13 NASB

Privilege of Praise

to Praise You

What can I give You, O Lord, that You have not already given to me? You have provided me with life, salvation, and countless generous blessings. The only thing I can offer You in return is my praise. So here I am, lifting my hands and my heart to You in adoration and thanksgiving.

Thank You, dear Lord, for granting me the privilege of praising You. How grateful and humbled I am that You allow me to come into Your presence. Thank You for welcoming me as Your own.

To You, dear Lord, I bring glory and honor. I love to praise Your holy name. You are my Most High God. You are above everything else You have created. You are my very existence, the theme of my life. You cause my life to be fully complete. You cause me to have a beginning that is wrapped up in You. You cause my life to have no end. I find fulfillment in You, life everlasting and free from sin's grip.

How glorious, how wonderful You are, O Lord. I lift my praise to You all the time. With my every breath I revere You. My soul rejoices in You. With my whole being, with all my might, I exalt Your holy name.

Bless the LORD, O my soul:
and all that is within me,
bless his holy name.
Bless the LORD, O my soul,
and forget not all his benefits.

PSALM 103:1–2 KJV

Autumn's Miracles

A mysterious weather pattern fills the air, Lord. One minute the sun is shining. It hurriedly attempts to ripen the last of the crops. The next minute, the wind rages, rowdily proclaiming the entrance of autumn. Rains follow, soaking the soil in preparation for winter's chill.

Birds prepare to fly south. Flocks gather on telephone wires and in trees. Overhead, V-shaped feathered families take off, calling encouragement to one another. Squirrels scurry here and there, gathering acorns and nuts from trees. The animals act differently. They swiftly begin seeking shelter. How do they know to do this, Lord? It must be through the instincts You put within them.

Frost nips at flowers and leaves. I can almost see their life-giving sap gradually working downward, preparing for dormancy. They yield to the changes. Their leaves turn dazzling colors of yellows, oranges, and browns.

"Get ready for winter's rest," You seem to be telling nature.

The days shorten. I want to go outdoors less often. Instead, I wish to stay within the walls of our comfortable home and enjoy a hot cup of soup or relaxing tea.

I look around, amazed. How do all these extraordinary events happen so perfectly? I wonder. What a marvelous autumn mystery. Thank You, Father. I praise You for it.

> *"Let us now fear the LORD our God,*
> *Who gives rain in its season,*
> *Both the autumn rain and the spring rain,*
> *Who keeps for us*
> *The appointed weeks of the harvest."*
>
> JEREMIAH 5:24 NASB

This Day

It's early morning, Father. Although it's still dark outside, my alarm shrills. Even before I hear its wake-up call, a song of praise to You revolves in my mind: *"Holy, holy, holy! Lord God Almighty! Early in the morning, my song shall rise to Thee."* I hit the snooze alarm and blink to focus my gaze on the clock. Ten more minutes. My groggy mind slowly acknowledges Your warm presence. I praise You for remaining with me through the night. My alarm sounds again. I get up and shuffle down the hall. I still hear the sweet refrain: *"Holy, holy, holy!"*

I finish preparing for work. Then I take a few treasured moments with You in my living room recliner. O God, thank You for being my God. I love to seek You during this early morning. Please lead me. Help me. Bless me throughout this day.

As I drive to work, I organize some of the day's events. Go before me, Father. Grant me wisdom and quick thinking. Guard my tongue against saying wrong things. Align my attitude to Your will.

My workday has ended, Father, and I'm driving home. Thank You for helping me. I praise You for how this day has belonged to You.

In the morning, O LORD,
You will hear my voice;
In the morning I will order my prayer to You
and eagerly watch.

PSALM 5:3 NASB

Evening Masterpiece

It's late afternoon, Father. I've finished running a few errands and am pulling into our driveway. I climb out of my car. I notice the trees in our yard are bright red from the reflection of the setting sun. I look toward the western horizon and gasp. I can barely take in the beauty.

Layered colors of pink, coral, blue, blue green, gray, and silver are filling the sky. I unlock the door, go inside, and sit by the window. I'm filled with wonder as this masterpiece You are creating before my eyes floats across the heavens like steady waves.

How can anything be so big and beautiful, Father? It's as though You are moving Your mighty hands from west to east, and the whole sky follows. I can almost hear You say, *"See, My child. This moving masterpiece is especially for you."*

The sun sinks behind the western hills. Everything turns dark, except for the streetlights. I lean back in my chair. I lift my heart in glory and honor to You, O Father God. Let my praise be lifted to You as a sweet incense. Thank You for being with me today. Thank You for these few moments of quiet that I can share with You. Praise You for Your glorious, breathtaking evening masterpiece.

> *Yours is the day, Yours also is the night;*
> *You have prepared the light and the sun.*
> *You have established all the boundaries of the earth.*

PSALM 74:16–17 NASB

Sing Praises

Here I am, Lord, at Your footstool, lifting my heart in songs of praise and thanksgiving. Day in and day out, no matter what time it is or where I am, I sing to You my adulation. How good it is to glorify Your holy name! How delightful it is to acknowledge You in Your sacred presence. I sing out my thanks to You, O Lord God. Here I give You my all.

How marvelous You are. When I think of the wonders You have shown me, I cannot count them all. Because of who You are, my soul fills with gladness. I sing praises to You, the Most High.

Although I'm alone right now and my voice holds little talent, I want my praises to sound like a grand choir, with harps and violins and drums and cymbals. See my heart, my love for You, O Lord? Take delight, I pray, in my sacrifice of praise.

I pay tribute to You. From my rising in the morning, to my working through the day, to my resting at night, I sing praises. Some songs may be at the top of my voice. Others, I hum continually in my heart and mind. To You, Lord God, I sing praise.

Oh, sing to the LORD a new song!
Sing to the LORD, all the earth.
Sing to the LORD, bless His name.

PSALM 96:1–2 NKJV

NOVEMBER 6

Your Church

This is the day of worship, Father. I look around and praise You for Your thriving church, this body of believers. It baffles me to consider the way Your church goes beyond these walls, this city's borders, even this country. I praise You for believers who are a part of Your church around the world. I realize culture, color, male or female, money or status matter nothing to You. Neither do doctrines or creeds. We are all Your children when we trust and obey You.

Thank You for making us different parts of Your church body. We each have our own abilities and personalities, our own strengths and weaknesses. Yet You still love us, and we are important to You.

Praise You, Father, for building Your church on a strong foundation—the foundation of Your Son, Jesus Christ. We face times of struggle, but we are constantly growing. Every day new baby Christians are born into Your family. Many of those who love You are thrilled about what You are doing in their lives.

As Your Spirit moves among us, we experience Your cleansing power. Old selfishness and hatred fall away and are replaced by harmony and love for You and one another.

How grateful I am to be a part of Your family, Your church.

> *We who believe are carefully joined together*
> *with Christ as parts of a beautiful,*
> *constantly growing temple for God.*

> EPHESIANS 2:21 TLB

Your Word

Thank You, Father God, for Your sure, true Word—Your Bible. When I read Your words and apply them to my heart and mind, I have complete confidence in You. Fears and doubts shatter, exposing the real truths—truths of Your love and faithfulness.

It is You I believe and trust. It is You who safely guards me. Everything I have, all my goals and dreams, I commit to You. My past, my present, and my future are in Your hands. I praise You that through the promises of Your Word, nothing can ever separate me from Your love. During good or fearful times, whether I'm here at home or far away overseas, You are with me every single minute.

Thank You for guiding me each day through Your Word. Thank You that I can tuck away Your lessons in my mind. When I'm confronted with temptations and trials, all I need to do is remember one of Your promises, and the devil flees. Your decrees are my greatest weapon against wrong. They are sharper than a two-edged sword.

How I praise You, Father God, for using Your Word to teach me. Thank You for anointing Your Word with Your Spirit for comforting and encouraging me as I walk with You.

For the word of the LORD is right and true;
he is faithful in all he does.

PSALM 33:4 NIV

For Carrying Me

When the things of this world crushed in and caused me to crumble, You carried me, Father. When I poured out my troubles to others and could find no one to really understand, You carried me. When I faltered and lost my way and struggled to put one foot in front of the other, You were the One who carried me.

Now I know not to lean on my own abilities. Although my friends and loved ones are dear, You are the One I can completely depend upon. I no longer try to be strong, for my strength lies in You. Thank You, dear Lord, for stooping down, picking me up in Your loving arms, and carrying me.

Thank You for helping me never to give up. No matter the circumstances, I praise You for being with me and showing me the way. When I'm unable to see around the next bend and wonder if there really is light at the end of the tunnel, Your light leads the way. I praise You, Father, for still carrying me.

Someday these troubles and trials will be over. I look forward to the day when You carry me once more to be with You in heaven. In the meantime, Father, I'll keep trusting, serving, and leaning on You.

> *[God said,] "I am with you;*
> *that is all you need.*
> *My power shows up best in weak people."*

2 CORINTHIANS 12:9 TLB

Praise You for Hope

I praise You, O Lord, for giving me hope. When I was lost and had no way to turn, You saved me. You turned my life around and gave me a positive anticipation for the future. You gave me hope not only for the future here on this earth, but for the future into eternity.

I seek Your wise guidance, Lord. Let my mouth praise You. Let me honor You with everything I do. Through You I experience a spiritually rich life filled with enthusiasm and joy. As I synchronize my walk with Yours, I know I can't lose. You, dear Lord, are my desire, my existence, my entire being.

Some say You don't care about Your children. But I know that isn't true. You cause Your favor and love to shine upon me—not only upon me, but on all who love and serve You.

I praise You for being my tower of refuge, my place of safety when things go wrong. How grateful I am for the way You bring me through countless challenges and bless me beyond measure. You have a way of weaving Your blessing of calm assurance in and out of everything in my life. Hope in You proved true yesterday. Hope in You still abides today. And Your certain hope shall remain tomorrow.

Thank You, Lord. How I praise Your name!

May your unfailing love rest upon us, O LORD,
even as we put our hope in you.

PSALM 33:22 NIV

Your Holy Ways

Holy are Your ways, Lord Jesus. Pure and faultless are You! Nothing in heaven or on earth can compare to You. No one can measure up to Your purity. The sun, the moon, and the stars are only inanimate objects and a part of Your creation. They can't begin to compare to You. What of humankind with our faults and frailties? In no way do we measure up to Your hallowed righteousness.

You set a perfect example when You lived here on earth. You were tempted. You were misunderstood and mistreated. You faced stress far greater than I can imagine. You were bruised and afflicted. Through all of this, Jesus, You never wavered in Your purity and obedience to Your Father. You were true and faithful, even during Your last moments on the cross.

How can I be holy, Lord? My heart longs to be like You. Lead me along the right paths, I pray. Share Your holiness with me. Fill and surround me with Your sweet presence. Teach me to walk in the footprints of Your righteousness, dear Lord. Let my heart be united with Yours. Grant me the power to overcome evil with good and reflect Your holy ways.

Teach me Your way, O LORD;
I will walk in Your truth;
Unite my heart to fear Your name.
I will give thanks to You,
O Lord my God, with all my heart,
And will glorify Your name forever.

PSALM 86:11–12 NASB

Your Faithfulness

Words ring out through history, telling of the veterans who faithfully fought for freedom. Along with those in the armed forces, we find police officers, firefighters, and even volunteers helping make our country and world a better place in which to live. Many have died while serving. Some carry scars—both inside and out—from the conflicts they have endured. Thank You, Father, for those who sacrificed themselves so we can be free.

When we hear bad news about war situations, we cringe and wait—hoping and praying for those we know who are in the line of battle. Father, please help change hearts and provide peace. Thank You for our leaders. May their hearts be pliable to Your will and their decisions be wise.

There are other kinds of soldiers I praise You for, Father. They are veteran Christian soldiers, who daily put on Your armor and steadfastly endeavor to win souls for You. Few are famous. Yet many of these men and women and boys and girls carry Your banner high, bringing hope and freedom to the hearts of those who don't yet know You.

Praise You, Father, for steadfastly loving every one of us, no matter who we are, where we live in the world, or what we have done. Thank You for continually calling to every lost soul.

O Jehovah, Commander of the heavenly armies,
where is there any other Mighty One like you?
Faithfulness is your very character.

PSALM 89:8 TLB

NOVEMBER 12

A Sweet Fragrance

Lord God, I come to You with my heart and hands lifted in praise to Your holy name. Hear me as I call to You. Guard my mind, my intent, and my mouth as I come to You in prayer. May the words of my mouth and the most inner parts of my heart bring praises as a pure, sweet fragrance to You, O God.

I want to glorify Your name throughout my day, from the rising of the sun in the morning to its setting at day's end. When I awaken, You hear my praises. I sense Your glorious presence. I ask that every word I speak be lifted to You. Oh, I praise You with all my being. You feed and satisfy my soul all day long.

When my head sinks to my pillow at night, I think of You. I lift sweet fragrances of praise and thanksgiving to You again for Your wondrous help and guidance. Uplifting songs of adoration flow through my mind. I nestle in the shadow of Your wings. My soul clings to You while You hold me with Your right hand. I fall asleep, knowing Your warm comfort and protection. How dear, how sweet You are, my God.

My voice You shall hear in the morning, O LORD. . . .
Let my prayer be set before You as incense,
The lifting up of my hands as the evening sacrifice.

PSALMS 5:3; 141:2 NKJV

Your Kindness

How I praise You, dear Lord, for loving me and constantly being so kind. Thank You for calling me by name. Thank You for making me Your own. Along with giving me Your love, You assure me in Your Bible that I am precious in Your sight.

Thank You for being patient with me and for giving me a chance to start over again and again. I never cease to be amazed by the way Your tenderhearted caring meets my needs. Your love, dear Lord, is so faithful. When I mess up, You still urge me to try again, and You assure me of Your help and encouragement. Thank You for being kind enough to look for the best in me.

There is no one as totally understanding and kind as You. I praise You for always listening to me, whether I'm happy or sad. Thank You for rejoicing with me over the good things in my life. How grateful I am for Your comfort and strength during times of adversity and discouragement— for helping me when I'm faced with temptations.

Praise You, Lord. Your love and kindness are with me forever. Your compassion continues all the days of my life and into eternity.

Oh, give thanks to the Lord, for he is good;
his lovingkindness continues forever.

PSALM 136:1 TLB

NOVEMBER 14

My Advocate

Fresh memories come to me about the times my children brushed against the threshold between life and death, Lord Jesus. At times I bolted from a sound sleep and felt Your warning of something about to happen—and Your assurance that You would be with us. Often when I prayed, I felt as though I rattled the gates of heaven, pleading on their behalf.

I'm amazed that I knew some things would happen. Was it because I love and identify with my children so closely? Or was it because I'm close to You? I just know I praise You for allowing me to be their advocate. When I became so fearful that I ran out of words to pray, You, Lord Jesus, became my Advocate and carried my urgent prayers to the heavenly Father.

Praise You, Lord, for dying for my sins and becoming my defense before our Father in heaven. Because You love me, I can come directly to Your throne of grace and ask for Your help. Then in accordance with what You perceive is best, You bring my needs to the Father. Thank You also for speaking to the hearts of others on my behalf. As I trust in You, my joy is complete. Praise You for being my Advocate.

In the same way,
the Spirit helps us in our weakness.
We do not know what we ought to pray for,
but the Spirit himself intercedes for us
with groans that words cannot express.

ROMANS 8:26 NIV

My Heritage

How can I comprehend Your adopting me as Your child, Father? There is no way. Still, I can completely trust You and the promises in Your Bible. Thank You for giving me Your marvelous heritage—one filled with peace of heart, deep inner joy, and a certain hope for the future You have planned for me.

Praise You for being my beloved Father and giving me Your Son, Jesus. You are my all in all. You are the strength of my heart. In You I have a fulfilling life here on earth and eternal life awaiting me with You in heaven.

Thank You for safely guarding everything I give You until the day of Your return. You love and care for me like a devoted parent. No matter where I am, I'm grateful You are only a prayer away. Thank You for being more than near. Thank You for living within my heart.

I'm grateful that I can place my identity in You. I've taken on the name of Your Son, Jesus Christ. I'm a follower of Christ. Yes, Father, thanks to You, I'm a Christian. I count it a privilege of being Your child—a child of the King of Kings! Thank You for giving me the greatest heritage ever, a heritage in You.

Yet to all who received him,
to those who believed in his name,
he gave the right to become children of God—
children born not of natural descent,
nor of human decision or a husband's will,
but born of God.

JOHN 1:12–13 NIV

NOVEMBER 16

My Buffer

I hear of many heroes who have been hurt or killed while snatching children or adults from harm's way. Some heroes carry scars from their courageous actions for the rest of their lives. Often the rescuers have been family members. However, others gave of themselves for total strangers.

Is that the way it was when You died to save me? Is that the way it is now, when You are my constant buffer against the dangers I face each day? Thank You for being my safeguard and defense, for cushioning the blows of life that come my way.

When I'm in need, I shall not worry, for You are looking after me. When I'm overwhelmed and desperate, You absorb the shocks and help me to find peace and rest. How I praise You for being my protector, my sentinel, my arbitrator. You are my refuge, the firm Rock I can cling to in life's storms. You are a shadow in the stifling hot deserts of my life.

No matter what comes my way, I will praise You for faithfully going before me and helping me overcome the obstacles in my path. No matter what happens, I know You are in charge. Thank You for being my buffer. I praise You, O God, with all my heart.

> *For who is God except our Lord?*
> *Who but he is as a rock?*
> *He fills me with strength and*
> *protects me wherever I go.*
>
> PSALM 18:31–32 TLB

Stepping-Stones of Courage

When I read in the book of Genesis about the way Joseph's brothers threw him into a deadly pit, I thought of how frightened he must have been. I'm thankful for Your helping him and giving him courage. Although Joseph was pulled from the pit, it didn't solve his problems. You helped and guided him during the following difficult years. Thank You for being with him and for his faithfulness to You. No one had the power to break Joseph. During his years in bondage, You gave him countless blessings. When he was falsely accused, You gave him honor. You helped him step over the stones of cruelty and stand firmly on a foundation of compassion and love.

When I was in the pit of despair, Lord, I felt like I was being buried under trials. Like huge rocks, my troubles piled up around me. Hurts and hopelessness were breaking my heart. The only way I could see was up. When I looked up, You were there.

I praise You for showing me how to take those terrible boulders and change them into stepping-stones toward victory. Each time I took a step, I could sense Your holding my hand, steadying me and giving me courage.

Thank You, Lord, for providing me stepping-stones of courage so I could experience numerous victories in You!

The steps of a good man are ordered by the LORD,
And He delights in his way.
Though he fall, he shall not be utterly cast down;
For the LORD upholds him with His hand.

PSALM 37:23–24 NKJV

NOVEMBER 18

Your Assurance

When I gave my heart to You, Lord, You established a never-ending covenant with me. You promised to be with me all the days of my life and into eternity. That step of faith I took—choosing life with You over spiritual death and destruction—released Your power to make me pure in the sight of God, my Father. I praise You, O Lord, for the assurance that You are my Lord and my Savior. Because of Your loving assurance, I know in whom I believe. I'm convinced, without a doubt, that You are totally able to keep everything I commit to You. Everything I place in Your hands is safely guarded and protected by Your unfailing love.

Thank You for Your abiding presence day and night. Praise You for Your promise that You will never leave me or abandon me. No one or no thing can keep Your love from me. Absolutely nothing has enough power to separate me from Your love. Not hardship or famine, not sickness or danger. Neither will life nor death. Evil cannot. Certainly the angels will not. Nor will the past, the present, or the future. Thank You, my Lord, for Your constant assurance and abiding love. Thank You for being with me all the days of my life.

> *For I know whom I have believed*
> *and am persuaded that He is able to keep*
> *what I have committed to Him until that Day.*

> 2 TIMOTHY 1:12 NKJV

The Treadmill

Good morning, Lord. It's six o'clock and time to get on the treadmill—not the one I step on in our garage, but the treadmill of life. Thank You for it and for the good that comes from walking on it each day.

I praise You for giving me the health and ability to get up each morning, have some quiet time with You, then scurry through a few housekeeping duties. Thank You for giving me the opportunity to make phone calls or write letters to those I care about. I praise You for the car You provide so I can get to work.

I pull into the parking lot and walk toward my job. How grateful I am to work here. I refuse to think I'm going back to what some folks call "the old grind," but eagerly look forward to laboring with my boss and coworkers. Thank You for the way You urge me to put pride in my work and to do so wholeheartedly. When I do, I'm also serving You. Thank You for showing me some fruits of my labor and blessing me with a feeling of a job well done.

I'm grateful for this treadmill of life, Lord. Praise You for guiding my steps and helping go in the way You lead me.

May the favor of the Lord our God rest upon us;
establish the work of our hands for us—
yes, establish the work of our hands.

PSALM 90:17 NIV

Rest

My day of work is ended, Lord. My body and mind are weary. After dinner, my husband and I share the good and bad events of the day. We pray together for situations and people. Then we purposefully leave our worries in Your hands and relax. We settle in our chairs with good books. Once in a while my beloved reaches over and takes hold of my hand. Thank You for my husband. Thank You for rest.

When it's time to sleep, we pray again, asking God to bless our loved ones, to keep watch over our thoughts, and to give us a good night's rest. Though heaven's ebony shroud hovers outside, we feel Your protecting presence. You gather us to You as a hen collects her chicks beneath her wings. There is no fear of night, for You are always near.

My head sinks into my soft pillow. Quiet breathing comes from my loved one at my side. The window is open a crack. I can hear refreshing rain falling. The air smells clear and clean. The tree next to our house lazily swishes its boughs in rhythmic song. An unusual soft twitter comes from winter birds in the tree's branches.

"This is the day the Lord has made," I replay in my mind. *"I will rejoice and be glad in it."*

Thank You, Lord, for rest.

I will lie down and sleep in peace,
for you alone, O LORD,
make me dwell in safety.

PSALM 4:8 NIV

The Way You Listen

Here I am, Lord, taking this block of time to just talk with You. There is so much I want to share. I realize You know everything, but it means a lot for me to pour my heart out to You. I love telling about the good, the bad, and even the funny things happening in my life.

I appreciate the way You hear my prayers. I'm grateful when the answers come. I want to talk to You with inward and outgoing breaths. I praise You for how You bend down and pay heed.

No matter how I feel or what's happening in my life, You listen. No matter what the circumstances, I still give my praise to You. You don't laugh at me. Instead, You understand exactly how I feel. Praise You, O God, for being here with me. Praise Your holy name for caring about everything in my life, no matter how big or small. When I pray, You encourage me and give me the vitality I need. Praise You for being my dearest Friend.

When I'm out of words, I still feel Your presence. Thank You, Lord, for listening. Now it's time for me to stop talking and hear You.

I love the LORD, because He hears
My voice and my supplications.
Because He has inclined His ear to me,
Therefore I shall call upon Him as long as I live.

PSALM 116:1–2 NASB

Your Friendship

How blessed I am, Lord Jesus, to have good friends. They warm my heart with a phone call or letter. Thank You for their encouragement. Thank You that I can be a good friend to them.

Even though they are valued, Lord, You are the dearest Friend of all. Thank You for always being with me. Unlike Old Testament times when common people weren't allowed to enter the Holy of Holies, I can now walk and talk with You anytime, anywhere.

Thank You for loving me, Lord. Whenever I pray, I feel Your warm presence surround me. I praise You for how Your Holy Spirit fills my heart and restores my soul. Because You call me friend, I give You my friendship in return. I give You my whole self, completely trusting in Your love. My body has become the home of Your Holy Spirit. Through this, I am joined with You, and we are one.

In the same way You know me so well, I want to know You. I want to recognize what pleases You in everything I think, do, and say. I want to praise You by being the kind of friend who gives You joy. Thank You, Lord, for Your friendship.

Mary sat on the floor,
listening to Jesus as he talked. . . .
[Jesus said,] "There is really only one thing
worth being concerned about.
Mary has discovered it—
and I won't take it away from her!"

LUKE 10:39, 42 TLB

Abundant Life

Because You are my Lord, my life is filled with joy and fulfillment. How blessed I am for putting my trust in You. To You, O Lord, I lift my praise with all my heart. In all my ways, I want to bless Your holy name.

Thank You for choosing me to become Your child. I praise You for looking for the best in me, for giving me certain talents. Thank You for handpicking what You want for me and helping me realize ways I can serve You. Praise You, Lord, for filling my life with purpose. Because of Your love for me, I have a reason to be here—a reason to love and serve You with all my strength and might.

I don't want to waste my life making material things my first love. Instead, I want to spend my life loving and trusting You. In You, Lord, I grow and thrive and have my motivation for living. It's an exciting life that's driven by Your divine will. It's a life of joy, everlasting and free from sin.

I praise You for the glorious plans You have for me. Your plans fill me with anticipation and hope. Thank You for putting me here to serve You, now and forever. Praise You, Lord, for coming to this earth and giving me abundant life.

[Jesus said,] "I have come that they may have life, and that they may have it more abundantly."

JOHN 10:10 NKJV

NOVEMBER 24

Restoration

My soul offers praise to You, O God, for how many times You have wrapped Your healing arms around me and restored me to wellness. I can't count the number of days of illness, heartbreak, and mental and emotional despair I've experienced. I occasionally wondered if there was any way back to recovery. Some sicknesses were so overwhelming I couldn't see the light at the end of the tunnel—only impossibilities. Yet deep within my heart, I knew all things were possible when I turned my needs for restoration over to You to work out in Your own way.

Several struggles with illness were severe enough to where I couldn't let them go. Whenever this happened, You helped me realize I was claiming sickness as a part of me. Little by little, You taught me how to let it go and quit nursing my injured being. When I learned to allow You as my Great Physician to take these things away and renew me, I was on my way toward being healed.

Thank You for comforting me. Because of Your love, You bound up my brokenness and gave me strength to overcome all that I went through. I praise You for the way You took my damaged body, mind, and spirit and restored me to wholeness in You.

He heals the brokenhearted
and binds up their wounds.

PSALM 147:3 NIV

My Family

Father, I come to You in thanksgiving and praise this morning for the wonderful family You have given me. Tantalizing aromas fill our home from pies I pulled from the oven. I just finished making the fruit salad. (The recipe was passed down from my mother-in-law.) As usual, it will be enjoyed by the whole family. As I pack everything for traveling, my heart is warmed by the love these dear ones share for each other.

This year, we will pick up my dad and travel over the mountain pass to our son and daughter-in-law's home, where lively grandchildren await us. I've been counting the days, Father. Thank You for making this possible. We will sit around the table, enjoying love-filled conversations and watching children who are like willowy, sprouting trees. Thank You for phone lines buzzing with calls between those of us who can't be together because of distance.

I praise You for Your mercy, which continues from one generation to the next, to every family member who loves You. Great is Your kindness toward those I love. How grateful I am for Your storing up vast blessings for them. Thank You, Father, for enveloping my loved ones in the protection of Your presence and keeping them safe in the hollow of Your mighty hand.

"His mercy goes on from generation to generation, to all who reverence him."

LUKE 1:50 TLB

NOVEMBER 26

Your Provisions

What a pleasant evening we enjoyed tonight, Father. We had friends over for dinner. I set a pretty table with a candle in the center. The meal was simple, but we all enjoyed it. Thank You for Your provisions.

When we settled in the living room with cups of tea after dinner, our friends said something I shall never forget. They mentioned how they felt at home because our house radiates Your love. I can't imagine anything that matters more to me than this.

Everyone has gone home now. My husband and I relax in our chairs, aligned side by side. I glance around at our furniture and other belongings. Most are simple. We received some as gifts. Our children made some priceless treasures. Others have been handed down through generations. They all tell a story of Your generosity and care.

Thank You, Father, for keeping us warm, dry, and safe. Thank You for the comfort of my simple recliner, for my cozy slippers—given to me by my friend. Thank You for my soft, warm lap robe—a gift from one of our sons. Each time I use these simple things, I think of my friends and loved ones. Praise You for Your warm love that wraps around us and for Your provisions in our home.

> *Trust in the LORD, and do good;*
> *Dwell in the land,*
> *and feed on His faithfulness.*

> PSALM 37:3 NKJV

Childlike Faith

Thank You for children—my grandchildren, the youngsters I teach in church, and my students at school. I love their openness. I enjoy their unhampered ability to show love. I praise You for giving me the wisdom and strength to teach them. The greatest lesson these children lay on my heart is the way they trust me completely. The trust shown in their eyes and their warm hugs are a constant reminder.

Thank You for repeatedly proving Yourself faithful to me, for building up my confidence in Your love and care. I know You are always here for me, Father. I trust that You will never abandon or deceive me. You are my heavenly Father. You are One I can totally rely on.

I praise You for my childlike faith in You. It isn't a faith I have to conjure up. Instead, it's something You have given me. The more You are in my life, Father, the more my love and trust in You grows. As we draw closer, my childlike faith flourishes in joy and assurance. When things are difficult and I don't understand why they are happening, I can draw from this faith You give me and trust in You. Thank You, Father, for this faithfulness—a gift of faith, full of Your endless love and care.

[Jesus said,] "Whoever humbles himself like this child, he is the greatest in the kingdom of heaven."

MATTHEW 18:4 RSV

NOVEMBER 28

Making Life Count

I praise You, Lord, for showing me I'm not here by chance. I'm here because You want me, and I really matter to You. Thank You for making my life count. You give me direction and purpose. You help me visualize Your reasons for putting me here. You provide me with dreams for my future—a future in which Your will and mine are carefully knit together as one. It doesn't matter whether I'm eight years old, eighteen, or eighty. Through the stages of my life, You call me to do special things for You. What an adventure it is—going through each day together!

The things You accomplish go far beyond my imagination. Through Your life-giving power working within me, little things I do will ripple out to others and down through generations. What You accomplish through me affects lives for eternity.

Someday when age causes me to slow down, I pray for You to help me look beyond bitterness and disappointments and think on how You have made my life count. Let me always see the big picture of Your purpose and savor memories of dear ones brought into Your family. Keep my mind and heart steadfastly fixed on You, my eternal Rock. In all circumstances I trust in You, Lord. Thank You for giving me a life that really counts.

The LORD will accomplish what concerns me;
Your lovingkindness, O LORD, is everlasting.

PSALM 138:8 NASB

Victory in You

Thank You for the hope and confidence You place within me, Lord. Thank You for helping me shed the life of being a victim. You are the One who makes me a victor. Because I trust in You, I gain Your wisdom to make right decisions that are within Your will and are best for me.

I praise You that I need not worry about anything. Instead, I pray about what comes my way and seek Your direction. I trust You, Lord, to work things out for the best.

I praise You for helping me with daily decisions. When I'm confused and don't know how to pray, You are near, beseeching Your Father for me. Oh, You understand me so well.

As I seek Your will and walk in Your ways, I'm grateful that You go with me and give me triumph. Thank You for helping me to be stalwart and courageous in times of difficulty. With You by my side, I can overcome fear, trusting You to banish it. Should it return, I know You will remove it again.

This victorious life doesn't come from weak efforts on my part. Instead, I praise *You* for being the conqueror over wrong and for providing me with victory.

[Jesus said,] "I have told you these things,
so that in me you may have peace.
In this world you will have trouble.
But take heart! I have overcome the world."

JOHN 16:33 NIV

NOVEMBER 30

A Small Sample of Heaven

It was a time when there were no distractions, no ill feelings for anyone, no bad attitudes. It was a time when we, a group of people, united in fervent prayer. We felt stronger than the three-stranded cord mentioned in Ecclesiastes. We were a united body praising, praying, experiencing Your honorable presence in our midst. It was more than a regular prayer time, dear Lord. It was a time when not one ounce of sin could enter our midst. It was a small sample of heaven.

We lifted our hearts to You in praise and petition—not for our needs, but for the salvation and the needs of those we love. Someone could have dropped a coin, and it would have been heard. Different ones prayed. One by one, first names only were voiced all around the room and brought to Your heavenly throne.

The air was so thick with Your holy presence, I felt as though I could have reached out and grabbed hold of it with my hands. Yet I was too awed to stir.

You were there in our prayer group, O Lord. We communed with You, our Almighty God, our Savior, our Holy Spirit, our King of Kings, our Lord of Lords. How I praise You for Your small sample of heaven.

Praise the LORD, O my soul.
O LORD my God, you are very great;
you are clothed with splendor and majesty.

PSALM 104:1 NIV

to Worship You

The Beginning and the End

If You were to roll out the scroll of time before me—the past, the present, the future, eternity—I wouldn't be able to take it in. If You showed me the secrets You revealed to John about heaven and time without end, I still could not comprehend them. How measureless, how everlasting You are, O God.

I bow down and worship You, the Alpha and the Omega, the Beginning and the End. You were, before all else began. You were in the beginning, You are with me now, and forever You shall be. You, O God, are the primary cause of everything. You are head over all, in and through all.

You set up the heavens and shaped the great rivers and the deep parts of the seas. You established the confines of the waters, instructing them to remain within their boundaries.

I worship You, O God, O Three in One. You were here as my Father, forming the plan for my life. Born a baby, You sacrificed Yourself for my sins. You became my Savior and my King. You are here as my Comforter, always with me.

O God, Alpha and Omega, the Beginning and the End, how I worship You.

"I am the Alpha and the Omega,
the Beginning and the End," says the Lord,
"who is and who was and who is to come, the Almighty."

REVELATION 1:8 NKJV

DECEMBER 2

The Word

I bring honor to You, my God. You are Logos, the Word. You are the very existence of wisdom and power. Through the Word, I am learning to understand how wonderful and marvelous You are. Through the powerful Word, You came into my life and changed me.

Even before the world was, the Word was with God. You, the Word, *are* God. Through You, life was given. You are the light of life that shines brightly into the darkest corners. In Your mighty wisdom and power, You embarked on a course driven with purpose, down through the ages, to come to earth.

How grateful I am for the way You humbled Yourself and became a little human baby, born of a virgin, cradled in a straw-filled manger. It is through this that humankind was able to see Your glory. You are the magnificent one and only God, who came from the Father, filled with truth and grace.

How can such a thing be possible? I only know it is true, because the Bible says so and You live within my heart. Thank You for providing me with a new life in You.

Glory be to You, God, the living Word who dwells among us.

> *In the beginning was the Word,*
> *and the Word was with God,*
> *and the Word was God.*
> *He was in the beginning with God.*

JOHN 1:1–2 NASB

Strong Creator

Glory, laud, and honor I bring to You, my strong Creator, for You made the heavens, the earth, the oceans, and all that is in them. So marvelous is Your craftsmanship, even creation itself tells of Your magnificence. You spoke a righteous command, and outer space was fashioned. Countless stars fell into place at Your command. You made the waters and caused them to pour into immense rivers and lakes. You spoke again and set the world into motion.

I look at this vast creation and how glorious it is. It's nothing compared to You, the Lord of all creation. What of humankind? We are only a fleck of dust.

You pick up a desert island like a feather and reposition it from one place to another. You restrain the oceans with Your capable hands. You measure the universe. You weigh the mountains.

Every time I look into the darkened skies and see the work of Your fingers, I'm filled with wonder. I am amazed at how You made the moon and countless stars. I'm dumbfounded by Your love and care for a mere person like me.

I praise and honor You, God, for creating all of this, and for creating me.

When I consider Your heavens,
the work of Your fingers,
The moon and the stars,
which You have ordained,
What is man that You are mindful of him,
And the son of man that You visit him?

PSALM 8:3–4 NKJV

Righteous God

Here, I come before You on bended knee, O righteous God. Holy, holy, holy are You, God Almighty. How pure and honorable You are. Your presence surrounds me to the point I feel I'm on holy ground and should remove my shoes. Every day I see Your just dealings as You help me make right choices. You fill my heart with security and love because I can completely depend on Your holiness. Even the heavens can't compare to Your devout ways. There is no one like You, Most Holy God.

Who else do I have in heaven but You? No one matters more to me. You are the certainty I can look to, O God. When I'm faced with temptation, You provide the power I need to live victoriously. When I stand before You, the deeds I consider righteous will be only like filthy rags, for I am not just and good on my own. You washed everything in my life and made me clean. Because of Your love for me, You have forgiven my sins and clothed me with the attire of Your salvation. You have draped Your cloak of righteousness over my shoulders.

I praise and thank You for being my righteous God forever and forever.

> *"And there is no God apart from me,*
> *a righteous God and a Savior;*
> *there is none but me."*
>
> ISAIAH 45:21 NIV

Daddy

The time has finally come when I have a chance to talk with You, my Lord. I steal away to my quiet spot to worship You with my love and praise. Your tender presence surrounds me like a warm, comforting blanket. You're not far away on some pedestal. You are here with me, right now.

I worship You, my Abba Father. Abba means "Daddy." How true it is. You are my heavenly Daddy. You are like a caring father; I can talk with You for hours, and You never tire of listening. You are tender and sympathetic each time I come to You in prayer.

Your loving care for me is endless. Your watchfulness begins anew each day. I will never forget the mercy and grace You bestow upon me. You give me food. You always keep Your promises. When I start to waver, You remain near and keep me from stumbling. You watch over me all night long while I sleep. You spread Your wings over me like an eagle does over her young. You know me so well— inside and out. You understand my strengths and weaknesses, my concerns, my wants and dreams.

I lift my hands in praise and give tribute to You, my dear Daddy God. Thank You for loving and caring for me.

For you did not receive the spirit of bondage again to fear,
but you received the Spirit of adoption
by whom we cry out, "Abba, Father."

ROMANS 8:15 NKJV

DECEMBER 6

Merciful and Gracious God

I come before You filled with adoration, Jehovah Elohim, my merciful God. I can only begin to thank You for Your kindness and mercy. You are gentle, patient, slow to become angry. The love You show to every person lasts beyond any measure of time. Amazingly, no matter if we deserve it or not, You keep loving us and desperately want all of us to know You as Savior and Lord.

Thank You for forgiving my sins and demonstrating Your steadfast love. Because of Your tenderhearted compassion, I am grateful to You and will honor You in every area of my life.

I offer my thanks to You, my God, for Your goodness, for Your mercy and graciousness that will remain with me forever. I give You my will, because You have given me a new life, and Your mercy and graciousness remain with me forever. I will follow You all the days of my life because of the mighty wonders You show me. In all things, I will trust You and not be afraid, because You keep and protect me with Your outstretched arms.

How I adore You, my Jehovah Elohim, my merciful, gracious God!

> *"Praise the LORD of hosts,*
> *For the LORD is good,*
> *For His mercy endures forever."*

JEREMIAH 33:11 NKJV

Provider

My God, my Provider, I hold You in highest regard for all You do to care for me. I bring my needs to You and trust You with them. No matter what I face, it's never too difficult for You to handle.

I am so glad to be Your child. You provide for me. You have an amazing way of knowing what I require even before I do! I possess nothing in myself. In You, Jehovah Jireh, I benefit from everything. In light of the miracles I have experienced during my walk with You, I lift my heart in worship. My help truly does come from You.

You are constantly watching over me. In famine You feed me. In sickness You restore my strength. Somehow You supply my needs. Your blessings come directly from Your riches in heaven to me, Your child. Thank You for Your promise that You will never leave me nor forsake me. When I consider the way You are the strength of my life and how You shield me from danger, I am filled with gratitude. I trust in You, and You help me. As a result of Your love, a new joy bubbles within my soul.

Thank You for being Jehovah Jireh, my Provider.

Blessed is he whose help is the God of Jacob,
whose hope is in the LORD his God.

PSALM 146:5 NIV

DECEMBER 8

Wonderful

How can I thank You enough for being my wonderful Lord? Deep gratitude fills me when I think of how You set salvation's plan into motion before time began. You knew we would fall into hopeless, sinful lifestyles. Sadness, self-destruction, and despair resulted from evil's snare. Yet You still loved us and followed through with Your plan. Prophets, kings, and great leaders came and went through the ages. Then You came to earth and dwelt among us.

What a wonderful way You stepped from eternity into time. You were born of a virgin, took on humility and self-denial, and became one of us. Only then could we better understand and follow Your example. You became our Teacher and Savior. You conquered evil by dying, rising from the grave, and ascending into heaven. What wonderful love You showed by sacrificing Yourself for this world. Your holy and righteous ways caused You to stand alone, shatter sin's hold, and free humankind from despair.

You, dear God, are separate, distinguished greater than anyone else. You are exalted above creation. You are magnificent! Your glory goes beyond compare. I can't begin to imagine Your infinite power.

I worship You. I love and adore You, my wonderful Lord.

And His name will be called Wonderful.

ISAIAH 9:6 NASB

Counselor

Once again I come to You, and we work through tough problems together. Here at Your feet I seek Your guidance and find wise answers. Thank You for being my Counselor, my Guide. Your words are filled with wisdom. You give me good advice and common sense. Your teaching lights the course ahead of me. As I heed Your instructions and obey, You keep me from stumbling.

How wise and all-knowing You are, my God. Without Your help, I don't always make right choices. You perceive things far beyond my abilities, and I trust You to guide me in everything I say and do. It's becoming easier to put You first. I experience Your peace and joy. Each time I listen and obey, I thank You for crowning my efforts with success.

I don't have the insight to plan what course in life I should take. When I become anxious and get ahead of You, I praise You for whispering to me, *"Go this way. Follow where I lead."*

I worship You, my God, my Counselor. I commit my endeavors to You. I honor and trust You, even when I don't understand why things are happening the way they are.

Thank You for guiding me through my whole life. Thank You for being my Counselor.

[Jesus said,] "And I will ask the Father,
and he will give you another Counselor
to be with you forever—the Spirit of truth."

JOHN 14:16–17 NIV

DECEMBER 10

Mighty God

Praise and honor be to You, O Mighty God, for doing great and marvelous things for me. No one is as strong and powerful as You. You are awesome—filled with splendor and wonder. Your miracles have no boundaries. Your abilities are unlimited. Let everyone who comes into Your presence acknowledge Your greatness. Your magnitude goes beyond measure. You alone are holy. To You I bring glory and honor and praise.

Praise You, O Mighty God and Strong Warrior, for giving me victories each day. Thank You for Your mighty arms that reach out and protect me. You are in all and over all. As You march before me in Your greatness and strength, I shall not fear. Each day I place my confidence in You while You keep me safely in Your care.

Glory be to You, O God, for how Your almighty power works Your purpose for one such as I. How grateful I am that You do far greater things in my life than I ever envisioned. Your love and help go way ahead of my prayers, my needs, my thinking, or my expectations. To You I give glory forever.

Trials and heartaches happen. Wrongs appear to prevail. Yet through it all I know You, my Mighty God, are in charge. Praise You! You are the victor now and through eternity.

> *Great is our Lord, and mighty in power;*
> *His understanding is infinite.*

PSALM 147:5 NKJV

Everlasting Father

Hear my words of worship, O God, my Everlasting Father. You and You alone are my Father God. There is no other before You. You are everything to me. May all I say and think and do glorify You. Let me be joined to Your ways, that we may be one.

You are all-encompassing. You have always been here and forever shall be. I praise You for being my Father now and my Father of all time. Your years shall never cease.

Thank You for never changing. Circumstances and people change, but You remain steadfast and sure. Praise You, Everlasting Father, for being the same yesterday, today, and forever. I can depend on You and Your promises. Your Bible says You never go back on Your word. You are trustworthy. You are Truth. Your love and compassion never end.

Praise You, Father, for Your unfailing love and kindness. You hide me in Your presence and snuggle me beneath Your strong hand—safe from sinful ways. I'm grateful for the way You store up blessings for me. Thank You for guiding me into the future. Your mercy passes on from one generation to the next, to those who trust and obey You.

O Everlasting Father, I worship You. O Everlasting Father, I give You my life, my all.

But the lovingkindness of the Lord is from
everlasting to everlasting,
to those who reverence him;
his salvation is to children's children of those
who are faithful to his covenant
and remember to obey him!

PSALM 103:17–18 TLB

DECEMBER 12

Prince of Peace

I lift my worship to You, O Prince of Peace. I praise You for the way You took my life of turmoil and strife and turned it around. You called me by name, and I followed You, instead of the selfish, uncertain things of this world. Thank You for cleansing my heart from wrongdoing and refilling it with boundless peace and contentment. Never has my life been fuller or happier. You, dear Lord, give me an inner calm that remains with me every day.

I praise You for Your just treatment, for shielding those who trust in You against heartless oppressors. How merciful and tender are Your ways. They are like heaven's sunrise breaking forth, bestowing light to those who struggle in darkness. Peace You offer every soul. It's a peace that comes only through You, the Messiah, the Lord of life. It's not a fragile peace like many seek from the world, but a tranquility of spirit and common sense that comes only from You.

Thank You for a sound, permanent peace. It doesn't hinge upon circumstances, but fully depends upon Your lasting care. Thank You for giving an inner harmony far more wonderful than any human being can comprehend— one that keeps my thoughts and heart confident and at rest.

May You, O Prince of Peace, reign forever. Glory be to Your name!

> *[Jesus said,] "I am leaving you with a gift—*
> *peace of mind and heart!*
> *And the peace I give isn't fragile*
> *like the peace the world gives.*
> *So don't be troubled or afraid."*

JOHN 14:27 TLB

DECEMBER 13

God with Us

Emmanuel. Dear Emmanuel, how I praise You for being with me every single day. You are so great. Even the heavens cannot contain You. Is there a way to measure Your love for humankind, when You left Your throne and came here to live among us? Thank You for Your loving forgiveness and truth, for becoming my Savior and Lord.

Thank You for Your promise that You will never abandon me nor disown me. You are my Helper. I will not be afraid, because I know You are protecting me wherever I go. Praise You for Your strength and steadfastness. No matter what comes my way, I know You boldly stand by my side, helping and guiding me.

When everything seems against me, You are here. Should others forsake me, You welcome and comfort me as Your own. I know You will always remain close to me during life's storms. You were here for me in the past, You are here for me now, and You shall be here for me beyond the end of time. You are the First and the Last. You are the One who died and the One who lives, now and forevermore.

I worship You, Emmanuel. I praise You for being near and abiding in my heart.

The LORD Almighty is with us;
the God of Jacob is our fortress.

PSALM 46:7 NIV

Deliverer

I exalt You, Lord God, for You are my Deliverer. You found me running down a one-way path toward utter despair. When You called me, I cried out for You to rescue me. I could see no way out. But You did. You broke my shackles caused by sin, and You delivered me from a sad, aimless existence.

Thank You for rescuing me, dear Lord. Thank You for lowering Yourself and actually dying like a criminal on a cruel cross. Though You are God, You didn't command Your rights as God. You handed Yourself over as a ransom, and set me free.

How victorious is the way You were elevated to the loftiness of heaven and then sent to be my rescuer! How marvelous is the way You still show Your great love and bring good news to the anguished and afflicted. How excellent is the way You comfort the despairing, liberate hostages of sin, and open the spiritual eyes of those who seek You. How consoling is the way You reach out to those who mourn, wrap them in Your loving arms, and assure them of Your abiding love.

At the mere mention of Your name, I bow, proclaiming You my Deliverer.

> *"Offer to God thanksgiving,*
> *And pay your vows to the Most High.*
> *Call upon Me in the day of trouble;*
> *I will deliver you,*
> *and you shall glorify Me."*

> PSALM 50:14–15 NKJV

Bright and Morning Star

It's the middle of December already, Lord. Every year I try to prepare in advance, but I find myself caught up in the Christmas hustle and bustle. This year is no exception. I'm up early, writing Christmas cards to friends and loved ones. It's still dark outside. I enjoy sitting by the living room window, waiting for the sun to rise while I work.

I pull back the drapes in order to catch a first glimpse of the sun. Twinkling stars hang like tiny lanterns in the clear, vast blackness. They wink good-byes and fade from view as the sky slowly turns from ebony to slate gray. One star remains. It shines brighter than all the rest. Could it be the morning star, Lord?

When I see it, I think of You, the Bright and Morning Star. It precedes the rising sun, welcoming a new day. Each time I see this star, it draws my thoughts to You as You prepare my heart for another day.

I worship You, O Bright and Morning Star. Let me honor You this day with my attitudes and endeavors. Thank You for reminding me whom these Christmas cards commemorate. It is You, my Savior and Lord, my Bright and Morning Star—You who prepares the way for another celebration of Your birth.

[Jesus said,] "I am both David's Root
and his Descendant.
I am the bright Morning Star."

REVELATION 22:16 TLB

DECEMBER 16

Solid Rock

Thank You, Lord God, for establishing my feet on Your solid, sure pathway rather than allowing me to stumble aimlessly on a foundation of shifting sand. You are my Lord, my mighty Rock, the basis for an unwavering life in You. You are the Messiah, the Son of the living God. My entire life is securely built on You, my Rock. The powers of hell can't even prevail against You.

You, mighty Rock, are the source of my salvation. There is no other who can save me from sin and wrong. I call on no one but You, the Son of the living God.

I am thankful that I can totally trust You, O Lord. Because of Your faithful love, I will allow no room in my life for mistrust. A mind unconvinced of Your faithfulness is as restless as debris on the ocean that is tossed to and fro by blustery weather.

I worship You, the One who loves me all the time. When anxiety or stress assails me, when scarcity of income strikes, when danger daunts, I will continue to trust in You. When these things happen, I still find surety and victory in You. On You, my solid Rock, I shall always stand!

The LORD lives!
Blessed be my Rock!
Let the God of my salvation
be exalted.

PSALM 18:46 NKJV

Master, Teacher

I love sitting at Your feet, Lord, constantly learning new things from my Bible about You and Your wondrous ways. The more I study about You, the more I want to learn. It's like tapping into a life-giving, spiritual river of endless delight. The more I drink, the more I want to dive in and immerse myself in Your wise, sure resources for my life.

You, my Master and Teacher, are the certain truth that guides me to make right choices. What great and marvelous lessons You bring me from Your Father in heaven. When false leaders attempt to sway me toward careless ways, I measure what they say by Your sure, true Word. If it doesn't pass the test, I turn my back on such misguided teachings. Your Word is given by the inspiration of Your Father. Thank You, Lord, for how it straightens me out and helps me follow what is right. Thank You for preparing me for whatever comes my way. Your positive teachings bring sunshine to my soul.

You are so astounding, my Master and Teacher. I am grateful for Your farsighted wisdom. Forever teach me Your holy ways so I may walk in Your truth.

[Jesus said,] "You call Me Teacher and Lord,
and you say well, for so I am. . . .
For I have given you an example,
that you should do as I have done to you."

JOHN 13:13, 15 NKJV

DECEMBER 18

Good Shepherd

I come before You in reverence and adulation, my God. I love You so much for being my Good Shepherd. I love the way You keep me near, leading me throughout each day. I love the way You whisper wise words to my heart and give me love and encouragement. Because I know You so well, I recognize Your voice when You speak to my heart.

Once You stood at my heart's door and constantly knocked, calling my name. I'm glad I finally opened that door and invited You into my life. You, O Lord, are my Good Shepherd. Thank You for providing me rest and strengthening my soul. Praise You for guiding me along the right way, like a shepherd guides his sheep. You use Your rod to lead me away from wrong, for I am Your name's sake. Your staff protects me from evil and harm. Thank You for filling my spiritual cup to overflowing with Your cleansing, healing oil.

When I face my final days of this earthly life, I know You will still be with me, and I shall have no fear. I will trust You, my Good Shepherd, to walk with me every step of the way through the valley leading from death to eternal life. I look forward, my Good Shepherd, to dwelling in heaven with You forever.

> *[Jesus said,] "I am the good shepherd;*
> *I know my sheep and my sheep know me—*
> *just as the Father knows me and I know the Father—*
> *and I lay down my life for the sheep."*

JOHN 10:14–15 NIV

Light of the World

O Lord, my Light in this dark world, how I adore You. You are the Light of my salvation, illuminating my way and directing me to a life of peace, hope, and joy. I no longer fear the darkness surrounding me. I trust in You and focus on Your presence. You keep my heart and mind in perfect peace. As I remain on Your lighted pathway, You make my feet sure on the treacherous curves. Thank You for leveling the uphill roads I'm forced to travel, for constantly smoothing out the bumps and potholes.

When bad news comes, I need not dread what lies ahead. Instead, I'm fully confident that You, my loving Lord, are taking care of my concerns every single day. You are the holy Light shining in my world. You are my refuge. No amount of darkness can hide Your glorious light.

I praise You for picking me up when I stumble and fall. Thank You for continually watching over me and caring for me, for being my defender. Thank You for protecting me day and night. Thank You for preserving my life and keeping me going in the right way.

Oh, how I worship and praise You. You are the wonderful Light of the World, the Light of my life.

Then Jesus spoke to them again, saying,
"I am the light of the world.
He [or she] who follows Me shall not walk in darkness,
but have the light of life."

JOHN 8:12 NKJV

December 20

Friend

You are dearer to me, Lord, than mere words can describe. I praise and adore You for being my Friend. I'm grateful for the way You love me all the time. What a comfort to know You are always with me and will never desert me. Thank You for loving me and looking for the best in me. Thank You for encouraging me as we walk through each day together. Thank You for listening to me and helping me with my daily decisions.

I can't imagine going through life without You as my Friend. I long for others in this world to experience the wonderful friendship You have to give. This friendship isn't limited just to me, but extends to everyone who willingly comes to You.

Lord, it's so good to know Your closeness and love. Everywhere, all the time, I feel Your warm presence surround me. The more we commune Friend with friend, the more You fill my thoughts and heart with Your love. The more I yield my will to You, the more my life is united with Yours. In all my ways, let me honor and glorify You. Let my actions and even my thoughts give You joy. I want my heart to be Your home.

How I love You, Lord, my most treasured Friend.

> *And now just as you trusted Christ to save you,*
> *trust him, too, for each day's problems;*
> *live in vital union with him.*

COLOSSIANS 2:6 TLB

Servant

Today is designated to give our church a good cleaning, Lord. There are many things I need to do to prepare for our family Christmas celebration at home, but they are put on hold. Now is the time to get Your house—the church—ready for worshiping You.

You know we are a small congregation. We don't have paid employees, but we all help out to get things done. When we do, I feel a warmth in my heart in serving You. Here I am, Lord, scrubbing the bathroom sinks and toilets, sprucing up the church kitchen, and mopping floors. I can hear my husband vacuuming the sanctuary and singing praises to You at the top of his lungs.

The back door springs open. It's Sherry, Lord. She's armed with cleaning supplies, ready to lend a hand. Only a few days ago, she and her family helped put up Christmas decorations. What a blessing! Thank You for them.

While I work, I consider how many times You are a Servant to me. You provide me with food and clothing. You restore my health when I'm sick. You comfort me when I'm sad. You give me strength for each day. How unworthy I feel, benefiting from Your care.

Scrub brush in hand and on bended knees, I worship You, O holy, loving Servant.

Give your burdens to the Lord.
He will carry them.

PSALM 55:22 TLB

DECEMBER 22

Intercessor

There are only a few days left before Christmas, Lord. Christmas songs play everywhere. Children practice carols of Your birth to sing in school and church. Bells ring from church steeples, doorways, and stores to remind us of Your love and to help those in need.

Although this time is special, I realize many are facing critical situations, depression, and anxiety. Sometimes I don't know how to pray for them, Lord, but You do. Thank You for interceding to my heavenly Father on behalf of each one. Bless them, I pray. Help with their needs, and comfort them.

My heart fills with gratitude as I bow before You, my Intercessor. When I'm incapable of knowing how to pray, You take my petitions to the Father and speak words to Him that can't be uttered by anyone else. Sadly, I can't meet all of their needs. This is when I depend upon the unlimited power of prayer in Your name. Thank You for caring for each person, for going where I can't go, and for accomplishing things within Your will that I am unable to do. I simply pray; then I trust You to work things out in Your way.

During this holy time of year, I worship You for being an all-loving, all-powerful Intercessor of my prayers.

In the same way, the Spirit helps us in our weakness.
We do not know what we ought to pray for,
but the Spirit himself intercedes for us with
groans that words cannot express.
And he who searches our hearts knows the mind of the Spirit,
because the Spirit intercedes for the saints
in accordance with God's will.

ROMANS 8:26–27 NIV

Defender

Here I am, Lord, driving home after a busy day of work. Traffic is thick, and I'm waiting for countless stoplights—sometimes through two cycles of changes. The awesome thing about all of this is how You cause me to slow down and think on Your wonderful ways.

This is supposed to be a time of year when peace and goodwill are expressed to everyone. But today I was tested. I was forced to face pressure no matter which way I turned. I had to deal with misunderstandings, hurt feelings, and some false accusations, Lord. Thank You for giving me an awareness of Your presence and helping me to remain calm. I'm amazed at how I didn't even have to defend myself. You did that in ways that still baffle me.

Here in gridlock traffic, I lift my heart to You in worship, my Lord, my Savior, my Defender. I praise You for being with me all the time. When the tempter throws troubles in my path and tries to trip me up, You help me make sound decisions and show me how to overcome problems with goodness, understanding, and kindness. Thank You for being with others who were stressed and for helping them sort things out in the right way.

I worship You, my loving, compassionate God, my Defender.

He is always kind and loving to me;
he is my fortress, my tower of strength and safety,
my deliverer. He stands before me as a shield.

PSALM 144:2 TLB

DECEMBER 24

Potter

Our church school class went smoothly today, Lord. My students listened to directions, stayed on task, and did a wonderful job in Bible memorization. We had a lot of fun in the process and finished ahead of time. As something extra, I brought out some clay. For the next few minutes, the students busily formed whatever they wanted to make.

At first the clay was cold, and their fingers had trouble getting it to yield. I encouraged them to keep working the clay to warm it up. Before long, the children successfully pressed their sculptures into desired shapes.

Now, at day's end, I reflect on You, my Potter. Sometimes when You work with me, my attitude is cold, hard, and unyielding. Yet You never give up on me. You gently keep warming my heart until I surrender to Your loving touch.

At times I thought I was in charge until You turned my life upside down and around and showed me You are the Potter. I give honor and glory to You, Lord, for I am the clay. You have a plan for me. Although I often feel chipped and broken from disappointments and heartaches, You form me into a new pot, beautiful in Your sight.

I worship and yield to You, my Potter, as You mold me to Your will.

> *"Behold, like the clay in the potter's hand,*
> *so are you in My hand."*
>
> JEREMIAH 18:6 NASB

Redeemer

Everyone in the family is excited as we gather around the Christmas tree. A hush settles over great-grandparents, grandparents, grown children, and grandchildren as my husband quietly opens the Bible. He reads the story of Your birth, dear Lord. We sing a Christmas carol in worship to You, our Savior and Redeemer. I ponder the small blessings our family enjoys sharing with those in need, as we would do for You. Finally, little ones and adults chime out the beloved "Happy birthday, dear Jesus!" Gifts are passed out. Squeals of delight break forth from newly acquired treasures. Hugs and thank-yous follow.

I worship You, my Redeemer! I am grateful You came to this earth as a baby so You could redeem us from our sins and bring eternal life. Through this act, I see what real love is—more than tangible presents. It comes from Your wonderful gift of forgiveness. Thank You, Lord. It is too excellent for words to even describe. It is all because You are my Lord. Praise You for forgiving me of my past, granting me a loving family, and assuring me of never-ending, faithful care.

I want to present You with a gift, my Redeemer. It is an uninhibited offering of my worship and love for You.

I, the LORD,
am your Savior and your Redeemer.

ISAIAH 60:16 RSV

Messiah

I come before You, my Messiah, with a reverent heart. In humility I give You praise. You are the Anointed One—the One who delivers us from sin. Praise You, Prophet, Priest, and King. You are not an earthly prophet, not a priest or pastor of a church, not a political king or president of a nation, but our true Messiah—the Son of the living God.

You fulfilled the prophesies that foretold Your coming. You were born the Messiah, Jesus Christ the Savior. You grew in wisdom and stature from baby, to child, to the Son of Man. You were baptized and tempted. You overcame temptation. You became a servant, filled with humility and compassion. When You suffered and died on the cross, You were the very power and wisdom of God. My soul wells with gratitude for how You also became my Savior.

You, the divinely appointed King, bring God's salvation plan to all who are willing to receive You. Your followers are known as Christians—those who belong to Christ now and forever.

Thank You for bringing victory over sin. You don't bring this victory through physical force or violence, but through Your love, humility, and kindness. Truly the Father has anointed You with the oil of joy and gladness.

I bring honor and praise to You, my Messiah, my Lord!

The woman said to Him,
"I know that Messiah is coming (He who is called Christ);
when that One comes, He will declare all things to us."
Jesus said to her, "I who speak to you am He."

JOHN 4:25–26 NASB

Lamb of God

Lord, remember the little cardboard nativity scene Bob and I purchased when we first married? It held a manger with a ceramic baby Jesus in it, Mary and Joseph hovering near, and a small terra-cotta lamb. I placed the lamb just outside the stable.

Years went by, Lord. Our children grew up. The nativity scene wore out, except for the lamb. Our friend made a beautiful ceramic nativity scene for us. I placed the lamb outside the stable. Remember when our grandson Ian was big enough to peer in, Lord? He moved the lamb inside the stable. He's done that ever since.

You came here as a baby to a stable. When You were grown, Your cousin John recognized You as the lamb of God, who would take away the sins of the world.

I worship You, O Lamb of God. You were browbeaten and ridiculed. You never complained. You came as a lamb to the slaughter. You stood silently before Your condemners. You did Your Father's will and laid down Your life for humankind.

I worship You for paying my ransom—not with money, but with Your precious, pure life's blood. Now I can completely trust in Your saving grace.

Worthy are You, O Lamb who was slain. How worthy are You to receive power, wealth, wisdom, might, reverence, majesty, and blessings eternal!

"To him who sits on the throne and to the Lamb
be praise and honor
and glory and power,
for ever and ever!"

REVELATION 5:13 NIV

DECEMBER 28

Lord of Hosts

Glory be to You, O God, my Lord of Hosts. You are Creator and Ruler of everything: the heavens, the earth, and the entirety of that which exists through time and space. You made it all and are Ruler over it all. The stars, the moon, and the galaxies were created by You. Although these things are lovely, they aren't made for us to worship. Only You are my Lord God. Although angels and heavenly hosts reflect Your glorious miracles and handiwork, You did not create them for us to pray to or to consider divine. You reign over the angels, as well.

When spiritual or physical battles are fought, You are the Mighty God of warriors. When victories are won, You are in charge. You are strong and mighty in battle. You are the Lord of Hosts, the King of Glory. Through turmoil, uncertainty, and despair, You are my refuge and strength. How blessed I am, trusting and obeying You. You are the Most High God.

In my quiet place, I worship You. In Your church sanctuary, I love bowing before You. I adore You, my Lord God. Praise I bring to You. Reverence and honor I lift to You! I look forward with longing to worshiping You, Lord of Hosts, when I someday meet You in heaven.

> *"Holy, holy, holy is the LORD of hosts;*
> *The whole earth is full of His glory!"*

ISAIAH 6:3 NKJV

Comforter, Helper

I come into Your presence, my Comforter and Helper, to worship and praise You. Thank You for being with me all the time. I love the way You speak to me deep within my heart and tell me I really do belong to You. Thank You for giving me confidence. I need not cringe or be fearful of troubles surrounding me, for You are always with me.

Truly You are my Sustainer, the One who keeps me going when I become weary. When spiritual battles rage, You rescue me. When I face daily problems, You help me. Thank You for teaching me how to pray when I can't express how I feel. Thank You for giving me hope and joy and Your power. Because of Your abiding presence, I can hold my head up with surety and confidence. No matter what happens, I trust in You. All is well, for I am in Your care.

You are so dear to me, my Comforter. I enjoy Your friendship all the time. I take pleasure in sharing good happenings with You. I'm grateful for Your reassuring love and help when I face trouble. When I feel alone, You are my Advocate. Thank You for encouraging me and cheering me on.

I worship You, my Comforter, my Helper. My words of praise can't begin to describe Your loving-kindness.

[Jesus said,] And I will pray the Father,
and he shall give you another Comforter [the Holy Spirit],
that he may abide with you for ever.

JOHN 14:16 KJV

Jehovah

I kneel before You at the church sanctuary altar, Lord God. No one else is here. Only the *whoosh* of warm air from the furnace breaks the silence. A sunbeam shimmers through the windows, casting its ray across the altar. It looks like a golden blessing, coming to me straight from heaven.

I adore You, Jehovah. How grateful I am, because You are my God. Your holy presence surrounds me. You fill me with a certainty of Your enduring love and care. You were in the beginning, You are now, and You shall be forevermore.

You are my Jehovah, my Yahweh. Many times You have whispered Your comforting words, *"I AM who I am. I will be who I will be."* Each time You do, I enjoy Your faithful, loving care.

You are above all else in heaven and earth. I love no other more than You, my God. When my health fails and my spirits sink, You still remain. When I become discouraged, You encourage and remind me that You *are* without end the great I am. You are the strength of my heart. You are my God. Because You claim me as Your own, I know my inheritance with You forever is my heavenly prize.

I worship and adore You, my Jehovah, my Yahweh, my Everlasting God.

> *"Behold, God is my salvation,*
> *I will trust and not be afraid;*
> *'For YAH, the LORD,*
> *is my strength and song.'"*
>
> ISAIAH 12:2 NKJV

King of Kings

Exalted are You, O King of all kings. I kneel in awe of Your holy name. When I consider Your glory, I tremble in Your presence. You alone are everlasting, surrounded by a pure, sweet light. There is no one as magnificent as You. You are Ruler and Creator of everything that exists. You place boundaries on the ocean edges. You declare their uninterrupted incoming and outgoing rhythm. Whenever they pitch and bellow, You are still in charge. Holy, holy, holy are You, O King of Kings and Lord of Lords.

You are my God, whom I worship and revere. I give thanks to You, my Lord, for Your love endures forever. You alone understand all things and do great wonders. You alone recognize the prayers of those who love and obey You.

You, my King of Kings, can place people in honor and give them authority according to Your will. You care about world events, and they are in Your capable hands. You have power to appoint kings or presidents. You have power to remove them and set others in their stead when we call on Your name for help. You give wisdom to those who seek You and reveal truth to those who study Your Word.

How blessed You are, my Redeemer, King of Kings, and Lord of Lords.

"He is Lord of lords and King of kings;
and those who are with Him are called,
chosen, and faithful."

REVELATION 17:14 NKJV

May the Lord Bless You

"The LORD bless you and keep you;
The LORD make His face shine upon you,
And be gracious to you;
The LORD lift up His countenance upon you,
And give you peace."

NUMBERS 6:24–26 NKJV

Scripture Index